STARTING AND BUILDING
YOUR OWN
ACCOUNTING BUSINESS

THE WILEY/NATIONAL ASSOCIATION OF ACCOUNTANTS
PROFESSIONAL BOOK SERIES

Denis W. Day • *How to Cut Business Travel Costs*

Harry L. Brown • *Design and Maintenance of Accounting Manuals*

Gordon V. Smith • *Corporate Valuation: A Business and Professional Guide*

Henry Labus • *Successfully Managing Your Accounting Career*

Ralph G. Loretta • *The Price Waterhouse Guide to Financial Management: Tools for Improving Performance*

James A. Brimson • *Activity Accounting: An Activity-Based Costing Approach*

Jack Fox • *Starting and Building Your Own Accounting Business, Second Edition*

STARTING AND BUILDING YOUR OWN ACCOUNTING BUSINESS

Second Edition

JACK FOX

JOHN WILEY & SONS, INC.

New York • Chichester • Brisbane • Toronto • Singapore

Library of Congress Cataloging in Publication Data:

Fox, Jack.
    Starting and building your own accounting business / Jack Fox.–
2nd ed.
       p.   cm.–(Wiley/Ronald-National Association of Accountants
professional book series, ISSN 0741-1010)
    Includes bibliographical references and index.
    ISBN 0-471-52643-6
    1. Accounting firms. 2. New business enterprises.   I. Title.
II. Series.
HF5627.F69   1991
657'.068'4–dc20   90-37154
                                           CIP

Printed in the United States of America.

10 9 8 7 6 5 4 3 2 1

To my parents,
Benjamin and Rebecca Fox

my wife,
Carole Olafson Fox

PREFACE

There can be no business without clients. I learned very early that although I was about to establish an independent accounting practice I would never succeed until I had built up a clientele. The best way to win clients is to moonlight before leaving a full-time job, but this I found impossible to do because of the constraints on time and the pressures of being the budget director of an organization with annual expenditures in excess of $60 million.

With expectations of assets I telephoned friends and acquaintances and informed them of my new status as an entrepreneur in accounting and asked for referrals. I was looking for any kind of accounting jobs at first, for in any new enterprise you rely on what you do best. My specialty was the preparation of Small Business Administration loan packages. This became the opening wedge for acquiring new accounts.

Initially, only a few leads came my way, and none of them panned out. In retrospect, I have come to believe that people are reluctant to recommend a beginner, even an experienced one. One primary reason—and a major consideration of potential clients—is that the stability of the practice rather than the professional competence of the practitioner is in question. Will the new accountant be around in a year or will another job be the answer? These are the questions they ask. I found it more effective to emphasize my qualifications and experience than the newness of my practice.

While I was searching for clients I began to participate in the Active Corps of Executives (ACE), a program of the SBA. ACE works in conjunction with SCORE (Service Corps of Retired Executives) to provide advanced education for prospective and fledgling business people. I taught a number of classes, which enabled me to meet potential clients. More productive, however, were several classes I held at the local community college, two of which, "Taxation for Small Business" and "Financing the Smaller Business," attracted considerable potential client interest. A teacher commands certain professional status that lends credibility. In my case it helped me to secure valuable new clients. Referrals became secondary. I learned that you cannot draw a sufficient number without a large enough client base.

I started planning more than a year before I established the practice and cut off the "security" of a paycheck. I actually decided to go into business for myself after attending a two-weekend program at The School for Entrepreneurs in Tarrytown, New York. About 30 people performed various business exercises, and, at the end of the program, presented their plans to a group of professional venture capitalists and to the entire class. The time had come for me to stand on my own.

I approached several accounting franchise operations, studied their printed materials and brochures, met with company representatives (salespeople), interviewed local franchisees, and analyzed their programs as best I could. I found that in return for sizable franchise fees, which ranged from $11,500 to more than $40,000, little was being made available to an aspiring practitioner with a good accounting background. Most franchises are designed for the nonaccountant who wants to become an accountant or, as some term it, a business consultant. I learned that most of the people who buy franchises have been in the military or have held government positions and are supported by a pension or some sort of guaranteed income.

The most alluring aspect of the franchises was the offer of marketing assistance because, in addition to being familiar with the accounting process and its concomitants, you have to know how to sell your services to potential clients. Fee-paying clients are vital to your business, but selling is often anathema to the accountant. Yet some sellers of franchises try to transform the accountant into a salesperson for their services rather than into an independent marketer. It seems that the bottom line on some of the proposals is that for a not inconsiderable fee you would be trained to sell these services. The write-up work would be processed by their computer facilities and the tax-return preparation would be performed by their specialists from data gathered by the franchise salesperson. I found that nearly everything the franchise offered could be duplicated at a much lower cost and with no franchise fee. A desire to share this knowledge and experience with others led me to write this book.

For me it has been worth all the effort. There is no substitute for being in charge of your own business future. The promise of rewards is always present, as is an awareness that the extra effort is directly beneficial to you and your family. There is no more exciting activity in the marketplace than working for yourself.

JACK FOX, M.B.A.

San Diego, California
March, 1991

CONTENTS

CONTENTS

CONTENTS

CONTENTS

CONTENTS

CONTENTS

CONTENTS

STARTING AND BUILDING YOUR OWN ACCOUNTING BUSINESS

1

HOW TO SUCCEED IN THE ACCOUNTING BUSINESS . . . BY REALLY TRYING

THE ACCOUNTANT AS AN ENTREPRENEUR

Always do whatever you really want to do—whatever you are good at, something for which you have talent.

Entrepreneurship is not easy. In your own business you will work harder than you ever have before. There will be times when you will feel like throwing in the towel—critical times when mistakes in judgment are generally made, but if you like what you are doing, if you have the talent for it, you will carry on through the difficult periods.

A great deal of research on the personal qualities and behavior of the entrepreneur has been done, but the precise identification of entrepreneurial talent remains elusive. At present, however, this identification process, in which psychological and related methods are used, remains imprecise and is more of an art than a science. Although numerous studies have yielded important insights into entrepreneurship, it is important to recognize that the knowledge available may represent only the tip of the iceberg. Drawing on this current data base can yield a substantial improvement over a mere seat-of-the-pants estimate of your own entrepreneurial potential. The key to improvement lies in a realistic and thorough self-evaluation by the prospective entrepreneur. Louis L. Allen, an experienced capital investor in small ventures, shares this view of the importance of the role of self-selection:

> Unlike the giant firm which has recruiting and selection experts to screen the wheat from the chaff, the small business firm, which comprises the most common economic unit in our business system, cannot afford to employ a personnel manager. . . . More than that, there's something very special about the selection of the owners: they have selected themselves. . . .

But how can you self-select wisely when you are not sure what to look for and what, in this case, is important to the entrepreneurial role? This dilemma, common to many job and career choices, must be faced by the accountant who is deciding to start a business.

One useful way is to view the self-selection and decision-making process as a matter of the fit or suitability of the various entrepreneurial characteristics in relation to the demands and pressures that apparently accompany an entrepreneurial accounting career. In addition, other complex factors go beyond your control—business conditions, political and regulatory changes, even providence—can undoubtedly affect the development of a new accounting business. This reality tends to lend further support to the importance of assessing and managing well the matters you can control, in particular to assessing the likely fit between entrepreneurial characteristics and role requirements.

4

Today it is a relatively easy matter to start an accounting business, but it is not so easy to build it to a substantial size. Indeed, the kind of people who have started and maintained their own accounting business runs from the small practitioner to the large multi-office operation. The intent here is by no means to demean the sole practitioner who can be successful and have an extremely lucrative business. American accounting entrepreneurs have come from widely varying backgrounds in terms of education and experience. Most accounting businesses in this country are small when compared to the statistics for all businesses in general. Most businesses in the United States are marginal—the classical "mom 'n pop" or the single proprietorship. One survey estimates that among the 10 to 11 million businesses in the United States perhaps fewer than 4000 have annual sales of more than $20 million. Another 1.5 million show sales between $5 and $20 million a year; perhaps 7 million of the remaining 8.5 million gross less than $100,000 and may employ fewer than eight people. Another authority notes that only about 10,000 of the 60,000 U.S. companies listed on the nation's stock exchanges are traded actively.

CHARACTERISTICS OF SUCCESSFUL ENTREPRENEURS

The wide range in the nature of the businesses and in the entrepreneurs who run them makes across-the-board generalizations regarding their characteristics risky at best, somewhat misleading at worst. For example, product-oriented businesses differ from those that are service-oriented. The educational backgrounds of technical entrepreneurs are different from those of nontechnical and service entrepreneurs. Thus, if we are to provide meaningful definitions of entrepreneurial characteristics in an economical and manageable way, we must make some generalizations at the risk of oversimplification. In so doing, it is useful to acknowledge that it would be an overkill to suggest that the same personal characteristics needed for the building of a multimillion dollar enterprise were also requisite in launching a small single proprietorship. In addition, study and personal development are essential to the growth of a business. This is probably the best way for many to discover how they can excel or where they are weak. Some entrepreneurial skills such as goal setting can be developed; certain role requirements such as knowledge of a particular business can be learned. Persons in their twenties about to embark on their first part-time or full-time ventures may form a small proprietorship or partnership. Early success provides not only valuable experience but also a platform on which to build a larger, more complex, and demanding venture later on. Therefore, you will have to judge for yourself where you are, where you are headed, and what you can do to develop your entrepreneurial potential from, say, a moderate fit to a high fit (Exhibit 1) vis-á-vis the entrepreneurial characteristics and role requirements presented here.

For the entrepreneur, prospective partner, and investor alike the question of the nature and extent of entrepreneurial potential is paramount. In the material presented here we have made an attempt to help you to recognize any major shortcomings or fatal flaws that could make your pursuit of an accounting business a program for failure. Do not expect that this book will enable you to decide whether you are capable of building an Arthur Andersen, Coopers & Lybrand, or Price Waterhouse. On the other hand, we do believe we can help you to determine whether, in fact, you have a reasonable chance of succeeding in an accounting business that will suit your own goals, values, and needs. In developing these entrepreneurial characteristics we examined the available research on the behavioral characteristics of successful entrepreneurs. We also reviewed the current practices of venture capitalists in their assessment of the per-

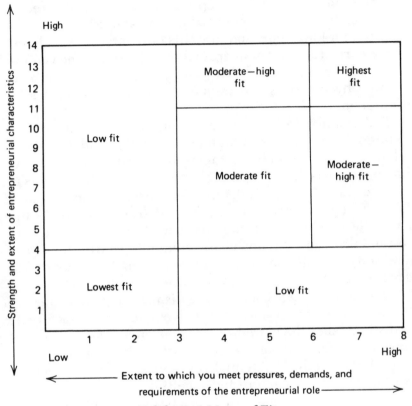

Exhibit 1. A Matter of Fit

sonal characteristics of entrepreneurs in whom they invested. We found that considerable effort had been expended to determine whether persons wanting to start a new venture and applicants for venture capital did in fact possess the necessary qualifications. Enough agreement at least was implicit in our investigation to identify 14 dominant characteristics of successful entrepreneurs:

7

1. Drive and Energy. Entrepreneurs are generally recognized as having excessive personal energy and drive—a capacity to work for long hours and in spurts of several days with less than the normal amount of sleep. Our examination of the venture capital industry confirmed drive and energy as characteristics mandated by investors and frequently observed in successful entrepreneurs.

2. Self-confidence. Agreement is also general that successful entrepreneurs possess a high level of self-confidence. They tend to believe strongly in themselves and their ability to achieve the goals they have set. They also believe that events in their lives are mainly self-determined, that they have a major influence on their personal destinies, and that they depend little on luck. Researchers often cite this characteristic. Further, venture capitalists and the financial community as well look for a strong sense of self-confidence before placing their money but regard overconfidence, subtle arrogance, or absence of humility, all of which may suggest a lack of realism, as negative traits.

3. Long-term Involvement. Involvement is a characteristic that distinguishes the entrepreneur—the creator and builder of a business—from the promoter or fast-buck artist. Entrepreneurs who create high potential ventures are driven to build a business. They are not interested in getting in and out in a hurry; their commitment to long-term projects and to working toward goals that may be quite distant is total.

One venture capitalist has said: "The lemons ripen in two or three years; the plums take seven or eight years." On the basis of their own experience, venture capitalists know that a successful growth business requires complete concentration on the attainment of objectives. This involvement, so characteristic of successful entrepreneurs, has also been confirmed by research.

4. Money as a Measure. Money has a special meaning for the professional entrepreneur; it is a way of keeping score. Salary, profits, capital gains, and net worth are seen as measures

8

of how well self-established goals are pursued. The entrepreneur is involved in a continuous process of making money, of investing it in other companies, and then starting all over again. This cycle never seems to end and the money accruéd is a way of measuring performance.

5. Persistent Problem Solving. Entrepreneurs who build new enterprises possess intense levels of determination to overcome hurdles, solve problems, and complete the job. They are not intimidated by difficulties. Rather than self-confidence and general optimism seem to translate into the fact that the impossible takes just a little longer. Yet they are neither aimless nor foolhardy in their relentless attack on obstacles that can impede their progress. Although they are extremely persistent, they are also realistic in recognizing what they can and cannot do and how they can get help to solve difficult but necessary tasks.

6. Goal Setting. Entrepreneurs have the ability to set clear goals for themselves—goals that tend to be challenging but always realistic and attainable. Entrepreneurs are doers—action oriented—with a clear and direct purpose. They know where they are headed.

7. Moderate Risk Taking. The successful entrepreneur prefers to take moderate, calculated risks in which the chances of winning are neither so small that they become a gamble nor so large that they represent a sure thing. Risks that provide a reasonable chance of success are preferred in a situation whose outcome is influenced as much by ability and effort as by chance. This entrepreneurial characteristic is one of the most important, because it indicates how decisions are made and implies the success or failure of the business.

8. Dealing with Failure. The use of failure as a way of learning and of understanding not only your own part but that of others in the cause of failure so as to avoid similar mistakes in the future is another significant entrepreneurial characteristic. Success and failure are not opposites. Rather they are companions—like the hero and the sidekick. The trial-and-error nature of becoming a successful entrepreneur makes serious setbacks and disappointments a part of the learning process. The most effective entrepreneurs are realistic enough to expect difficulties. They are not disappointed, discouraged, or depressed by setbacks—at least not for long. More typically, they seek opportunity in difficult times and victory in situations in which most people see only defeat.

Entrepreneurs are not afraid of failure. Being more intent on succeeding, they are not intimidated by the possibility of failing. Those who fear failure will neutralize whatever motivation for achievement they may possess and tend to engage in easy tasks in which there is little chance of failure or in chance situations in which they cannot be held personally responsible if they don't succeed.

9. Use of Feedback. Entrepreneurs, as high achievers, are especially concerned with doing well. This concern is responsible, in part, for another entrepreneurial characteristic: the use of feedback. Without this information the entrepreneur cannot know how good or bad the performance is. Successful entrepreneurs demonstrate a capacity to use feedback in order to improve or to take corrective action.

10. Taking the Initiative and Assuming Personal Responsibility. Historically the entrepreneur has been viewed as an independent and highly self-reliant innovator, a champion of the free-enterprise economy. Considerable agreement has been reached among researchers and practitioners alike that effective entrepreneurs take the initiative by placing themselves in situations in which they are personally responsible for the success or failure of the operation.

11. Use of Resources. Several studies have shown that successful entrepreneurs know when and how to obtain outside help in building their companies and will follow the best advice they can afford. They are not so ego-involved in independent accomplishment that they will refuse to allow anyone else to help. This trait, at first glance, appears to be at odds with a popular stereotype of all entrepreneurs as highly individualistic loners. The willingness to take advantage of outside resources is a key characteristic that distinguishes the high-potential entrepreneur from the rest of the pack.

12. Competing against Self-imposed Standards. Competitiveness can be a misleading attribute. It is most important to distinguish between competition directed toward others, without any objective measure of performance, and an internalized kind of competition with a self-imposed standard.

13. Internal Locus of Control. The entrepreneur does not believe that the success or failure of a new business depends on luck or fate or other external, uncontrollable factors. Rather the belief is that personal accomplishments as well as setbacks lie within personal control and influence.

14. Tolerance of Ambiguity and Uncertainty. Entrepreneurs have long been viewed as having a special tolerance for the ambiguous and for making decisions under conditions of uncertainty. In contrast to the professional manager, they are able to live with modest-to-high levels of uncertainty in job security. Job permanency is considerably lower on the entrepreneur's list of preferences as compared with a managerial counterpart. This toleration for insecurity is generally recognized as an important characteristic.

These 14 characteristics were extracted from the literature on entrepreneurship, research with venture capitalists, and personal experience. Their dimensions constitute what is currently believed to be the most significant aspects of entrepreneurial behavior, but the biggest gap in existing knowledge is how to measure and identify many of the psychologically oriented characteristics accurately and consistently. Probably no single entrepreneur possesses all 14 characteristics to an extremely high degree. In principle, more are better than fewer, but weaknesses can be complemented by other strengths. Thus, it is important to recognize these strengths and weaknesses with respect to each of the characteristics. By the same token, the absence of several key characteristics, many modest ratings, and few, if any, high ratings, suggest a low suitability for high-potential entrepreneurship.

ROLE DEMANDS AND REQUIREMENTS

It is not enough to possess an intense level of entrepreneurial characteristics. Certain conditions, pressures, and demands are inherent in the role requirements which are important to the fit of the entrepreneurial task and to the eventual success or failure of the venture. Although successful entrepreneurs may share several characteristics with those who succeed in other careers, their preference for and tolerance of the combination of requirements unique to the entrepreneurial role are a major distinguishing features. Research has suggested eight dominant role requirements. (See Exhibit 2.)

1. Accommodation to the Venture. The entrepreneur lives under constant pressure—first to survive, then to stay alive, and always to grow and withstand the thrusts of competitors. The entrepreneur's time, emotions, and loyalty are top priority demands in a high-potential venture—demands that are important to decisions relating to marriage, raising a family, and community involvement. To do all of these things well is not a realistic burden for most people. The cooperation and understanding of your spouse is essential and cannot be overemphasized. In fact, many owners of small businesses are probably dominated as much by personal and family considerations as by the profitability of the business.

	Successful Entrepreneur	Unsuccessful Entrepreneur	Professional Manager	Promoter
Personal attributes and characteristics	Personal drive (highly dedicated to business) Persistent Strong character Competitive Independent Takes educated risk Builder Has realistic goals Ethics	Self-centered Unwilling to listen to others Takes big or small risks Unclear goals Money more important than building a business	Proved skills and expertise Can establish goals Can direct and motivate Self-confident Decisive Competitive Thinking about next job Cautious risk taker	Fast-buck artist Short timer Shotgun approach Ego motivated Not a builder Gambler Least ethical Super salesman
Role and job demands	Own values and standards Hard work Sacrifice Business comes first Knows the business Team builder Long hours in early years Five to 10 years to build business Innovation and creativity	Same as successful entrepreneur but doesn't meet many of the demands	Oriented to organization's values, status, rewards More routine work pattern Security builds up Less risky Management skills crucial Maintenance and efficiency oriented	Quick entrance and exit Short bursts of activity Not a builder High risk High return Boom-and-bust pattern

Exhibit 2. Perceptions of Characteristics and Role Demands

2. Total Immersion and Commitment. Launching and building an accounting business is not a part-time proposition. Building a profitable accounting business requires total immersion in and commitment to that end. The managerial role can be delegated—the entrepreneurial cannot.

Building a new business is a way of life. Unless it is a way on which you can thrive it can be intolerable. Perhaps Joseph Conrad captured the meaning of this kind of work, although unintentionally:

> I don't like work—no man does—but I like what is in work—the chance to find yourself. Your own reality—for yourself, not for others—what no other man can ever know.

3. Creativity and Innovation. The entrepreneurial role has long been recognized as a prime source of innovation and creativity. Recent studies of entrepreneurial careers have identified the "career anchor" with which it is associated. Once again, the entrepreneur's career anchor is creativity and innovation. Managers, on the other hand, find their career anchors in competence and efficiency; whereas college professors prefer autonomy—or control over one's time.

4. Knowledge of the Business You Want to Launch. Venture capitalists stress the importance of the track record—business experience and accomplishments—of the entrepreneur and the team in which they invest. Most strongly prefer that a potential venture be headed by an individual who has a thorough operating knowledge of the business to be launched.

5. Team Building. High-potential ventures are rarely sole proprietorships. One-person operations are extremely limited in upside potential.

6. Economic Values. Business entrepreneurs must share the key values of the free-enterprise system: private ownership, profits, capital gains, and responsible growth. These dominant economic values need not necessarily exclude social values, but the realities of the competitive market economy seem to require a belief in or at least a tolerance of them.

7. Ethics. Historically, the entrepreneur has possessed what is referred to as situational ethics. Personal ethics tend to be defined by the needs and demands of the situation rather than by some external, rigid code of conduct applied uniformly, regardless of the conditions and circumstances.

8. Integrity and Reliability. Not to be confused with situational ethics, integrity and reliability are paramount qualities for the aspiring accountant who is trying to raise conventional venture capital and debt financing. A reputation for dependability, reliability, and honesty is essential.

Except in the area of personal values, no tests or other instruments exist that can help you to assess your fit to a particular role requirement. Induction and inference, coupled with hard-nosed reality testing with those who know you well, are required to arrive at realistic self-assessments in relation to these requirements. Do not be dismayed if you don't meet them all. Perhaps nobody does. It is more important to understand your own attraction and aversion to these role demands and their implications and the alternative ways of compensating for them.

The accounting professional can look forward to an increasingly significant role in the country's economic future. The last several years of economic upheaval have done much to emphasize the growing value of professional support at the small and medium-sized business level. Managers of all types of business have learned that out-of-date, shoe box accounting systems will no longer do. CPAs and non-CPAs are being sought more and more, for their expertise in systems design and analysis and for their ability to install new account control mechanisms.

Indications are that the small accounting business will move away from the attest function to the write-up engagement and advisory consultation.

In keeping with the times, the accounting profession can expect the numbers of women in its ranks to increase. Once an all but exclusively male pursuit, accounting has at last opened its doors to women and has begun to encourage female colleagueship. The American Women's Society of Certified Public Accountants in Marysville, Ohio, reports that its membership has jumped from fewer than 600 in 1973 to currently more than 1200. A spokeswoman for the organization emphasizes that the trend is likely to continue.

At the turn of the century—just four years after the first public accounting certificate was issued—certified public accountants numbered 500 nationwide. Getting its start at a time when more Americans than ever had direct stakes in the country's burgeoning industries, the new profession filled a need for standardized financial reporting to the investing public. As a result, the ranks of public accounting continued to grow. Today there are more than 165,000 CPAs in the United States and more than 100,000 other accountants.

Public accounting offers a wide range of career paths: the large accounting firm, the middle-sized partnership, the professional corporation, the small partnership, and the individual practice. The large firms give newcomers the advantage of the experience and advice of older partners, association with a professional group, and specialization. The medium-sized CPA firm provides interesting work with experienced professionals and a chance to specialize or to vary assignments.

The professional corporation, a relatively new development, offers its members many of the advantages derived from the middle-sized partnership and certain corporate advantages—tax benefits, profit-sharing opportunities, and insurance options.

Small partnerships generally offer staffers and partners many incentives to show individual initiative and creativity, but sole proprietorships allow the independent thinker the greatest amount of flexibility.

Practitioners currently engaged independently or in partnership often describe the satisfaction of working with a less structured environment, setting their own time schedules, choosing their own clients, and, in general, making their own decisions.

Accountants who strike out alone, however, to form a small partnership or individual accounting business ultimately face the most demanding challenges. To establish yourself you must first choose the type of practice, select its location carefully, set up the office physically, develop the business' contacts personally, manage the business skillfully, and continue to update your professional knowledge of accounting.

TYPES OF SMALL ACCOUNTING BUSINESS

Sole Proprietorship

To the free-thinking professional, the individual accounting business presents many possibilities. Easily formed and free from the obligations of partner association, single proprietorship can result in considerable personal gratification to the accountant-entrepreneur sufficiently motivated to make it work.

On the other hand, the solo practice lacks the "review" emphasis that contributes to the quality of the work of a partnership. Moreover, a problem common to the individual practice is the limited ability to stay up to date with massive amounts of information—tax laws, procedural regulations, and theoretical professional data—all of which affect the profession directly.

Because a successful small practice is usually a busy one, an independent's time for acquiring new knowledge can be constrained.

Small Partnerships

Small practice partnerships frequently offer new accountants the opportunity for professional independence and affiliation with peers. Partnerships can give professionals the chance to broaden their expertise in accounting areas into which the sole proprietor may consider it a luxury to penetrate. Two partners may favor different aspects of the profession: one may prefer to handle tax procedures; whereas the other may enjoy serving clients in a consulting capacity. Partnerships also provide the opportunity to expand. Unlike the sole proprietorship, which is restricted in size for obvious reasons, the ability of a partnership to enlarge is almost unlimited. Many of today's large accounting firms began as two- or three-member partnerships.

The establishment of a partnership, of course, can sometimes be tricky. Accountants who wish to enter into partnerships should know and understand their prospective colleagues well before agreeing to "hoe the same row." After the business has been established is not the time to discover an inability to get along. Bear in mind also that professional rules bar partnerships between CPAs and non-CPAs.

One of the best ways of ensuring the success of a partnership is to acquire experience as a sole practitioner, build a practice, and then merge with another sole practitioner. Remember that sole practitioner status and partnerships are not mutually exclusive.

Accountants experienced in partnerships recommend that prospective partners ask themselves the following questions before making a commitment:

Do we share professional objectives?

Are our skills complementary? Does the professional expertise of one fill the gaps in weak areas of the other?

Do we relate well to others?

Are our lifestyles too different for us to share common interests?

Do we really like each other?

How much volume can each of us provide?

What promises can we make concerning the probability of obtaining clients?

Sometimes professionals who are not ready to enter into partnership decide instead to form a trial partnership, often referred to as a loose association. This arrangement provides the professional atmosphere of the partnership without the legal obligations. In such instances two or three accountants may rent office space together and share the overhead expenses. Participants do not usually share clients or work loads but are available to one another to compare notes and exchange ideas on technical problems. If successful, a loose association can provide the basis for forming a permanent partnership.

CHOOSING A LOCATION

Site-seeking accountants are naturally drawn to locations that provide unique business potential or access to the kind of lifestyle and cultural setting in which they feel most at home. Ideally, the best place to locate an accounting business is one that serves professional and personal needs equally well.

Achieving the ideal becomes a formidable task for many accountants who quickly find that every location option carries its share of compromise and occasional sacrifice. Veteran accountants stress that newcomers who wish to avoid big city trappings by establishing near suburban or provincial communities or small towns most often forego the income potential and professional stimulation usually available to practitioners situated in thriving urban centers.

Location plays a definite part in determining the kind of work the accountant will perform. A matter of miles can often mean the difference between a practice geared toward write-up and tax work and one that is involved in budget preparation, consulting, and auditing. In one area a practice may derive most of its clients from small businesses—retailers, service vendors, and doctors or dentists. In another region customers may be large firms, government contractors, and others requiring specialized professional help.

Site seekers may wish to consider the types of location available.

Small Town in a Rural Area

Small-town locations can provide independent or partner accountants excellent opportunities to establish useful and highly personal accounting businesses. Seasoned practitioners, however, caution that unless a town or the area around it shows an obvious trend toward economic development the choice is often impractical. An examination of all current data related to outside interests can be helpful. Positive speculation on the use of the area's natural resources, energy development, farming, and real estate activity by authoritative enterprises and institutions may provide a sound reason to establish in an economically placid area.

Accountants who have started businesses in small towns report on the pros and cons. Some say they have found local residents skeptical of accountants; others report appreciative acceptance. An advantage of the small-town practice is that it permits personal involvement with the community and its members.

Others report that building a client base is extremely difficult in small-town locations. Many would-be clients avoid local practitioners because they feel a higher degree of expertise can be obtained by traveling the extra distance to a large city.

It is also important for practitioners who are considering a semi-rural area to determine what kind of backup is available. Is access to computer service bureaus easy? Is staff support available for bookkeeping and clerical work? After establishing their businesses, some accountants have found themselves swamped with nontechnical paperwork that leaves little time for professional development.

Industrial Counties and Urban-spillover Areas

Midway between bustling city centers and small towns are heavily populated spillovers in which many small businesses thrive and manufacturers churn out goods. Some accountants regard these outlying areas as the best potential for a new accounting business. They cite as advantages the variety of clients, access to service bureaus, proximity to other professionals, and probability of available housing.

Some accountants who have established businesses in urban outlying areas report initial difficulties in attracting clients and warn newcomers to prepare for long waits before an adequate amount of work is forthcoming. Unlike the small town, in which the new accounting business is usually visible to community inhabitants, the overspill location frequently makes the new practitioner seem like an anonymous ant in a sugar mill.

Although at first the going is often rough, accountants who are willing to stick with it can usually build a healthy business within three years. Normally, the first clients are gained during the tax season. After that, it is a matter of marketing.

Downtown and Financial Center Locations

Accountants who choose to locate their businesses in downtown areas, specifically those sites close to or in financial districts, face a particularly demanding challenge. These urban centers—in which banks, insurance and stock brokerages, large corporations, and professional firms thrive—produce an atmosphere of quick-paced competition.

The downtown accountant is more likely to develop a specialty than is the practitioner located in a small town or spillover area. Because so many other accountants are operating in the city, small practitioners often try to develop a particular expertise and establish a good reputation. If an accountant is successful at a specialty, referrals will follow—from attorneys, present and former clients, other accountants, and financial advisors.

GUIDES FOR LOCATION RESEARCH

Whatever the accountant's preference, the decision to locate should be backed by sound market research. A number of tools are available for this purpose.

Real Estate Reports

Real estate reports that deal with regional commercial and residential construction activity—building costs, wage rates for construction tradespeople, market activity based on deed recordings, and trends in housing and office space costs—are published in locations throughout the United States. Frequently these reports are sponsored by interested members of the business community such as banks, investment corporations, or real estate firms with a direct stake in the future of the surrounding area. For the site-seeking accountant this kind of report can be useful in projecting costs of office space and emergence of new businesses while providing a fair idea of residential areas and house prices.

These publications may be found in local public libraries or, in some instances, real estate offices.

Chamber of Commerce Reports

Accountants may also wish to consider the reports published by city, county, and state chambers of commerce, which often provide detailed information on population growth, types of local businesses, including accounting businesses, and average income data for residents.

"Survey of Buying Power"

Sales Management magazine's annual, another standard marketing guide, lists per capita incomes and retail sales figures for cities across the country. It is available at major public libraries and from Sales Management, 630 Third Avenue, New York, New York 10017.

Important Contacts

An accountant with a potential location in mind should not depend entirely on published data. Statistics and census tracts, although helpful, may also be misleading. Knowledgeable individual sources often provide a key to the flexibility of an area—or lack of it.

CPA and Public Accounting Societies

State societies and their local chapters can be helpful to accountants who are uncertain about a particular location. By speaking with members new practitioners can learn a lot about an area's professional atmosphere and its need for new accountants.

Service Bureaus

Data processing and computer service bureaus are important to accountants who are speculating on the use of computerized backup. A telephone survey of local bureau representatives for price quotes, descriptions of the services offered, and time in process should prove beneficial.

Business Schools

Local colleges and universities are good sources of information on continuing education programs and teaching opportunities.

Bankers

During an informal interview a local banker may provide valuable insight into community businesses.

Real Estate Brokers

Representatives of local real estate firms can give advice on office-space availability and local housing costs.

SELECTING OFFICE SPACE

After deciding on the geographic location of the new business, the accountant faces the question of office space. As professionals, accountants are careful to select quarters that reflect the position of public trust they represent. Exterior as well as interior design should be used to project an image of professionalism, good taste, and respectability. Experienced accountants often advise fledglings to lease space in well-known professional buildings in which the public is likely to seek specialized services.

Small-town or suburban offices should be as visible as possible—on a main street, in a shopping center, or near municipal buildings. Any site in which there is heavy pedestrian traffic is likely to be a sound choice.

To combine living quarters with working environment, some accountants have established offices at home. An advantage associated with this arrangement is that the accountant can claim a portion of the cost of the dwelling as an overhead expense, thereby gaining a tax deduction. In addition, working at home obviates any necessity for commuting—an attractive fantasy for those facing heavy traffic after breakfast and before dinner. However, many who have attempted to mix the two worlds caution newcomers to think long and hard. "It just doesn't work," conceded an accountant who recently moved from a home office to a downtown site. "The distractions are ever-present and the will to submit to them is strong."

SETTING UP THE BUSINESS

"Finding the location and office site is just the first step," warns one veteran accountant. "Once that's accomplished it's bound to take another two to three months before you can even open your door."

The numerous details of building a new business—legalizing the lease, purchasing office supplies and furniture, creating attractive decor, hiring an office assistant, and sending out announcements—are bound to overwhelm the beginner. Attention to details at the outset can save time later on when the main concern is professional service, and the time spent setting up a business gives the accountant an excellent opportunity to flex managerial muscles. All talents must come into play: individual judgment, intelligent buying, skillful negotiation, and wise application of funds. Well used, these attributes can help to ensure the quality of the new business.

LANDLORDS AND LEASES

Negotiation of a lease for office space is usually the accountant's first priority. Striking an equitable agreement on lease terms, costs, and optional provisions takes a bit of bargaining, and those unfamiliar with these documents should keep in close touch with their attorneys. The basic "bone of contention" is the rent. Is it consistent with the area and/or building norms? Will the landlord allow a discount for leasehold improvements? What extra services are covered by rent? Who handles office maintenance, painting, and refuse collection?

Those experienced in negotiating lease arrangements often recommend that prospective lessees press landlords for the right to sublet and for the use of adjacent space for expansion. Lessees should also be aware of lease renewal terms, penalties for early termination, required deposits, total floor space, and exact areas of the building covered. Some accountants have been surprised to find that they are paying rent for hallways between offices and elevators.

SPACE REQUIREMENTS

The space needed can be gauged in relation to the number of persons who will be working there. A small business with two partner accountants, a receptionist/typist, and a junior staff assistant will generally require 800 to 1200 sq ft. This allows each partner a roomy office of 175 to 250 sq ft and leaves 200 to 300 sq ft for the staff and reception area, plus additional space for a library, files, duplicating equipment, and work surface for assembling reports and returns.

LAYOUT AND DESIGN

The professional office should be attractive, yet as functional as possible. The reception area, which generally measures approximately 100 to 150 sq ft, must provide visitors with comfortable seating—either cushioned chairs or a sofa—and because it most likely forms the potential client's first impression, it should reflect the accountant's taste and personality. Suitable art, plants, a table for professional publications, and perhaps a handsomely framed CPA certificate or diploma will give the waiting client a favorable picture of a professional even before introductions are made. Some accountants have found that an automatic coffee maker is a welcome addition.

Adjacent to the reception room, but preferably out of sight, is the work area. This space, 100 to 200 sq ft, contains files of client records, the staff assistant's desk, a photocopier, and shelves for reference books and other materials and supplies.

The professional's office is itself a matter of personal taste. Generally speaking, large desks of fine wood, carpeted floors, paneled walls, comfortable seating, and tastefully arranged personal objects are favored.

Adequate lighting in all office areas is highly conducive to good working conditions.

FURNITURE, SUPPLIES, AND EQUIPMENT

Furniture

An accurate projection of the requirements for furniture can be an involved task for the new practitioner. A systematic and realistic appraisal of each need and the specific item necessary to fill it is made in the following chart:

Furniture (New or Used)	Cost Range	
Desks (1 for the accountant, 1 for the office assistant)	400	$2000
Desk chairs (2)	150	400
Client chairs (1 for the waiting area, 1 for interviews)	300	600
Coffee table (for the waiting area)	150	350
Lamp (for the waiting area)	95	145
Bookcase (reference materials)	300	850
Locking file cabinet	225	500
Cabinet for supplies (closet will suffice)	200	450
Art/Pictures	300	800
Total	$2,120	$6,095

Accountants who have the available resources can, of course, spend thousands of dollars on furnishings and decoration. Commonly, however, the new accountant's cash reserve is thin, and those who have "been there" advise tyros not to go overboard. Local newspaper advertisements, garage sales, and weekend flea markets often yield attractive bargains. In some areas repossession warehouses do a thriving business in nearly new furniture at considerable savings, and office-furniture leasing companies offer good values in used furniture that is in excellent condition.

Before shopping for new furnishings, accountants are advised to send for catalogs from supply houses that do mail-order business. Catalog shopping can save time and is a handy guide to average costs.

Supplies

Veterans suggest a check of the following list of supplies:

Postal Accessories

Large envelopes for tax returns

Mailing labels for large envelopes

Return address labels or stamper

Printed stationery (letterhead, billhead, envelopes)

Postcards

Postage stamps

Postage scale

Rubber stampers ("Taxpayer's Copy," "First Class Mail," "For Discussion Purposes Only," "See Attached Sheet," "Confidential")

Desk Supplies

Pencil sharpener
Scratch pads
Paper clips
Stapler/staples
Cellophane tape and dispenser
Scissors
Ruler
Rubber bands
File folders and stick-on labels
Loose-leaf binder
Punch (two- or three-hole) for binder sheets
Columnar sheets or cards for accounts receivable/work in process
Form for keeping track of long-distance and toll calls
Tax forms for IRS and various states
Adding machine or calculator tape
Carbon paper
Stamp pad
Desk blotter
Wastebaskets
Desk calendar
Three-prong adaptor for various office machines

Miscellaneous

Nameplate for office door
File trays (in-out, pending)

Index cards and file box

Yearbook for keeping track of time and appointments

Monthly time record sheets

Clock

Briefcase

Coffeepot and supplies

Experienced accountants also advise new practitioners to obtain as many forms and form letters as possible from other accountants to guide them in the design of engagement letters, time sheets, tax-return transmittal letters, audit programs, and routing slips.

Again, when shopping for furnishings, buying office supplies from mail-order houses is usually an easy way to obtain the necessities.

Equipment

The need for equipment in a small accounting practice is modest. In general, a typewriter, a pocket calculator, a tape-fed adding machine, a personal computer, and perhaps a photocopier are sufficient. The total cost of these items, excluding the personal computer, should not run more than $3000.

A personal computer is essential. Shop carefully for the computer after selecting your accounting software programs so that you will have the proper equipment capable of running your programs with the capacity for growth. A major decision will be whether to select an IBM and/or clone or MacIntosh. The overriding rationale would be to insure that the equipment will run your software. A dot-matrix printer and/or laser printer are also necessary. Shop carefully for your equipment, and keep service availability in mind. The total cost for the items above with the appropriate software should be in the $12,000 to $15,000 range.

A CHECKLIST FOR SETTING UP AN ACCOUNTING BUSINESS

Obtain Permits and Licenses

1. Certificate and license from the State Board of Accountancy.
2. Zoning permit from the local permit bureau if zoning for professional office is in doubt.
3. State, county, township, or city professional or occupational license, if required. Call municipal information.
4. Federal and state ID numbers for self and employees. For federal number, call the local (or regional) IRS office—Form SS-4; for the state, call the district office of the state tax department.

Establish Professional Relationships

1. National, state, and local professional organizations. Apply for membership.
2. Other CPAs or accountants in the building or neighborhood (good referral source).
3. Bank manager or loan officer. Open business checking and/or savings account. Use at least two banks for greater chance of referrals.
4. Insurance broker.
5. Attorney.
6. Service bureau representatives.

Handle Business Details

1. Malpractice insurance. Check with state CPA society for details.
2. Telephone and professional listing in the Yellow Pages. Utilities.
3. Local IRS office. Ask to be put on the practitioner's mailing list.
4. Business cards and announcements.
5. Professional business-magazine subscriptions (see further sources).

2

CPA . . .
TO BE OR NOT TO BE

Life is full of decisions. Some people meet those decisions with enthusiasm and anticipation; others try to avoid making choices. The avoiders fool only themselves, because a decision not taken is, in fact, a decision to do nothing.

If you hold a CPA certificate, all to the good. On the other hand, do not allow the lack of a certificate keep you from launching a successful accounting business.

The CPA certificate does not guarantee success. To build a business you must be hard-working and self-motivated. You must like working with people and be able to plan. You must enjoy selling and be able to make firm, no-nonsense decisions. You must have sufficient financial resources, and the desire to be a respected member of your community should be sincere.

An outside accountant retained by a company is usually more involved in its day-to-day operations and knows more about it than almost anyone except senior management. Unlike the company's outside lawyers, who, as a rule, are consulted only when a specific problem must be dealt with, the accountant is concerned with the company's business on a continuing basis.

Moreover, the accountant has access to internal financial data that are closely guarded by top management and is often privy to information that is given to no one else, not even the board of directors. William James, who wrote, "The greatest discovery of my generation is that men can alter their lives by altering their attitudes of mind."

Start to make your plans at once by making one of W. Clement Stone's favorite self-motivators, "Do it now!" your principle. Take a three-by-five card and write on it "Do it now!" Read these words aloud repeatedly. You'll be making use of the scientific principle that learning is reinforced when the senses are focused on a single task. See it, hear it, say it, but "Do it now!"

Keep the card with you for at least a week. Look at it before you go to bed and when you get up. Stick it on the mirror when you're shaving or brushing your teeth. Take it with you everywhere you go. Every time you touch the card repeat the words—aloud, if possible. Keep repeating the self-motivator until "Do it now!" pops into your head every time a job presents itself.

Are you willing now to devote the time and effort necessary to put your business life into high orbit? Are you willing to make use of the tested principles that have worked for others?

Remember, no decision is a decision not to act. Remember the self-motivator: "Do it now!" Take a pen and write in your notebook, "Business Plan for a Successful Accounting Business." This will be a visible sign of your commitment to adopt this planning system.

Do it now!

Congratulations! You've taken the first step to success.

OVERVIEW

This planning system provides the framework for your success. Like any structure, it must be built on sound foundations; therefore it is designed as a step-by-step process. First is a series of exercises that will help you to set your goals by taking stock of yourself, to discover how you see your physical self, to evaluate your risk-taking inclinations, your management strengths and weaknesses, and your entrepreneurial bent. In the next step you'll begin to think about priorities in your business and personal life.

You will then be ready to write down your goals, after which we will help you to build belief in your own ability to achieve these goals. Finally, step-by-step systems will help you to maximize your efforts and monitor your progress toward ultimate success.

YOUR PERSONAL INVENTORY

The Physical You

Psychiatrists tell us that every person carries a mental self-image. Often it is in conflict with reality.

EXERCISE 1

Stand in front of a full-length mirror and take a long, hard look at yourself. Turn sideways to the right and left and use a hand mirror to get a rear view.

Now pretend you're going to meet a stranger who will give you $1 million if he can identify you in a crowded room. In your notebook write a description of yourself for your benefactor. It must be so accurate that in no way could he ever mistake someone else for you and inadvertently give that person your money. Tell it like it is!

EXERCISE 2

Using a scale of 1 to 10 (10 is the best), rate yourself on the following items. Be as objective as you can.

General appearance ____   Smile ____
Neatness of clothing ____   Posture ____
Appropriateness of clothing ____   Weight-to-height ratio ____
Neatness of hair ____   Overall rating ____

EXERCISE 3

In your notebook write specific things about your physical appearance that you would like to change. Do you need to lose weight? Does your wardrobe need a lift?

Don't worry for now about how you can accomplish these goals. Just write down everything you'd like to improve.

The Inner You

Put the first section aside. We'll get back to it later. Now let's concentrate on exploring the inner you.

Psychologists tell us that most people never take the time and trouble to figure out who they are and what they want in life. Indeed, the world is full of people who hate their jobs because they stumbled into them.

How much are you willing to risk to become the architect of your self? This is a difficult and private question that only you can answer. To find out more about yourself as a risk taker omplete the following exercise.

EXERCISE 4. MY RISK-RATING INDEX

Write the letter that best reflects your attitude. If your choice is not clear-cut, write the letter that comes closer. Answer all questions.

1. When I play cards I like
   A. high stakes;
   B. penny ante.
2. When I go swimming I
   A. plunge in;
   B. test the water and then wade in.
3. If I were down to my last quarter I'd
   A. flip for double or nothing;
   B. save it to make a phone call.
4. When I'm driving I like to
   A. push the car to its limits;
   B. take it easy and get there.
5. I'd rather be
   A. a test pilot;
   B. an airline pilot.
6. I'd rather be a
   A. surgeon;
   B. dermatologist.
7. If I could I'd like to live my life
   A. in a new town every few years;
   B. in the same town always.
8. At an amusement park I'd rather ride in a
   A. roller coaster;
   B. ferris wheel.

9. I'd rather play
   A. blackjack;
   B. poker.
10. If a neatly dressed stranger asked to borrow $10 which he'd mail to me later, I'd
   A. give him the money;
   B. tell him to call Travelers Aid.
11. When making friendly bets I most often take the
   A. underdog;
   B. favorite.
12. I'd rather take a lesson in
   A. skydiving;
   B. flying
13. I'd rather travel by
   A. motorcycle;
   B. automobile.
14. If I could be an animal I'd be a
   A. wild stallion;
   B. racehorse.
15. If I could be a professional athlete I'd be a
   A. hockey player;
   B. speed skater.

Scoring

Give yourself one point for each (a) and zero for each (b). Add your total and enter the answer in your notebook.

Analysis

13–15. You're willing to take a high degree of risk in your life.
6–12. You're a moderate risk taker.

1–5. You tend to play it safe.

Risk is often a crucial element of success. When, however, it is not tempered with good judgment it is a liability. If you are willing to consider a high degree of risk take extra precautions before you leap.

If you are a moderate risk taker you are more likely to make sound, practical decisions when faced with risk.

ENTREPRENEURSHIP

For many people success means managing a business of their own. Nicholas Murray Butler, former president of Columbia University, referred to three types of person—doers, onlookers, and the uninterested. The doers are the few who make things happen; the onlookers are the many who watch things happen; the uninterested constitute the large majority who have no idea what is happening.

The entrepreneur, who plays a critical role in our society, is definitely the doer—a practical creator who makes things happen. Businesses, industries, cities, even nations take form largely because of the decisions made by individual entrepreneurs who turn ideas into realities.

EXERCISE 5

Take a few moments to think back to your childhood. Write a brief account of a successful entrepreneurial activity you engaged in as a youngster. Describe in detail what you did, how the project developed, and to what degree it was successful.

Now close your eyes and try to recreate in your mind your feelings when you completed the project. Did you feel exhilarated? Feel it again. Did you feel satisfied? Feel it again. Enjoy the moment once more by reliving it.

Not everyone is the entrepreneurial type. In fact, few of us are. The following exercise is designed to help you decide if you belong in that group.

EXERCISE 6. MY ENTREPRENEURIAL INVENTORY

Circle the letter opposite the statement that describes your attitude best:

1. (a) I'm comfortable retaining responsibility
   (b) I'm comfortable sharing responsibility.
2. (a) I like to use tried-and-true methods.
   (b) I like to be the first to try a new method.
3. (a) Most people need to have their work checked.
   (b) Most people can be trusted to do their jobs correctly.
4. (a) When I make a good decision I want full credit.
   (b) I'm happy if a subordinate gets credit for my decision.
5. (a) Top managers deserve the best offices and perks.
   (b) The best reward is the thrill of completing a project successfully.
6. (a) I like running an established concern in which we know what we're doing.
   (b) I like opening a new branch in which we write the rules as we go along.
7. (a) Management is a shared responsibility.
   (b) The buck stops with me.
8. (a) Most good ideas come from the same few places.
   (b) Good ideas are everywhere and I'll use them regardless of the source.
9. (a) Finding good people is our biggest problem.
   (b) Using people wisely is our greatest challenge.

10. (a) I like to stick to the prescribed routine.
    (b) I like to experiment to improve results.
11. (a) I like to bring my projects in on time.
    (b) I like to win the race and get done early.
12. (a) People create problems for the company.
    (b) Solve these problems and you'll solve the company's problems.
13. (a) It's better to be safe than sorry.
    (b) A turtle doesn't make any progress until it sticks its neck out.
14. (a) If I double my output I'll be earning much more.
    (b) If I double my output I'll be the top man in my division.
15. (a) Too much pressure will break a person.
    (b) If you can't stand the heat get out of the kitchen.

Add up your score.

(a): _____
(b): _____

Research indicates that successful entrepreneurs tend to rank high in the qualities presented in the (b) entries. How did you fare?

David McClelland of Harvard University concludes that certain characteristics are shared by successful entrepreneurs. Among them are a compelling need for personal achievement; a tendency to be conservative in games of chance but daring in games of skill; a strong self-confidence, almost to the point of overestimating the chances of doing well; an ability to thrive on the pressure of competition; a feeling that accomplishments are more important than power or belonging to the "right" groups.

Charlotte Taylor, who did research on successful entrepreneurs for the White House Task Force on Women in Business, lists some additional characteristics: physical stamina—the ability to work long and hard; a strong sense of responsibility; the emotional ability to handle worries, assume debts, and adjust to an irregular income; a strong desire to control one's own destiny; a sense of well-being and pleasure from making something out of nothing.

THE NEED FOR CHANGE

Many of us find ourselves in a dead-end situation or in a spot in which we're no longer comfortable. Change is required, but change is often difficult and we delay. After reading the material on entrepreneurs you may have decided that you lack what it takes. Don't be so sure. Remember your childhood experience as an entrepreneur? The reason for that exercise is important. Researchers have discovered that childhood activity is often a strong indicator of entrepreneurial ability. What often happens, however, is that we sublimate or bury this desire in our subconscious because we think we'll never have a chance to exercise it.

Of course, lack of entrepreneurial experience as a child does not rule out the possibility of entrepreneurial success as an adult. Other factors determine success as well and the greatest is desire.

You rank your priorities according to what you want most in life. If you want it badly enough you can get it.

3

THE SMALL BUSINESS MARKET . . . IT'S ALL AROUND YOU

The market potential for an accounting business is tremendous. Experience has demonstrated that the number of businesses closely follows population figures. Internal Revenue Service records show that approximately 17 million business tax returns are filed annually. This is almost one business tax return for every 13 people in the country.

Accountants have long wrestled with the question of what to do about the small business client. No one is taking proper care of the needs of small businesses—a major reason why so many fail. They lack adequate record keeping procedures and timely financial statements. Most small business owners take the attitude that they must keep records only because the government requires them for tax purposes. We know that this is the wrong reason.

Records should keep a business person informed of the financial situation at any given time—to warn of impending danger. With adequate records the business person can detect the trouble before an irreversible point is reached.

The provision of accounting services for small businesses presents a wonderful opportunity for those willing to satisfy the need. Visit any number of small businesses and you will learn quickly that most of them can boast little solid accounting assistance. Typically the owner's spouse handles the bookkeeping—or the owner does it—whenever there is time to get around to it. Low-cost accounting services are needed— obviously—and a virtually untapped market awaits the accountant entrepreneur.

We know, of course, what small businesses do not want. Large-scale financial statements aren't necessary, nor do small businesses require an outsider to write their checks. What they do need, first of all, is a monthly profit/loss statement. This report is a vital tool for determining ongoing financial and operating conditions. It is most important to provide percentages in all categories to ensure the clarity of the statement.

Also necessary is a balance sheet—a list of assets, liabilities, and net worth—to preclude the practice of making decisions based solely on how much cash is in the bank.

In addition, a detailed general ledger that itemizes all expenses listed in the operating statement is important. Bank reconciliation, payroll records, income-tax preparation, and occasional business consultation are also included in the accounting services required by small businesses.

The key to your success as an accountant is low cost. If you can offer your services at a price small businesses can afford, your earning power will be unlimited. Similarly, the higher fee structure of traditional CPAs opens vast possibilities for building a successful accounting business.

Financial services and the accounting profession are literally a wide open field. The need for talented people to provide essential information grows stronger every day. A career in accounting will offer almost everything you could be looking for in a business or your own. The compilation and analysis of financially related data to provide management with hard facts on which to base their decisions is one of the fastest growing fields in the contemporary business world.

Nothing can match the security of filling the ongoing requirements of small businesses at a greater depth of service and at a lower cost than can be found anywhere else.

What could be more gratifying personally than to become a valuable management consultant and financial advisor to a hundred or more independent business people who turn to you for your specialized services?

Purely and simply, accounting is a lucrative field. A recent Dun & Bradstreet study revealed that the average public accountant nets nearly half the total fees taken in.

As if those reasons weren't enough, consider the following facts as well. More than 17 million business tax returns are filed every year. The Small Business Administration has stated that 48% of the nation's small businesses are struggling along without professional bookkeeping services. Among the remaining 52%, how many employ really competent financial consultants—at an affordable price?

Numerous government studies have pointed to financial mismanagement as the most pervasive reason for small-business failure. Accordingly, managers of small to medium-sized businesses are keenly aware of the need for accurate and timely financial data, and all indicators show that the demand for this information will increase sharply in the years ahead.

You can be the one to fill this ever-growing demand in your area.

You will be able to design a total system based on your client's unique requirements. You will start with an analysis of the new client's financial data. You will decide what raw information should be made available to you each month in a form that is as uncomplicated as possible. That raw information will be prepared by you for computer processing. Once it has been processed, the finished reports will be returned to you for review. You will then deliver them to your client. When your business becomes large enough to justify the fixed expense of a computer of your own, the system will be carried out completely in-house.

The programs you will offer are extremely flexible and adapt readily to virtually any kind of small business. They're designed to arrange accepted, double-entry accounting information into easy-to-comprehend, management-oriented financial reports that the small business person can use to enhance the profitability of the operation.

In short, you will be offering a total financial systems-control package tailored exclusively to the needs of each of your clients. From the time you approach a prospective client until you deliver the tax reports at the end of the first quarter, you will have everything mapped out for you. Because our system minimizes your clerical work, you will be able to invest your time in the more profitable areas of counseling and adding to your list of clients.

The internal procedures outlined in this book are streamlined to enable you, with the help of a single clerk, to bill approximately $9,000 to $11,000 in write-up work each month. When you figure processing costs of less than 20%, you've got what amounts to a very profitable and rewarding operation.

MICROCOMPUTER CONSULTANT

Assisting clients in automating or upgrading their accounting systems is a high-growth field, and accountants are increasingly finding that it can provide a new market for their services. There is no doubt that there is a growing demand for "computer literate" accountants who can provide advice about automating small business accounting systems and, in particular, help clients to select and apply appropriate accounting software.

The market for accountant microcomputer consulting consists primarily of small businesses that need to computerize to compete. They realize that now is the time to automate their in-house accounting procedures or to replace their existing accounting software and hardware.

The estimated size of this market varies. According to the United States Bureau of Labor Statistics, there are 17 million businesses in the United States, 98% of which are small (under 100 employees). More than one million new businesses start up each year.

Of the small businesses that would benefit from being computerized, 90% have not done so. In addition, according to Future Computing, the office software market is growing at a rate of 22% per year. Accounting software represents 31% of the total office software market and is expected to grow by 22% per year.

To add to this market, there are many small businesses that need to replace their existing hardware and software. Clients who are upgrading their computerized systems are more receptive to your firm and services. They understand that choosing and installing a computer system requires professional service and an investment of time and money.

It is a given that the accountant has a comprehensive knowledge of accounting and of the client's business. But where do you go to become knowledgeable about hardware and software?

SELECTING HARDWARE

First (and most difficult) is hardware. It would be best to tell you where not to go, or who not to rely on.

You should not rely on the manufacturer's telephone-based technical support service (you frequently cannot get through over the telephone) or the average computer retail store.

You need a basic knowledge of the hardware yourself. Fortunately, this basic knowledge is not hard to come by. Classes are available for accountants to learn hardware. In addition, knowledge can be gathered from experience with your own computer system.

Get to know a dealer—a good one. Work out arrangements for the dealer to fully install the hardware. Also, make certain that the dealer has the ability to have everything working on site before you go to your clients to install the software. Protect yourself in an engagement letter to the client in which you state that the hardware is not your responsibility. Keep one thing in mind. When something goes wrong, hardware people frequently blame software people and vice versa. This is one major reason for supplying both the hardware and software.

SELECTING SOFTWARE

Getting to know accounting software is easier—you are trained for it. Added to this is the fact that many of the software publishers are courting your business—as dealers, consultants, advisors or installers.

Accounting software publishers understand that this market belongs to the accountant, or at least to the aggressive accountant. To attract this market, they offer accountants low-price software and usually excellent support via separate accountant, or dealer, phone lines. Training which ordinarily qualifies for continuing education credits is also available.

No less than two—and no more than four—accounting packages should be selected for support by your firm. Two packages give you some flexibility. Learning more than four packages (and keeping up with their updates) would be too time-consuming.

When selecting accounting software packages, you should keep a few pointers in mind:

Ask the publisher questions. How long have you been in business? What is your research and development policy? How often do you release updates? What is your policy on selling updates? What is your installed base?

Always be open to investigate new accounting packages.

Make sure the publisher's telephone support is accurate and timely. There is nothing worse than being at a client's office when an error message occurs, and then placing a call to support, only to wait several hours—or days—for an answer.

Select software that best matches the industry of the majority of your clients. For example, one package would be fine for manufacturing, while another would be better for retailing. Therefore, if a large portion of your client base is in manufacturing, you should support software that targets manufacturing. Also, specific software for types of industry make additional strong points for supporting several different accounting packages.

Concentrate on "high-end" accounting packages (packages retailing for $500 or more per module). There are two reasons for this. First, if clients do not want to spend more than $500 to $1,000 for software, then they would probably not want to pay for your installation and training fees. Second, you must emphasize that the cost of computerized accounting is not the hardware and software. It is the investment that management makes in time for the conversion and training.

Further, there could be another cost, a hidden one that is hard to quantify. Lower-end accounting packages will be sparse on management reports. For example, some higher-end packages will produce reports on inventory turn by item or group of items; gross profit by inventory item and by customer; the number of times a customer has been charged finance charges; amount of payable discounts taken and discounts loss, and so on. Lack of this information can be costly to management.

Other features are also factored into the cost of the system, such as the speed, ease of use and flexibility of the software.

Specialized software is also available that can help you to select appropriate accounting software for clients. There are several programs that quantitatively match the attributes of many accounting programs to your or your client's needs. One is *A Guide to Accounting Software for Microcomputers*, available from Computer Training Services, Inc. Contact Sheldon Needle, 5900 Tudor Lane, Rockville, Maryland 20852 (301) 468-4800.

The product asks a series of questions regarding the features desired in a software product. These requirements are weighted by importance and compared with all or a selected group of software. A report is produced quantitatively showing which software meets the specified requirements.

The *Guide to Accounting Software* analyzes the top 18 accounting software packages, both through a written review and a Lotus template.

Another avenue to consider for acquiring knowledge is to get involved in a computer user group, as well as in professional organizations or committees that deal with microcomputers. Most state CPA and public accounting societies have microcomputer user groups and committees.

After you are comfortable with the hardware (and support of the hardware) and have made your software selection, you should consider establishing your firm as a dealer to buy wholesale. Most of the time all you need is a resale certificate.

Buying wholesale enables easier entry into the accounting software market by packaging your services in the cost of software and hardware. This is important. The business microcomputer market appears price sensitive. Having the "CPA" after your name may help, but so does the bottom line. Since small businesses are becoming more competitive and are monitoring their costs, you need to come close in cost to your competitors.

Currently your competitors are largely the retail stores. The smart retailer is hiring your expertise to help their sales staff sell accounting software, and some retailers are joining forces with accounting firms. The remaining retailers are trying to sell and support accounting software without the assistance of an accountant.

Buying wholesale, however, and marking up the product to your client is a controversial area. Many believe that the practice is acceptable if it is fully disclosed to the client. In addition, you can explain that your billable time is in the gross profit of the software and the hardware.

If your firm is still uncomfortable being a "retailer," there are two alternatives. First, a firm could offer the software to its clients at their cost and charge for the time involved.

The other avenue is to participate in the varous accountant programs offered by software publishers. Since they understand that some accountants are uneasy about selling the software, they offer training and support for their product without requiring the accountant is sign up as a dealer. The publisher will also give the accountant leads generated for postsales support or requests from other retailers for support.

When it's time to start marketing your microcomputer services, you should begin by focusing on what you know best—accounting. Do not try to be an expert on hardware issues. Focus on your knowledge of accounting and accounting software. Be sure that you know your products.

Your first target market should be your easiest—your existing client base. Undoubtedly within your practice are clients that need to computerize their accounting systems, to bring their systems in-house (and thereby give managers better control over both financial and managerial reports), or to update their systems.

In addition, hardware sales can be directed to a retailer you feel comfortable with. These referrals from you can assist in receiving future referrals from the retailers.

However, using computer retailers for referrals can be tricky. On the one hand, they can produce viable and fast leads. Retailers need your expertise to give them more credibility when they talk about accounting software.

On the other hand, there can be drawbacks. The retailer referral market has already been exploited by accountants and other consultants. Retailers can only recommend a few accounting firms. In addition, the retailer could possibly view you as a competitor, especially if you provide hardware and software on a retail basis.

When working with a dealer, discuss and put in writing the exact relationship you will have. Who sells what? Who supports what? What should you do if, after a few months, the client wants to purchase additional software or hardware?

There are other ways to market your firm. These include seminars on "computerizing your accounting department," direct mail, yellow-page ads under "Computer Dealers" or "Computers: Software," and newspaper ads.

Direct mailings should always be followed by phone calls. Newspaper ads must be consistent and run often. It is much better to run a smaller ad 10 times than a large ad once. Also, do not expect wonders overnight. You are not selling a TV at the lowest price, but a service. Sometimes publishers will assist in the cost of advertising with co-operative programs.

The marketers are right when they state: "The best advertising is free advertising." Every effort should be made to get information about your firm published. Start with local newspapers and publications and work up to national coverage.

Word of mouth is also invaluable. Once an installation is complete with a satisfied client, ask for a letter of recommendation. Also ask the client as to whether they know of any other businesses that could profit from your service.

First and foremost, make sure that your client needs accounting software. It is true that most businesses can benefit from computerization, but are they ready? Some businesses cannot accept the technology, different responsibilities and job functions as well as the increase in work load.

Yes, there is an increase in the work load. The client needs to realize that for the first 6 to 12 months there will be an additional time commitment in the accounting function. In fact, as mentioned before, the cost of automating the accounting department doesn't involve just the cost of the hardware and software. There is a large cost in training personnel and inefficiencies involved when learning a new system of internal control. The return on this time and money investment comes through more timely and meaningful reports.

Before any accounting software package can be recommended, a needs analysis should be performed. Along with this, you should get a feel for the wants and desires of the client and how competent the staff is. Ask key questions such as:

Why do you want to computerize?

What reports would you like to see generated?

What benefits do you expect to result from an automated accounting system?

Many times you will find that client expectations are far greater than what the software and hardware can provide.

Before you attempt an installation and the training of the client's staff, it bears repeating that you must know your products. Study (yes, study) the software manuals and use the full running demo disk or the on-line tutorial. In fact, you might want to first use the software in your own firm for keeping your books and for your client write-up work.

Attend training either in town or at the publisher's location. Going to the publisher costs extra but allows you the opportunity to meet the staff involved with the software and shows the publisher your interest.

You will not make money on your first installation. In fact, you will probably lose money. There will be too much time involved. Keep in mind that what should go wrong won't, what couldn't go wrong will, and what doesn't even exist will give you an error.

Moreover, take your estimated time to convert to the new accounting system and triple it. Be prepared for an extended client learning curve.

Always use an engagement letter, mainly to avoid misunderstandings. Be very detailed on exactly what you are providing to avoid conflicts between software and hardware responsibilities.

The engagement letter should also state that payment for the hardware and software is due upon receipt and state the maximum time of training before additional charges occur. Charges for telephone support should also be dealt with.

Installation problems will occur that you will be unable to answer. Do not be afraid to ask for help, either from the software publisher or hardware manufacturer or distributor or a local "expert" that you know.

When the installation and training are finally complete, the client will still have a learning curve. Your firm will not appear to be a "hero" overnight. The new system needs time to integrate into the client's organization. However, once integration has been accomplished you should have a satisfied client and a good referral. You are now on your way to offer your newly acquired microcomputer expertise to other eager clients.

"In the future, CPAs can expect that virtually every activity will require computers. . .Computer literacy and the ability to use computers as tools are emerging as basic to the accounting profession." This quote, from a report title *A Look Ahead:*

Trends for Colorado CPAs for the '90s (published by the Colorado Society of CPAs), should have great impact on you and your firm. It is mandatory for the accountant to become efficient with microcomputers.

Expertise in this field can lead to increased revenue through a microcomputer consulting practice. There is a need for this expertise. As you complete installations and training, you and your staff will gain not only knowledge but confidence. Word will circulate about your ability. Revenues and profits from your newly formed microcomputer specialty will expand, and rightly so—you are providing your client with an invaluable management tool.

4

ESTABLISHING AND DEVELOPING THE BUSINESS PLAN

The careful preparation of a business plan represents a unique opportunity for the accountant to consider all phases of the new venture, to examine the consequences of different marketing, production, and financing strategies, and to determine what human and financial resources are required to launch and develop a business. All of this can be done on paper without the expense of an actual trial-and-error operation.

The business plan may be the only one on which to depend in the early months of a new business. One successful accountant told of using his business plan to guide his initial activities; he then updated it as his business developed. He also found the plan invaluable as a guide to obtaining bank credit. He added that once his business got going he lacked the time to plan activities and examine alternative strategies that he had had when he devised his business plan.

SOME DO'S AND DON'TS

Before delving into the details of what a business plan should contain, some important general do's and don'ts are worth keeping in mind as you read the guidelines and begin to write your own plan. These do's and don'ts are based on personal reactions to a great many business plans.

1. Do keep the plan as short as you can without compromising the description of your business and its potential.
2. Don't overdiversify your business. A new or young business will not have the depth of management to pursue a number of opportunities.
3. Don't have mysterious, unnamed people on your management team.
4. Don't describe technical products or processes in jargon that only an expert can understand.
5. Don't estimate your sales on what you can or would like to produce. Do estimate carefully your potential sales and from them determine the production facility you need.
6. Don't make ambiguous, vague, or unsubstantiated statements. They will make you look like a shallow and fuzzy thinker. For example, don't say merely that your markets are growing rapidly; determine and delineate past, present, and projected growth rates and market sizes.
7. Do disclose and discuss any current or potential problems in your business. If you fail in this your credibility will be badly damaged.

STEPS TO STARTING A BUSINESS

Each year in the United States more than 500,000 new businesses are launched by entrepreneurs eager to express their own ideas, to make their own decisions—to be the "boss." Each one hopes to achieve a better life-style, income, or community status—perhaps even amass a fortune.

The reality of business life is somewhat harsher. More than half the businesses that failed in 1989 did so in their first five years of operation. Survival is especially tough in today's roller-coaster economy, in which the small business is beset on all sides by fluctuating money conditions, rising costs, uncertain supply sources, and erratic markets. The new owner could lose everything—family car, life savings, even a home.

Then, too, owning a business, even a profitable one, is not so idyllic as it may seem. Being a boss is confining in a way that working for others is not. Far from being freer, the head of a business often works 15 hours a day, seven days a week, and is responsible to family, suppliers, customers, and employees. Gone are the days of the regular paycheck, 40-hour work week, paid vacations, retirement security, and reduced costs of life and health insurance.

Yet managing one's own business can be a personally and financially rewarding experience for an individual strong enough to meet the test. One with stamina, maturity, and creativity who is willing to make sacrifices may find making a go of a struggling enterprise an exhilarating challenge.

Your business plan should describe, in words and numbers, the proposed business and its products and services. It should also include an analysis of the market, a marketing strategy, an organizational plan, and measurable financial objectives. The plan will be used by prospective lenders and investors to evaluate your potential for success, and by you in a constant assessment of the strength of your operation.

The accountant must ask: What do I offer the marketplace? What does the marketplace offer me? What can I do to reach and adapt to this marketplace?

The nature of your products and services must be defined. What makes them better than others already on the market?

The market must be mapped out and described. Is there evidence of a need for the prospective products and services? Is the primary market a certain type of business of a certain age, sales level, or geographic area? Is the timing right?

The competition must be counted. Who and where are the competitors? How does the proposed business measure up to those now in existence? Is it of higher quality or lower cost? What are the marketable differences?

A thorough market study provides the best means of answering these questions. A rudimentary marketing study can be developed by securing information from newspapers, trade journals and associations, chambers of commerce, bank or utility companies, libraries, federal agencies, local universities or state colleges, and city, county, and state planning commissions.

Next, the expenses for setting up shop must be accurately computed. Insufficient financing is a major cause of small-business failure. Adequate funding must allow for the following expenses:

Down payment on the purchase of or deposit on the lease for business premises.

Fixture or remodeling costs.

Purchase or lease of needed equipment.

Telephone and utility installation fees.

Stationery and supply costs.

Taxes and licenses.

Professional services (attorney, consultant).

Advertising and promotion.

Insurance premiums.

Travel and dues.

Along with opening costs, such operating expenses as owner's draw and employees' wages must be covered until the business shows a profit. Because many enterprises take months to operate in the black, at the very least enough funds should be available to cover the first three months of operation and provide a cash reserve for emergencies.

To allow the plan to become a working tool all monthly income and expenses should be estimated for at least the first year. Without realistic projections to follow, rough periods that could have been predicted become crises that cause a new business to fail.

The projected operating statement will show the following:

Predicted sales volume and the rate at which it will expand.

How much it will cost to produce the services to be sold.

Fixed monthly operating expenses, including rent, utilities, and insurance premiums.

Controllable monthly operating expenses, such as advertising, salaries, and professional services.

Next the accountant can bring this on-paper profit and loss closer to reality by developing a cash-flow projection to forecast an actual cash surplus or deficit for each period.

During the first year of business, in a time of sharp expansion, or whenever finances require close scrutiny, these financial projections should be recorded and monitored monthly. Later, and during stable business periods, quarterly or annual profit-and-loss and cash-flow statements may be sufficient to keep management ahead of the action.

Planning need not be a guessing game. To arrive at realistic projection figures the business manager should consult trade associations, trade publications, suppliers, and other sources of information to determine the appropriate standards of efficiency for the type and size of business. Operating ratios common to various businesses are published by the National Cash Register Company (Expenses in Retail Business), The Robert Morris Associates (Annual Statement Studies), and Dun & Bradstreet, Inc. (Key Business Ratios).

The history of small-business failures reveals that many firms fail not from lack of capital or external economic forces but from the cummulative effects of substandard performance and ongoing cost leaks due to poor management.

To help choose among the options the business owner considers return on investment. Will the rate of return on the money invested in the business be greater than the rate of return on the same money invested elsewhere? Financial professionals consider return on investment (ROI ratio) a criterion of profitability, often the key measure of management efficiency. The ratio determined by dividing net profits (before income taxes) for a certain period by net worth at the end of the period is expressed as a percentage:

$$\frac{\text{net profit (before taxes)}}{\text{net worth}} = \frac{\$10,000}{\$40,000} = 25\%$$

Generally a ratio of 14 to 25% is a desirable return on investment and growth. If the return is too low, the money could be used better elsewhere. Robert Morris Associates also provide return-on-investment figures—yardsticks for determining the potential of a business in light of the performance of an industry.

The business operator with a realistic plan has the best chance of success. Decisions regarding financing and legal organization should be made only after every operating function of the proposed enterprise has been appraised.

ANNUAL WORK PLAN AND CASH FLOW PROJECTION

Make a step-by-step analysis of your situation and establish your goals. How much income do you want three years from now? How much leisure time do you want three years from now? Then work backward to establish intermediate goals for the second and first year. Reserve time in the first year for public relations to get your name known and to build a reputation in your community as a professional business counselor.

After setting your annual goals, plan intermediate objectives month-by-month and measure your progress day-by-day, using the working tools described in the following paragraphs.

Accountants who expect to be successful and credible as business counselors must regard their practices as profit-making businesses in the same way as they regard the business activities of their clients. You must establish goals and determine the steps necessary to meet them. You must review your cash-flow requirements to ensure that you are adequately capitalized to conduct your business until it yields the desired profit. The process requires analysis in three parts.

Part I—Development of Sales Objectives

1. Determine your minimum personal income requirements for the next 12 months.
2. Reduce them by the amount of capital set aside to meet personal expenses during that period.
3. Make provision for income and self-employment taxes.
4. The result is the net cash required from your business over the next 12 months.

5. Add expenses: estimated support fees, estimated business expenses, and repayment of debt. Include the increase or decrease in accounts receivable anticipated during the 12 months. This will affect the net available from sales income. Examine your accounts-receivable experience and planned credit policy for the year.

6. The result is the gross profit required for the year.

7. Compute gross sales. For estimating purposes assume that your gross profit will be 70% of gross sales, which will include annual fees, initial set-up charges, additional tax preparation charges, and charges for the preparation of financial statements, loan applications, and other one-time billings. Then divide gross profit by 0.70 to obtain the gross sales figure.

Part II—Develop a Work Plan

Directions follow that will enable you to complete the form in Exhibit 3 and devise an effective annual work plan.

8. Divide the required annual gross sales figure by the average charge per client, including annual fees and additional charges, to find the number of clients needed to achieve the desired gross sales goal.

9. Multiply the average number of presentations required to make a sale by the desired number of clients to obtain the number of presentations that must be made during the year. By keeping careful statistics the accountant will quickly determine the number of presentations that must be made

ANNUAL WORK PLAN AND CASH FLOW PROJECTION

1. Required net personal income
   for next 12 months. $_____

2. Less available resources planned
   for use.   _____
                                                                    $_____

3. Plus total income taxes   _____
        self-employment taxes   _____
                                                                    _____

4. Net cash flow required   _____

5. Plus estimated support fee   _____

   business expenses   _____

   debt payments   _____

   increase or (decrease)
   in Accounts Receivable   _____
                                                                    _____

6. Gross profit   _____

7. Required annual gross sales $\dfrac{\text{gross profit}}{0.70}$ $_____

8. Required annual gross sales $_____ + average

   revenue per client $_____ = number of clients

   _____ .

9. Number of clients _____ × average contacts

   per close _____ = number of presentations _____ .

Exhibit 3. Annual Work Plan

73

10. Number of presentations _____ × average contacts

    per presentation _____ = number of contacts _____.

11. Number of contacts _____ ÷ 46 productive weeks = contacts

    per week _____.

12. To achieve my required net income my time must be split:

Number of hours of servicing per week   _____

Number of hours of prospecting   _____

Number of hours of presentation   _____

Number of hours of travel time   _____

Number of hours of administration and office work   _____

Exhibit 3. (Continued)

per sale. In the absence of experience statistics use five presentations per sale.

10. Multiply the number of presentations by the average number of contacts per presentation to obtain the number of personal and telephone contacts that must be made for each sale anticipated. In the absence of experience statistics use five contacts to secure one presentation.

11. Assume 30 working days or six weeks for attending meetings and seminars, vacations, illness, and similar nonbillable time, 46 work weeks remain. Divide the number of contacts by 46 to find the number of contacts per week required to achieve sales goals.

12. Now time must be budgeted to service all clients properly; time must also be reserved for prospecting and selling, for administrative and office work, and for professional development.

Part III—Cash Flow Projection

The Annual Work Plan is completed and the number of client sales and required gross income have been established. In the next step these figures are projected on a month-to-month basis over the year to determine the adequacy of sales and resulting cash flow.

1. Estimate the number of sales you can make in each month; 2/week, 1–1½/week, 1/week. Be realistic.

2. Estimate the average annual fee based on your business plan. For illustration purposes use $950.

3. Experience indicates that payments are divided equally: one-third of the clients pay in advance; one-third pay one-third down with the balance spread over three months; and one-third pay one-third down with the balance spread over 10 months. Thus monthly billing is required. Project the cash received in your first month and carry the receivables into the second and succeeding months. Repeat this procedure for each succeeding month. Total the cash receipts from service agreements in each month and add the monthly cash receipts projected for other services, such as consulting or loan applications.

4. If separate initial set-up charges are made they should be added to fees for supplemental services at the bottom of the cash-flow projection form.

5. Subject your estimated support fees and business expenses to arrive at your net profit before taxes. Revise this cash flow from time to time but not sooner than every six months.

Work Plan Statistics

Organize your time carefully to achieve your income and public relations goals. The sales funnel shows that for every 10 personal contacts you will conduct two sales interviews and for every 10 interviews you should make two sales. To record planned and actual activities you must take the following steps:

Account Daily Call Schedule

1. This schedule is used to record daily activities such as telephone calls, sales presentations, direct mail sent, and sales.

Time and Charges Work Sheet

2. This work sheet is used to record the time and costs incurred for each client. It is a management aid on which you can base future charges and review activities.

Success requires sales knowledge and ability, product knowledge, and motivation. Most of all it needs a defined goal and a work plan.

5

BUSINESS VERSUS PRACTICE

You have now been thoroughly versed in one of the most important phases of successful entrepreneurship—effective, realistic goal setting. The effort may not have been so difficult as you anticipated. This rapid simulation of the process has demonstrated its fundamentals:

1. Setting goals.
2. Establishing priorities.
3. Identifying actions and obstacles.
4. Setting action steps.

WHAT DOES IT TAKE?

Make no mistake—goal setting and planning are a difficult, demanding, and time-consuming process. If you have not done it in a thorough manner you may find it a somewhat agonizing, although rewarding, experience. Few people are effective goal setters. Perhaps fewer then 10% have ever committed their goals to paper. Perhaps fewer than 50% of the adults you know do even mental goal setting and much of that may be labeled speculative thinking or fantasizing.

Effective goal setting demands four critical personal requirements:

1. Your time.
2. Self-discipline.
3. Commitment and dedication to it.
4. Practice and development of the habit.

More important, it can and must be mastered for entrepreneurial success.

STEPS TO EFFECTIVE GOAL SETTING

The goals set by successful entrepreneurs are neither the product of wishful thinking nor mere predictions of the future. Goals are far more concrete and specific—they are decisions or choices. Goal setting is a process by which uncertainties are controlled and risks are minimized. It is a process by which you decide where you want to go, how fast, how to get there, and what to do along the way. It also defines performance as a means of determining progress.

Goals properly set to chart your course must be carefully defined. Proper goals should meet the following criteria:

1. Goals must be specific and concrete rather than abstract and out of focus.

2. Goals must be measurable.

3. Goals must be related to time; that is, they must establish what will be accomplished over a certain period.

4. Goals must be realistic and attainable. Meeting the first three criteria is not enough; goals must be a challenge as well.

Once set, goals should not become static targets. Goal setting is not a task but a process, a way of dealing with the world. A number of distinct steps are involved, steps that must be repeated as conditions change.

Step 1. Establish your goals. (They must be specific, measurable, time-related, and attainable.)

Step 2. Establish priorities (from most to least important goals and action steps); identify potential goal conflicts and tradeoffs and how they can be resolved.

Step 3. Identify potential problems and obstacles that could prevent you from attaining your goals.

Step 4. Specify the tasks and action steps that must be performed to accomplish your goals.

Step 5. Indicate how you will measure the results you hope to achieve.

Step 6. Establish milestones for reviewing the progress you are making; for example, specific dates on your calendar.

Step 7. Identify the risks that are involved in meeting your goals and what must be done to avoid low chances of success.

Step 8. Identify and seek the help and resources that may be needed to obtain your goals.

Step 9. Review progress periodically and revise goals and plans as feedback and results indicate that revision is appropriate.

These are the basic components of effective goal setting. Of course, there are numerous ways of actually going about it. Research and practical experience have shown that these elements are common to almost all successful planning efforts. Become familiar with the process, adapt it to your needs as individually suitable and begin to practice the approach. It is by effective goal setting that the lessons learned will be translated into action, and only effective goal setting can produce a plan likely to produce a successful business.

PUTTING YOUR PLAN INTO ACTION

When your plan is as near on target as you can make it you will be ready to put it into action. Keep in mind that action is the difference between a plan and a vision. If a plan is not activated it is of no more value than a daydream that evaporates over the breakfast coffee.

A successful owner-manager does not stop after information has been gathered and a plan has been drawn up, as you have done in working through this material. You must begin to use your plan.

At this point look back over your plan. Look for things that must be done to put your plan into action. What is essential will depend on your situation; for example, if your business plan calls for an increase in sales, funds must be provided for expansion.

Once you put your plan into action look out for changes. They can cripple the best made business plan if the owner-manager lets them. Stay on top of changing conditions and adjust your business plan accordingly.

Sometimes the change is within your company; for example, several of your employees have resigned. Sometimes the change is in your customers; for example, their desires and tastes have shifted. Sometimes it is technological—when a new computer is put on the market to introduce new processes and procedures.

To make an adjustment in your plan to account for these changes consider the following:

1. Be alert to the changes that come about in your business, your market, and your customers.
2. Check your plan against these changes.
3. Determine what revisions, if any, are needed in the plan.

The method you use to keep your plan up to date to allow your business to weather the forces in the market place is up to you. Read the trade papers and magazines. Another suggestion concerns your time. Set some time–two or three hours or whatever is necessary periodically—to review your plan. Once a month, or every other month, go over it to see whether it needs adjusting. If revisions are needed make them and put them into action.

WHEN TO "FIRE" A CLIENT

One technique for upgrading an accounting practice is often overlooked—the elimination of undesirable clients. Painful though the process may be—and it is often painful even to contemplate—there are strong professional reasons for getting rid of such clients.

1. To protect a firm's reputation;
2. To minimize the problems of client relations;
3. To improve profitability.

Accountants who analyze their client relations often discover that most of the trouble stems from only a few accounts. A client

NAME OF CLIENT _____

PARTNER/EVALUATOR _____

DATE _____

Circle Only One Number

CLIENT'S INFORMATION

-2 Hopeless or always late
2 Scattered but workable
4 Client needs training
6 Good
8 Excellent

CLIENT'S POTENTIAL

-5 Terminating
-2 Decreasing
2 Level
8 Growing
15 Unlimited potential

COLLECTION OF FEES

-5 May never receive
-2 Always 90 days late
5 Pays within 45 days
10 Pays on receipt of bill

FEE STRUCTURE

-5 Always complains—too high
-2 Requires time and bill itemized
5 Usually accepts amount of bill
10 Wants service and will pay for it
15 Thinks we're the greatest— pays premium

CLIENT'S SELF-INDULGENCE

1 Spendthrift with self and family
2 Cheap
3 Frugal and economical
4 Liberal
5 Controlled first class

CLIENT'S ATTITUDE TOWARD OUR STAFF

1 Hostile
2 Lukewarm
3 Client wants a friend
4 Client is polite and businesslike

CLIENT'S ATTITUDE TOWARD IRS
1 Neurotic
2 Hostile
5 Apathetic
8 Wants things right

CLIENT NEEDS
2 Bookkeeping
5 Unaudited reports
10 Certified reports
12 Special services—estate, systems
15 "Big League"—unlimited future

CLIENT BEATS DRUM FOR US
-2 Never
1 Would if could
2 Not recently
5 At times
10 Every opportunity

CLIENT WANTS
1 Minimum service (low fee)
2 Security from IRS
3 Counseling
4 Timely service
5 Direction and tax planning

LIABILITY EXPOSURE
-20 Good chance of loss
-5 Possible
2 Not likely
5 Almost impossible

Scoring: Maximum = 100 points
Minimum = -33 points

Action: Below 30 points = Drop client
30 to 50 points = evaluate in 90 days (on trial)
50 to 70 points = make an attempt to upgrade client
Above 70 points = Retain client

Exhibit 4. Client Evaluation Form

who is difficult to get along with will usually take more than a fair share of the accountant's time. The time spent is often unbillable and detracts from the attention that could be given other clients. In addition, unnecessary client relations problems can pollute the overall climate of the practice.

Each business must develop its own criteria for evaluating and rating clients and for deciding what action to take with regard to those who have the lowest ratings. These criteria center on four areas:

1. The type and quality of the service required by the client.
2. The client's attitude toward accountants and their work.
3. The client's potential for growth.
4. The fees received from the client.

The client evaluation form shown (Exhibit 4) features a weighted scale for all rating categories. Positive or negative points are awarded, depending on the nature of the items and their effect on an accounting practice. Of course, a firm can add to, delete, or revise these categories to fit its own needs and goals.

One method of instituting an evaluation program requires all in-charge staff members to fill out an evaluation form annually or as a regular part of each major engagement. This is only the first step, however. Because the usefulness of the client evaluation process depends in the end on taking appropriate action, the program should be planned to its culmination. In other words, you must face the fact that some clients may have to be fired. Although it is an unpleasant prospect, "firing" a client is often important to a healthy growing business that intends to go on providing quality service to its desirable clients.

Many firms destroy the evaluation form after it has been filled in and appropriate action has been taken. There are at least two reasons for this: (1) the frank comments on the form might be embarrassing if the client saw it; (2) if a question of legal liability arises—quite possible with marginal clients—the form could be obtained by the plaintiff's attorney (through the discovery process) to the detriment of the accountant's defense.

6

THE ACCOUNTING FACTORY

Management is the "act, art or manner of managing, or handling, controlling, directing"; management is the function that establishes goals, creates a system to reach those goals, and controls the workings of that system.

The goal of the accountant should be maximum profits. This end is achieved by twin systems: (1) obtaining as many accounts as possible and (2) performing the best services for the least cost. Therefore, it is necessary for the accountant to acquire and retain clients. The way to this lies in setting up the business to handle all the client work in a standardized, routine, and cost-efficient manner.

RECRUITING AND MANAGING THE STAFF

In the early stages the accountant will gain valuable first-hand experience by doing all the processing. This is important because you must be proficient in training a staff.

During the interview, make note of the clarity and tone of voice because the new clerk will be expected to deal with clients by phone on a daily basis. An outgoing personality, of course, goes without saying.

It is good policy to check work history and references methodically. It is not good policy to hire on the first meeting. After an ample number of applicants have been interviewed, a second meeting should be arranged before a choice is made. At this particular interview, responsibilities and wages should be discussed, and, if all is in agreement, a starting date set.

When the recruit starts, all necessary papers, such as the tax withholding form and insurance application, should be completed. An employee file should be created to contain all necessary paperwork and kept in a confidential area not accessible to other employees. If the interviews have been conducted in a businesslike manner, the employee will gain confidence in your professionalism and in the new job.

You should pay a competitive hourly wage relative to your particular market. This figure, however, is susceptible to change, depending on the prevailing wage patterns in the area.

TRAINING

When you have reached this point in your business, you will be an efficient processor yourself. It is important during the early stages to scrutinize the new processor's work closely. At the same time you will be able to judge its quality during the probationary period. It is important not to expect the clerk to have contact with the clients during the early stages of training.

Needless to say, you should review all processed work before submitting it to the computer service bureau until you are confident that your processor is efficient.

There are two things that processing clerks are never allowed to do: set up new accounts and backwork. Even if they learn to do backwork as they progress, this will detract from their ability to process high volume.

STAFF DEVELOPMENT SUPERVISOR

As the business grows, a point will be reached when a second and third processor must be added to the staff. At that time you will experience the need for an administrative assistant to manage the staff. This person should be a graduate accountant or perhaps a night-school student who has completed all the required accounting subjects. A supervisor is essential if you are to continue to enjoy a successful growth pattern.

RECEPTIONIST

As your volume increases, you may want to fill this position. Before a full-time receptionist is hired, the processing clerks may assume some of the responsibilities. In general, they would do all those clerical jobs that fall outside the duties of processing, such as receiving and directing telephone calls and opening, date-stamping, processing, and distributing all incoming mail. Miscellaneous typing and administrative details will also be handled by them. You may find it advantageous to train the receptionist as a fill-in processor for assignment during vacations and sick leave. This employee could also assist in routine backwork such as sequencing checks and running tapes to relieve the higher paid processors.

The bulk of the work you get will consist of routine postings and payroll preparation. Basically, your clients' budgets will limit their accounting expenditures drastically. This necessitates the lowest possible charges for the work provided.

Typically, most CPAs charge for their services on an hourly basis. Billable hours become the focal point of production measurement and a means of facilitating planning. A better system for working with smaller businesses that need a retainer-fee arrangement is production per day, a system in which a daily report is compiled by each producing member of the staff concerning work done that day, the percentage of completion of the project, and the actual dollars earned, based on the billing arrangement.

The value of this system lies in stressing the importance of that day. When production is measured and analyzed on a per-day basis, the tendency is to maximize the contribution of that day toward the overall effort and to minimize the number of unproductive days or days when production was lower than it should have been.

On a daily basis each staff member, with the exception of clerical and marketing personnel, must submit a production report on which productive work for each client, time spent, and an estimate of earnings for that work are listed.

In a firm that is primarily concerned with small business write-up, the production-per-day system provides highly accurate cumulative information. It also indicates whether a given month, week, or day has resulted in a profit.

CLIENT HEADING INFORMATION

Exhibit 5 is set up to contain the information that must be gathered when a new client is added. This will serve the data-processing service bureau as a master information form with which to identify that client for computer processing. Consult the service bureau that will be processing your work to determine whether another form would be preferred or whether additional data are required.

CLIENT HEADING INFORMATION   PAGE _____ OF _____

AFFILIATE _____ CLIENT _____   ADD ▢   CHANGE ▢

CLIENT NAME _____ 30

ADDRESS 1 _____ 30

ADDRESS 2 _____ 30

ADDRESS 3 _____ 30

FEDERAL I.D. _____ 9

DEPARTMENTAL STATEMENTS   YES   NO

PRINT ACCOUNT NUMBERS ON STATEMENTS   YES   NO

PRINT ZERO BALANCES ON STATEMENTS   YES   NO

PRINT EVEN DOLLAR AMOUNTS   YES   NO

PRINT MULTI-STATE 941 REPORTS   YES   NO

STATE ID #1 _____ 15   STATE _____ 2 EXP. RATE _____ 3

STATE ID #2 _____ 15   STATE _____ 2 EXP. RATE _____ 3

STATE ID #3 _____ 15   STATE _____ 2 EXP. RATE _____ 3

GENERAL LEDGER DETAIL MONTHS _____ 2

Exhibit 5. Client Heading Information

JOURNAL ENTRIES

Exhibit 6 is a form to be used to record all journal entries, such as sales, purchases, general journal, cash receipts, and cash disbursements, for data processing. Debits are entered in black and credits in red for quicker and error-free processing.

95

THE ACCOUNTING FACTORY

JOURNAL ENTRIES

PAGE _____ OF _____

AFFILIATE _____ CLIENT _____

CLIENT NAME _____

Account Number	Dept Number	Date	Source 4	Description 25	Emp No.	Debit <Credit>	

Exhibit 6. Journal Entries

96

CASH RECEIPTS AND SALES JOURNAL

Exhibit 7 may be used by the client to record all cash receipts. If the client supplies this information in another format, such as a checking account statement or other list of deposits and sales, these data may be recorded and transmitted on this form for processing.

The form in Exhibit 8 is also useful for recording cash receipts and sales.

WEEKLY SALES AND CASH REPORT

The form in Exhibit 9 is particularly useful for clients who do a large part of their business on a cash basis. Restaurants and convenience stores, which must pay cash for many deliveries, fall into this category.

DEPRECIATION SCHEDULE

Exhibit 10 is used to record all depreciable and amortizable assets. This makes all necessary information for financial statements and tax returns.

NEW ACCOUNT SETUP

Exhibit 11 is a preprinted form on which to chart a new client's accounts and to record the opening balances for each of them.

PAYROLL FILE MAINTENANCE

Exhibit 12 must be filled out in order to enter each employee of your client into the payroll recording system for after-the-fact

THE ACCOUNTING FACTORY

DAILY CASH RECEIPTS

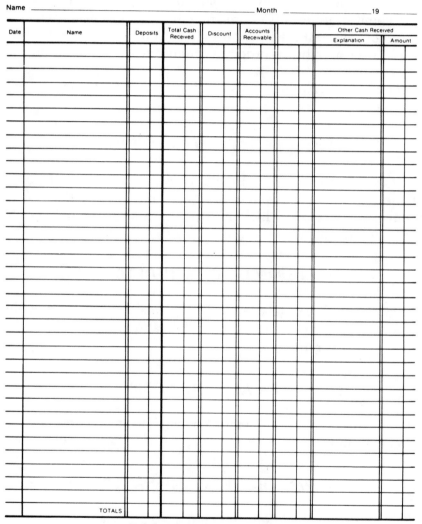

Name _____ Month _____ 19 _____

Date	Name	Deposits	Total Cash Received	Discount	Accounts Receivable		Other Cash Received	
							Explanation	Amount
		TOTALS						

Exhibit 7. Daily Cash Receipts

98

CASH RECEIPTS AND SALES JOURNAL

Exhibit 8. Cash Receipts and Sales Journal

THE ACCOUNTING FACTORY

NAME _____ WEEK ENDING _____

LINE	DESCRIPTION	DATE MONDAY		DATE TUESDAY		DATE WEDNESDAY		DATE THURSDAY		DATE FRIDAY		DATE SATURDAY		DATE SUNDAY		TOTAL	CODE
1	SALES (1)																
2	SALES (2)																
3	SALES (3)																
4	SALES (4)																
5																	
6																	
7																	
8																	
9																	
10	SALES TAX																
11	TOTAL SALES (ADD LINE 1 TO 10)																
12																	
13																	
14																	
15																	
16	CASH AT START OF DAY																
17	TOTAL TO BE ACCOUNTED FOR (LINE 11 TO 16)																
18	MDSE. (1)																
19	MDSE. (2)																
20	MDSE. (3)																
21																	
22																	
23																	
24	REFUND/RETURNS																
25	ADVERTISING																
26	CAR AND DELIVERY																
27	FREIGHT-POSTAGE																
28	LAUNDRY-LINEN																
29	MISCELLANEOUS																
30	OPERATING SUPPLIES																
31	REPAIRS AND MAINTENANCE																
32	TRAVEL-ENTERTAINMENT																
33	PERSONAL DRAWING																
34	NET WAGES (ATTACH SLIPS)																
35																	
36	TOTAL PAYOUT (LINE 18 TO 35)																
37	CASH DEPOSITED																
38	CLOSING CASH																
39	TOTAL CASH ACCOUNTED FOR (TOTAL LINES 36 TO 38)																
40	OVER OR SHORT (LINE 17 MINUS 39)																
41																	
42																	
43																	
44																	
45																	
46																	

Vertical labels: CASH RECEIVED (lines 1–16), CASH PAYOUTS (lines 18–35)

Exhibit 9. Weekly Sales and Cash Report

DEPRECIATION SCHEDULE

NAME

FOR THE YEAR

KIND OF PROPERTY	Date Acquired	Method	Rate	Cost or Other Basis	Investment Credit	Salvage	Amount to be Depreciated	Depreciation in Prior Years	Depreciation This Year	Reserve at End of Year	Depreciation This Year	Reserve at End of Year	Depreciation This Year	Reserve at End of Year
				$	$	$	$	$	$	$	$	$	$	$

Exhibit 10. Depreciation Schedule

THE ACCOUNTING FACTORY

NEW ACCOUNT SET-UP

AFFILIATE _____ CLIENT _____

CLIENT NAME _____

BEGINNING BALANCE DATE _____ YEAR END _____

Account Number	Dept. Number	Description 30	Paren Control	Payroll Code	Debit < Credit >	
0980		ASSETS	D		XX	
0990		CURRENT ASSETS	D		XX	
1020		CASH-IN-BANK	D			
1040		PETTY CASH	D			
1080		ACCOUNTS RECEIVABLE	D			
1110		EMPLOYEE ADVANCES	D			
1120		OFFICER ADVANCES	D			
1150		ALLOWANCE FOR UNCOLLECTIBLES	D			
1200		INVENTORY	D			
1230		PREPAID INTEREST	D			
1990		TOTAL CURRENT ASSETS	D		XX	
2500		PROPERTY, PLANT & EQUIPMENT	D		XX	
2510		LAND	D			
2520		BUILDINGS	D			
2530		MACHINERY	D			
2540		FURNITURE & FIXTURES	D			
2550		VEHICLES	D			
2800		ACCUMULATED DEPRECIATION	D			
2990		NET PROPERTY & EQUIPMENT	D		XX	
3500		OTHER ASSETS	D		XX	
3510		INVESTMENTS	D			
3520		SECURITY DEPOSITS	D			
3950		TOTAL OTHER ASSETS	D		XX	
3960		TOTAL ASSETS	D		XX	

Exhibit 11. New Account Set-Up

PAYROLL FILE MAINTENANCE

NEW ACCOUNT SET-UP

AFFILIATE _____ CLIENT _____

CLIENT NAME _____

BEGINNING BALANCE DATE _____

Account Number	Dept Number	Description 30	Paren Control	Payroll Code	Debit < Credit >	
3980		LIABILITIES	C		XX	
3990		STOCKHOLDERS EQUITY	C		XX	
4000		CURRENT LIABILITIES	C		XX	
4010		NOTES PAYABLE	C			
4020		ACCOUNTS PAYABLE - TRADE	C			
4040		FEDERAL & FICA W/H	C			
4050		STATE W/H	C			
4090		ACCRUED STATE UNEMPLOYMENT	C			
4180		ACCRUED SALES TAX	C			
4250		ACCRUED SALARIES	C			
4490		TOTAL CURRENT LIABILITIES	C		XX	
5000		LONG-TERM DEBT	C		XX	
5020		MORTGAGE PAYABLE	C			
5030		EQUIPMENT NOTES PAYABLE	C			
5050		OFFICER NOTES PAYABLE	C			
5300		TOTAL LONG-TERM DEBT	C		XX	
5500		STOCKHOLDERS EQUITY	C		XX	
5510		COMMON STOCK	C			
5580		RETAINED EARNINGS	C			
5590		CAPITAL	C			
5600		DRAWING	C			
5850		NET INCOME (LOSS)	C		XX	
5890		TOTAL STOCKHOLDERS EQUITY	C		XX	
5900		TOTAL LIABILITIES & EQUITY	C		XX	

Exhibit 11. (Continued)

103

THE ACCOUNTING FACTORY

NEW ACCOUNT SET-UP

AFFILIATE _____ CLIENT _____

CLIENT NAME _____

BEGINNING BALANCE DATE _____

Account Number	Dept. Number	Description 30	Paren Control	Payroll Code	Debit < Credit >	
6000		SALES	C		XX	
6980		RETURNS & ALLOWANCES	C			
6990		TOTAL SALES	C		XX	
7000		COST OF GOODS SOLD	D		XX	
7010		BEGINNING INVENTORY	D		XX	
7020		PURCHASES	D			
7030		FREIGHT-IN	D			
7040		DIRECT LABOR	D			
7070		DEPRECIATION	D			
7090		RENT	D			
7100		SMALL TOOLS	D			
7110		TAXES	D			
7120		REPAIRS & MAINTENANCE	D			
7130		INVENTORY CHANGE	D			
7800		CLOSING INVENTORY	D			
7980		TOTAL COST OF SALES	D		XX	
7990		GROSS PROFIT	C		XX	

Exhibit 11. (Continued)

NEW ACCOUNT SET-UP

AFFILIATE _____ CLIENT _____

CLIENT NAME _____

BEGINNING BALANCE DATE _____

Account Number	Dept. Number	Description 30	Paren. Control	Payroll Code	Debit < Credit >	
8000		SELLING EXPENSES	D		XX	
8010		SALESMEN SALARIES	D			
8020		COMMISSIONS	D			
8030		ADVERTISING	D			
8040		AUTO EXPENSE	D			
8050		ENTERTAINMENT	D			
8060		PROMOTION	D			
8070		MISC. SELLING EXPENSE	D			
8200		TOTAL SELLING EXPNESE	D		XX	
8500		GENERAL & ADMINISTRATIVE	D		XX	
8510		ACCOUNTING & LEGAL	D			
8530		AUTO & TRUCK EXPENSE	D			
8540		ADVERTISING	D			
8550		AMORTIZATION	D			
8570		BAD DEBTS	D			
8600		BANK CHARGES	D			
8610		CASH OVER/SHORT	D			
8620		CLEANING	D			
8630		COMMISSIONS	D			
8640		CONTRIBUTIONS	D			
8780		DEPRECIATION	D			
8790		DISCOUNTS	D			
8800		DUES & SUBSCRIPTIONS	D			
8810		EQUIPMENT RENTAL	D			

Exhibit 11. (Continued)

THE ACCOUNTING FACTORY

NEW ACCOUNT SET-UP

PAGE __5__ OF __6__

AFFILIATE _____ CLIENT _____

CLIENT NAME _____

BEGINNING BALANCE DATE _____

Account Number	Dept. Number	Description 30	Paren. Control	Payroll Code	Debit < Credit >	
8870		F.I.C.A. EXPENSE	D			
9040		INSURANCE	D			
9050		INSURANCE-GROUP	D			
9060		INSURANCE-OFFICER	D			
9090		GROSS WAGES	D			
9100		HEAT, POWER, LIGHT	D			
9160		MISCELLANEOUS	D			
9180		OFFICE EXPENSE	D			
9190		OFFICE SALARIES	D			
9200		OFFICER SALARIES	D			
9210		OUTSIDE SERVICES	D			
9220		OPERATING SUPPLIES	D			
9240		POSTAGE	D			
9250		PROPERTY TAXES	D			
9260		PERMITS & LICENSES	D			
9280		RENT-EQUIPMENT	D			
9290		RENT-REAL ESTATE	D			
9300		REPAIRS & MAINTENANCE	D			
9310		STATIONERY & PRINTING	D			
9410		TELEPHONE	D			
9420		TRAVEL & ENTERTAINMENT	D			
9430		UNEMPLOYMENT TAX	D			
9450		UTILITIES	D			
9480		TOTAL GENERAL & ADM. EXPENSES	D		XX	

Exhibit 11. (Continued)

106

PAYROLL FILE MAINTENANCE

NEW ACCOUNT SET-UP

AFFILIATE _____ CLIENT _____

CLIENT NAME _____

BEGINNING BALANCE DATE _____

Account Number	Dept. Number	Description 30	Paren. Control	Payroll Code	Debit < Credit >	
9490		TOTAL EXPENSES	D		XX	
9500		NET OPERATING INCOME (LOSS)	C		XX	
9550		OTHER INCOME & (EXPENSE)	C		XX	
9560		INTEREST INCOME	C			
9570		RENTAL INCOME	C			
9580		MISC. SALES	C			
9590		INTEREST EXPENSE	D			
9600		TOTAL OTHER INCOME & (EXPENSE)	C		XX	
9700		NET INCOME (LOSS)	C		XX	
9950		SUSPENSE	C		XX	

Exhibit 11. (Continued)

107

NEW ACCOUNT SET-UP

PAGE _____ OF _____

AFFILIATE _____ CLIENT _____

CLIENT NAME _____

BEGINNING BALANCE DATE _____

Account Number	Dept. Number	Description 30	Paren Control	Payroll Code	Debit <Credit>	

Exhibit 11. (Continued)

PAYROLL FILE MAINTENANCE

PAGE _____ OF _____

AFFILIATE _____ CLIENT _____

CLIENT NAME _____

□ ADD   □ CHANGE   □ DELETE
                     □ NO FICA

EMPLOYEE NO. _____ 4

S.S. NO. _____ 9

NAME _____ 25

ADDRESS _____ 25

ADDRESS _____ 25

TAXING STATE _____ LOCALITY _____ 5

PENSION   Y   N

	QTD	YTD
GROSS		
FICA		
FED. WT		
EIC		
STATE WT		
LOCAL WT		
SICK PAY		
TIPS		
MEALS		
DEDUCT 1		
DEDUCT 2		
DEDUCT 3		
1099		
NET		

□ ADD   □ CHANGE   □ DELETE
                     □ NO FICA

EMPLOYEE NO. _____ 4

S.S. NO. _____ 9

NAME _____ 25

ADDRESS _____ 25

ADDRESS _____ 25

TAXING STATE _____ LOCALITY _____ 5

PENSION   Y   N

	QTD	YTD
GROSS		
FICA		
FED. WT		
EIC		
STATE WT		
LOCAL WT		
SICK PAY		
TIPS		
MEALS		
DEDUCT 1		
DEDUCT 2		
DEDUCT 3		
1099		
NET		

□ ADD   □ CHANGE   □ DELETE
                     □ NO FICA

EMPLOYEE NO. _____ 4

S.S. NO. _____ 9

NAME _____ 25

ADDRESS _____ 25

ADDRESS _____ 25

TAXING STATE _____ LOCALITY _____ 5

PENSION   Y   N

TOTALS

	QTD	YTD
GROSS		
FICA		
FED. WT		
EIC		
STATE WT		
LOCAL WT		
SICK PAY		
TIPS		
MEALS		
DEDUCT 1		
DEDUCT 2		
DEDUCT 3		
1099		
NET		

Exhibit 12. Payroll File Maintenance

109

payroll. A word of caution is extended to the accountant not to take on the task of preparing payroll checks. This is a specialized activity that is best left to a computerized service firm. Several national companies market these services and will call on you soon after you establish your practice. Determine which of them offers the best service and prices and make your recommendation to your client.

TIME REPORT

Exhibit 13, on which you can record the hours spent for each client on a daily basis, will enable you to complete your billing arrangements and judge the profitability of clients you serve on a retainer basis. Analysis of the information entered on this form will allow you to set realistic retainer rates and justify necessary increases.

G/L ACCOUNT MAINTENANCE

Exhibit 14 is a form to be used to record general journal entries, debits, and credits.

INFORMATION FOR CLIENT

Exhibit 15 may be returned with the client's work to indicate action to be taken. By checking the appropriate boxes you will save a great deal of time that would ordinarily be required to write the client a letter.

TIME REPORT

OFFICE NO. _____

EMPLOYEE NAME _____

EMPLOYEE NUMBER _____

MONTH OF _____

PAGE _____ OF _____

CLIENT NAME	BILLING	1	2	3	4	5	6	7	8	9	10	11	12	13	14	15	16	17	18	19	20	21	22	23	24	25	26	27	28	29	30	31	TOTAL	CLIENT NUMBER	REMARKS

TOTAL ASSIGNED TIME

UNASSIGNED TIME

HOURS ABSENT

TOTAL HOURS

Exhibit 13. Times Report

THE ACCOUNTING FACTORY

PAGE _____ OF _____

AFFILIATE _____ CLIENT _____

CLIENT NAME _____

Account Number	Dept. Number	Maint. Code	Description 30	Paren. Control	Payroll Code	Debit <Credit>	

Exhibit 14. G/L Account Maintenance

112

FORM ENCLOSED and/or IN PAYMENT OF:

Quarter: 1 2 3 4
Month: 1 2 3 4 5 6 7 8 9 10 11 12

	FEDERAL	STATE
☐ F.I.C.A. & Withholding Tax (941)	☐	
☐ State Withholding Tax		☐
☐ Income Tax	☐	☐
☐ Estimated Tax Payment	☐	☐
☐ Unemployment Compensation Tax	☐	☐
☐ Sales Tax		☐
☐ Other: _____		

MAKE CHECK PAYABLE TO:

☐ Internal Revenue Service

☐ Director of Labor

☐ Retail Sales Tax Division

☐ Comptroller of the Treasury

☐ Other: _____

☐ Please sign attached form

☐ Mail with your check for $ _____

☐ No Check Required

☐ Enclose Depository Receipt Card

☐ Use Enclosed Envelope

☐ Affix Corporate Seal

DUE DATE: _____

Exhibit 15. Information for Client

ACCOUNTS RECEIVABLE

Customer Maintenance

When you maintain accounts receivable records for your clients, Exhibit 16 should be used to set up individual accounts or to make other changes shown on the form.

Cash Received

Exhibit 17 is used for all entries that concern the client's accounts receivable. Customer number, name, deposit, date cash received, discount granted, and accounts receivable credit are designated. Miscellaneous entries that relate to accounts receivable may also be entered.

A/R Changes

Miscellaneous entries that are not covered by Exhibit 17 should be entered on Exhibit 18, which is particularly useful for making corrections or adjustments to earlier entries.

NEW ACCOUNT CHECKLIST

Exhibit 19 serves as a checklist to ensure that all steps are taken to set up a new account. It also records the name of the person who fulfilled this function.

**ACCOUNTS RECEIVABLE
CUSTOMER MAINTENANCE**

AFFILIATE NO. |__|__|__| CLIENT NO. |__|__|__|

NEW CUSTOMER ☐	CHANGE CUSTOMER ☐	DELETE CUSTOMER ☐	CLIENT HEADING CHANGE ☐

Field	No.		
CUSTOMER NUMBER	1	|__|__|__|__|__| 5	
CUSTOMER NAME	2	|__|__|__|__|__|__|__|__|__|__|__|__|__|__|__|__|__|__|__|__|__|__|__|__|__| 25	
NAME OR ADDRESS	3	|__|__|__|__|__|__|__|__|__|__|__|__|__|__|__|__|__|__|__|__|__|__|__|__|__| 25	
ADDRESS	4	|__|__|__|__|__|__|__|__|__|__|__|__|__|__|__|__|__|__|__|__|__|__|__|__|__| 25	
CITY	5	|__|__|__|__|__|__|__|__|__|__|__|__|__|__|__|__|__|__|__|__| 20	
STATE	6	|__|__| 2	
ZIP	7	|__|__|__|__|__| 5	
TELEPHONE NUMBER	8	|__|__|__|__|__|__|__|__|__|__| 10	
SALESMAN NUMBER	9	|__|__|__|__| 4	
CUSTOMER TYPE	10	|__|__|__|__| 4	
* CURRENT	11	|__|__|__|__|__|__|__:__|__| 9	DATE |__|__|__|__|__|__|__|
* 30-60 DAYS	12	|__|__|__|__|__|__|__:__|__| 9	
* 60-90 DAYS	13	|__|__|__|__|__|__|__:__|__| 9	
* 90-120 DAYS	14	|__|__|__|__|__|__|__:__|__| 9	
* OVER 120 DAYS	15	|__|__|__|__|__|__|__:__|__| 9	
SALES TO DATE	16	|__|__|__|__|__|__|__:__|__| 9	
CREDIT LIMIT	19	|__|__|__|__|__|__|__:__|__| 9	

* INCLUDE IN AMOUNTS TOTALS

Exhibit 16. Accounts Receivable Customer Maintenance

ATTACH:
1—HASH TOTAL AMT TAPES
2—CUSTOMER NO. TAPES
PRINT CLEARLY

ACCOUNTS RECEIVABLE

CASH RECEIVED

CLIENT #

CLIENT NAME

CUSTOMER OR CLIENT NO	NAME / DEPOSIT	DATE	CASH DR	DISCOUNT DR	ACCOUNTS REC'BLE CR	MISCELLANEOUS DR	MISCELLANEOUS CR	EXPLANATION (MISCELLANEOUS)
TOTAL					(HASH TOTAL)			

Exhibit 17. Accounts Receivable (Cash Received)

CLIENT NAME _____

INVOICE OR MEMO NO.	CUSTOMER OR CLIENT NO.	NAME	DEBIT <CREDIT>		EXPLANATION

Exhibit 18. Accounts Receivable (A/R Changes)

THE ACCOUNTING FACTORY

NEW ACCOUNT CHECKLIST

CLIENT NO. _____   BOOKKEEPER _____

G/L SET UP COMPLETED   _____   _____

PAYROLL SET UP COMPLETED   _____   _____

CHECKS ORDERED   _____   _____

BANK ADDRESS FORM   _____   _____

WORK BOX   _____   _____

FILE FOLDERS: BOX   _____   _____

           CABINET   _____   _____

ROLODEX CARDS   _____   _____

REPETITIVE BILLING   _____   _____

TAX FILE CARD   _____   _____

Exhibit 19. New Account Checklist

7

A PROGRAMMED
ACTION PLAN

FIRST WEEK TO TWELFTH MONTH

First Week
Objective: Make New Contacts

1. Prepare your marketing plan and its implementation.
2. Follow up on replies to direct mail. Undelivered mail may mean that an address has been changed.
3. Telephone every addressee of the preceding week's direct mailing and ask for an appointment.
4. Call in person on all direct-mail addresses who could not be reached by phone.
5. Make appointments by phone or in person with referrals given to you during the week who are in your prospecting area.

6. Make get-acquainted calls until you have acquired 20 appointments from all sources. The appointments should yield a minimum of 10 interviews.

7. Visit the courthouse and city or town hall to become familiar with the registration and licensing requirements for new businesses. Obtain copies of all regulations and forms. Determine where and how lists of new businesses are maintained. Make lists of good prospects.

8. Send out at least 33 pieces of direct mail on Monday or Tuesday.

Daily (Each Week)

1. Check your briefcase each day to be sure that it contains all the required items.

2. Inform your office of your schedule or leave appropriate instructions with your answering service or on your telephone answering unit.

3. Check twice daily with the person who answers your telephone or pick up your messages from your answering device.

4. Ask all contacts (prospects, opinion leaders, clerks, friends, suppliers, and service providers) for referrals.

5. Maintain your Day-Runner.

Reports

1. Summarize your Day-Runner.

2. Summarize call reports.

3. Update prospect cards.

Second Week
Objective: Call on Opinion Leaders

1. Be sure that you have entered all appointments for the week in your Day-Runner.
2. Follow up on replies to direct mail. Telephone or call in person on every addressee of the preceding week's direct mailing and ask for an appointment.
3. Brief two opinion leaders, preferably your banker and Chamber of Commerce representative. Offer to put them on your mailing list for *Client's Monthly Alert*. Write thank-you and confirming notes to all of them. *Client's Monthly Alert* is a publication that is sold to accountants in bulk for distribution to clients. It is published by *The Practical Accountant* magazine.
4. Follow up in person or by phone on referrals given to you from all sources.
5. Follow up all call-backs and missed appointments.
6. Make 25 get-acquainted calls (more if needed) until you have arranged 10 appointments from direct mail and other sources. Your quota is five interviews a week, thus allowing for unkept appointments and leads that are obviously unqualified.
7. Send out at least 33 pieces of direct mail on Monday or Tuesday.

Reports

1. Summarize your Day-Runner.
2. Complete time and charges worksheets—daily.
3. Update prospect cards.

Third Week
Objective: Locate Local Tax Authorities

1. Be sure that you have entered all appointments for the week in your Day-Runner.
2. Follow up on direct-mail replies and telephone or call in person on every addressee in last week's distribution. Ask for appointments.
3. Return to the county/city/town hall and record new businesses. Call on them ASAP.
4. Brief two opinion leaders during the week.
5. Visit the local offices of the IRS and state income, sales tax, and unemployment offices. Brief the office chiefs; pick up new regulations, application forms, and instructional materials.
6. Make 25 telephone calls and get-acquainted calls (more if needed) until you have arranged 10 appointments. Your quota is five interviews a week, thus allowing for appointments not kept and leads that are obviously unqualified.
7. Send out at least 33 pieces of direct mail on Monday or Tuesday.

Fourth Week
Objective: Do All the Things That Should Be Done

1. Review your client sales and the interview and contact goals included in your annual work plan. Determine the necessary activity for the fourth week.
2. Be sure that you have entered all appointments for the week in your Day-Runner.
3. Follow up on direct-mail replies and telephone or call in person on every addressee in last week's distribution. Ask for appointments.

4. Follow up in person or by phone the referrals given to you from all sources.

5. Make 25 telephone and get-acquainted calls (more if needed) until you have arranged 10 appointments. Your quota is five interviews a week, thus allowing for appointments not kept and leads that are obviously unqualified.

6. Send out at least 33 pieces of direct mail on Monday and Tuesday.

7. Brief two opinion leaders and send notes to all on your list. Plan to call on them again in two weeks.

8. Call the opinion leaders you briefed two weeks ago.

9. If you've met your goals by the end of the fourth week, treat yourself (and spouse) to an evening out. If you failed, adjust your contact levels. Don't lower your sights.

Fifth Week
Objective: Identify Ways to Use Your Time and Contacts to Increase Number of Prospects

1. Schedule service calls to take the best advantage of your time and confirm all appointments.

2. Follow up direct-mail replies and telephone or call in person on every addressee in last week's distribution. Ask for appointments.

3. Brief two opinion leaders. Send them thank-you notes and plan to call them again in two weeks.

4. Return to the county/city/town hall and renew important contacts. Record new businesses for follow-up.

5. Follow up all call-backs and missed appointments.

6. Make 25 telephone and get-acquainted calls (more if needed) until you have arranged 10 appointments. Your quota is five

interviews a week, thus allowing for appointments not kept and leads that are obviously unqualified.

7. Send out at least 33 pieces of direct mail on Monday or Tuesday.

8. Call the opinion leaders you briefed two weeks ago.

Sixth Week
Objective: Get Some Help

1. Schedule service calls and confirm appointments.

2. Follow up on your leads—referrals, direct mail, and callbacks—and ask for appointments.

3. Generate new leads: search out new business listings. Be observant. Ask for referrals. Join a local business or professional association.

4. Make 25 telephone and get-acquainted calls (more if needed) until you have arranged 10 appointments. Your quota is five interviews a week, thus allowing for appointments not kept and leads that are obviously unqualified.

5. Send out a minimum of 33 direct-mail pieces on Monday or Tuesday.

6. Call the opinion leaders briefed two weeks ago.

Seventh Week
Objective: Identify Your Services and Build on Them

1. Schedule service calls and confirm appointments.

2. Follow up on your leads—referrals, direct mail and callbacks—and ask for appointments.

3. Generate new leads, new business listings, and personal observations. Ask for referrals.

4. Make 25 telephone or get-acquainted calls (more if needed)

until you have arranged 10 appointments. Your quota is five interviews a week, thus allowing for appointments not kept and leads that are obviously unqualified.

5. List the good things you have done for your clients. Speculate on what they would have done without your help. Then, if appropriate, ask for testimonial letters.

6. Visit the business editor of your local newspaper. Offer to provide a feature, tax tips, or a bottom line series or to give an interview to get your name in print.

7. Become active in a service organization. Offer to be a speaker or a committee member.

8. Send out at least 33 pieces of direct mail on Monday or Tuesday.

9. Call the opinion leaders briefed two weeks ago.

Eighth Week
Objective: Plan Your Work and Work Your Plan

1. Schedule service calls and confirm appointments.

2. Follow up on your leads—referral, direct mail, and call backs—and ask for appointments.

3. Make 25 telephone and get-acquainted calls (more if needed) until you have arranged for 10 appointments. Your quota is five interviews a week.

4. Send out at least 33 pieces of direct mail on Monday or Tuesday.

5. Talk to your current clients about suppliers, subcontractors, customers, or acquaintances to whom your services should be offered.

6. Brief two opinion leaders.

7. If you've met your goals by the end of the eighth week treat yourself (and your spouse) to a holiday or a night out.

Ninth Week
Objective: Make Yourself Known

1. Visit and brief the business editor of your local newspaper on your activity and the needs of small businesses. Offer to provide regular news articles.
2. Brief two opinion leaders, preferably SBA loan and bank loan officers on your business, and ask for referrals.
3. Send out 33 pieces of direct mail. Follow up on last week's mailing.
4. Make your 25 telephone or get-acquainted calls.

Tenth Week
Objective: Concentrate on What Works

1. Schedule service calls and confirm appointments.
2. Follow up your leads—referrals, direct mail, call-backs— and ask for appointments.
3. Analyze your direct mail returns and responses. Are your lead sources current?
4. Review the results of your efforts to reach propects by telephone. Try to make them more effective.
5. Are your get-acquainted calls as effective as you would like them to be?
6. Review your contact-to-appointment ratios. Have they improved since your first month? Role play to identify all negative factors, mannerisms, or failure to listen.
7. Study your close rate. Catalog the reasons why you made some sales and lost other. Did you ask enough questions and listen for the answers.
8. Practice exercises for improving your interviewing skills.
9. Review the materials you use during interviews.

10. Make your regular 25 telephone calls and secure five interviews.
11. Send out 33 pieces of direct mail.
12. Brief two opinion leaders. Follow up on those you briefed earlier.

Eleventh Week
Objective: Find the Hidden Business

1. Schedule service calls and confirm appointments.
2. Select the business areas you are least acquainted with. Canvass them on foot for hidden businesses. Try to make at least 25 calls and plan to complete your canvass.
3. Study the business service ads in your local newspaper for hidden business leads.
4. Ask your branch bankers for "hidden business" leads. Concentrate on those with which you are comfortable.
5. Send out enough direct mail to maintain your leads from these sources.
6. Follow up on all your leads.

Twelfth Week
Objective: Prospects

1. Schedule service calls and confirm appointments.
2. Follow up on leads.

Fourth Month

Make a special effort to close "hot prospects."

Fifth Month

Prepare a priority list for maximum use of your time. Then

consider step-by-step implementing actions. Use outside help to handle details.

Sixth Month
Objective: Expand Your Horizons

1. Develop a counseling program for each of your clients. Good records, cash controls, compliance with tax laws, and the preparation of estimated tax returns are a good start.
2. Cultivate new businesses and offer, for a fee, to prepare business plans for those who have none. Minimum service should include profit-and-loss projections, cash-flow projections, and sales break-even analysis.

Seventh Month

1. Review and list common business problems encountered by clients.
2. Discuss possible resources to solve these problems with knowledgeable people (e.g., opinion leaders).
3. Call on individual specialists who can solve these problems (e.g., advertising agencies, insurance brokers, and estate planners).

Eighth Month
Objective: Develop Expertise

1. Review your progress. Adjust your sales activities to meet your goals.
2. Continue to cultivate opinion leaders.
3. Concentrate on professional development activity to expand your knowledge of accounting and the preparation of financial statements.
4. Review your fee structure, accounts receivable, and cash flow.

Pre-tax Season

1. Obtain year-end tax forms and instructions from state and local agencies. Learn how to complete each form.
2. Order W-2 forms and tax information sheets.
3. Review payroll records, withholdings, and deposits. Verify accuracy and balance for each client. Get preceding year's tax returns from each client.
4. Have W-2 forms prepared for client's terminated employees.
5. Estimate profit or loss, adjusted for accruals if necessary, and prepare estimated taxes at year-end. Compute tax credits and tax bill. Review tax-planning approaches to defer or reduce taxes.
6. Send out taxpayer work papers to all clients.
7. Arrange tax-season selling.

Tax Season

1. Schedule selling time each week.
2. Prepare your checklist for visiting your clients.
3. Schedule and confirm appointments. Reschedule if clients are not prepared.
4. Keep track of time, costs, and meeting and return dates for every tax information packet handled.
5. Continue advertising, direct mail, publicity releases, and articles for posttax-season selling activity.

Post-tax Season

1. Clean up extensions on client tax-return work. Do preceding year tax-return amendments.
2. Prepare your post-tax season critique, using specific examples.

3. Catch up on service visits that you have neglected or delayed. Do not let your clients feel abandoned.

4. Mount a campaign with a post-tax-season theme.

5. Cultivate opinion leaders who know business people who have suffered tax-season distress—for example, bank loan officers.

6. Be sure to ask for referrals from every contact.

7. Celebrate a good tax season.

Twelfth Month
Objective: Review Your Clients

1. Review your time and charges worksheets, counseling notes, and tax work for all clients.

2. Prepare a brief note to outline what was accomplished during the year and what is planned for the next few months for each client.

3. Review and adjust your fees as needed.

4. Review your own first year's activity.

DAILY WORK PLAN

Just as you outlined your objectives for the first year, you should plan in detail your schedule for each day.

General

Get an early start each morning at a consistent time. Self-discipline is vital. Be at your desk by 8 A.M. From 8 to 9 A.M. make telephone calls, check your briefcase, get your car serviced, and pick up your mail.

Briefcase

Your briefcase, in essence, becomes a traveling office. It must contain all the materials required for each visit on a given day. Detailed information on scheduled stops will be shown on the daily call schedule or work record card for clients and on prospect cards for prospects. Review the day's plans carefully to determine whether any special forms or applications will be needed. If you call on a client or a prospect and fail to have at hand the necessary papers, another trip will be required. The value of your time can make this costly.

Briefcase for Sales Presentations

1. Sales presentation easel and aids. These aids may be a specially prepared system, leave-behind literature, or something of your own devising.
2. Client information record.
3. Application for employer's identification number (Form SS-4) for closing.
4. Application for social security account number (Form SS-5) for closing.
5. Employee's withholding exemption certificate (Form W-4) for closing.
6. Federal license applications (liquor license)—(Forms 11 and 11B) for closing.
7. Applications for state income tax withholding account numbers, unemployment tax account numbers, disability or other insurance numbers, and sales tax numbers.
8. County and city tax number applications.
9. Samples of direct mail and leave-behind pieces.
10. Comparison tax return.

11. Your business cards.
12. Client presentation folder.
13. Prospect cards.
14. Current year W-2 forms.
15. Carbon paper.

Briefcase for Service Calls

1. Time and charges worksheets for all clients listed on your daily call schedule.
2. Circular E.
3. *Your Federal Income Tax*, IRS Publication 17.
4. *Tax Guide for Small Business*, IRS Publication 334.
5. State and local tax regulations.
6. (a) Quarterly report of wages (IRS Form 941).
   (b) Statement to correct information (IRS Form 941c).
7. Withholding tax statement (IRS Form W-2).
8. Quarterly federal excise tax return (IRS Form 720).
9. Annual federal unemployment (IRS Form 940).
10. State income tax forms, when applicable.
11. State unemployment tax forms, when applicable.
12. State sales tax forms, when applicable.
13. Property tax forms, when applicable.
14. Local inventory, gross receipts, sales, and use tax forms.
15. Federal highway use tax (IRS Form 2290).
16. System for set-up with appropriate sheets.
17. Extra payroll sheets.
18. Estimated federal income tax worksheet (IRS Form 1040ES).

Briefcase for Tax Service Calls

1. Time and charges worksheets for clients on your daily call schedule.
2. *Your Federal Income Tax*, IRS Publication 17.
3. *Tax Guide for Small Business*, IRS Publication 334.
4. Equipment and property schedule.
5. Corporation/partnership tax information sheets.
6. Tax interview worksheets.
7. Tax information sheets and supplemental sheets appropriate to your state.
8. Applications for automatic extension of time to file income tax returns (IRS Form 4868 for individuals and IRS Form 7004 for corporations) and other applications for the extension of time to file state income tax returns.
9. Scrap paper and 16-column ledger paper.
10. Number 1 lead pencils and eraser.

Auto

Almost everyone needs an automobile to visit clients and prospects. Recommended is a late-model compact car to avoid the impression of ostentation or inadequate means. Much time is spent in your car. It must be comfortable (have an air conditioner for a warm climate or a heater for cold.) It is important to appear fresh and energetic when you arrive at your prospect's or client's place of business. Do not park your car directly out front. Find a place a few feet off where it will be out of the way.

Driving time is not productive time. Plan your itinerary carefully before you start your day. Be sure you have an updated map of the area and eliminate all unnecessary calls. Call in sequence to reduce driving time to a minimum. Always have some alternate stops in case you miss an appointment for any reason. Be extremely time conscious and plan the use of your automobile accordingly.

Important Note

If you are starting a business in another state be sure to get the correct license plates immediately. Nothing makes a more damaging impression or is more likely to affect a sale than your almost-convinced prospect's sudden awareness of an out-of-state car. The same applies to credit cards, driver's license, and all other items of identification that might tab you as a "foreigner."

Working Tools

An accountant's working tools are simple. A Day Runner is a must. Carry it with you at all times and note in it your pocket expenses and services performed.

No successful accountant would ever be caught without a good supply of cards on which to record information on possible prospects as he encounters them in his day's work.

A pocket calculator is a useful device for computing ratios of expenses to gross sales for counseling purposes. You are strongly urged, however, not to make *extensive* use of it, because clients will invariably begin to depend on you to do their calculations for them and you cannot affront them by refusing. If a client needs an adding machine, he should buy one. Recommend a good place for him to make the purchase.

Self-Evaluation

After each call take a moment to review your activity. Note your successes and capitalize on them. Determine also where you went wrong so as to avoid the same mistakes. Fill out your prospect card and note the price you quoted. If this has been a service call, note the activity and the time spent on it in your Day-Runner, daily call schedule, and/or time and charges worksheet.

Set aside a little time each week to record your calls, appointments, presentations, sales, and referrals. The statistics you accumulate will tell you how well you are progressing toward the achievement of your goals.

Appearance and Attitude

Most important of all, before leaving your office, consider your mental attitude. Are you enthusiastic? Are you positive? If necessary, give yourself a pep talk. Then check your dress. Look like the owner of a successful business. A professional appearance is essential.

Remember that success or failure depends on you. You are providing a professional service. Therefore, look and act like a professional. Be enthusiastic about your business in all contacts. Always try to have a positive attitude. A negative deadhead never signs anyone. Be sincere in your offers to help. If you are convincing, your clients will be your form of advertising.

Improving Personal Efficiency

The following basic rules may help to improve your personal efficiency. Practice them.

1. Study ways to save time. Route all calls carefully to cut down on driving distance.

2. Determine not to behave in a manner that will lower your efficiency. Don't eat or drink too much.

3. Don't skimp on your planning or study time.

4. Start early—you will be surprised that many calls can be made at 7 or 7:30 A.M. if you take the trouble to locate them.

5. Keep your sales talks as short as possible or practical. Cut down especially on all conversation unrelated to business. Don't take 30 minutes of a prospect's time if you can sign him up in 10.

6. Make your lunch light and brief.

7. Don't stop early if you've had a bad day.

8. Make night calls if you find yourself lagging. Prospects can be seen at night, on holidays and weekends, or whenever you are willing to spend the time.

9. Select the prospects you plan to call on and make sure that they are the best ones for that day. Practice selective selling.

10. Eliminate unnecessary calls and don't develop the habit of calling too often. Your clients may begin to expect you and feel offended if you don't continue the courtesy.

11. Always have alternate prospects to visit to take the place of those you may miss.

Daily Call Schedule

This schedule should be completed each day as you make your sales calls. The information should then be transferred to the individual lead or customer card you are maintaining for each prospect or client. These cards should be saved for future analysis to determine how to streamline your daily calls. Time can be saved by entering the follow-up call on your calendar to remind yourself to make the appointment. One method I have used with success is to place file cards behind dividers labeled 1 to 31. A follow-up call scheduled for the 15th is placed on a card behind the divider labeled 15.

8

HOW TO CHARGE
AND COLLECT

THE POSITIVE APPROACH TO QUOTING A FEE

There is one sure way to recognize an inexperienced or unsuccessful accountant. He or she is the one who usually tries to bypass or minimize the subject of fees. This negative attitude can give a client the impression that the accountant is afraid or ashamed to talk about fees because they are out of line.

The only approach to the establishment of fees is a positive one. They should be discussed early in the first conference with a new client with a full description of the benefits and services that you intend to provide.

By emphasizing the fact that you recognize the client's needs and can supply the necessary services, the fee will seem more reasonable. It all boils down to telling the client that you will provide "so much in value at so much in reasonable price."

Now suppose your client still expresses concern at the fee you quote. It's just as well to reach this point early in the discussion because it will give the client time to adjust to your fee basis. You must, however, avoid being put on the defensive. Instead, take the offensive. Act a little surprised by the client's attitude. Ask him why he thinks the fee is too high. Make him defend his position instead of rushing to defend your own. You will often discover that his objections are poorly conceived or based on some misunderstanding of the services you are going to provide.

Once you feel that the client has fully explained all objections, demonstrate again how the benefits you can supply more than justify the fee. If you create a recognition of need, your fee will appear to be reasonable and your services desirable.

The philosophy that you are offering your services solely because they are needed is, of course, simplistic. Basically, every business and professional person starts with the idea of making money. If the business person doesn't make money, survival will be short-lived. So it is with you. Your future, and that of your employees, depends on your efforts (and theirs) to earn an amount above the cost of providing those efforts, a cost that includes not only salaries but a sizable overhead.

However, the main thrust of your explanation (not defense) of any fee you quote is benefit. The client should want you for what you can provide in your area of expertise—and should be willing to pay for it.

The subject can be likened to buying oats, as an old friend of mine has pointed out. If you want nice clean oats, you must pay a fair price. If, however, you can be satisfied with oats that have already been through the horse, they come a little cheaper.

METHODS OF ARRIVING AT A FAIR FEE

So many conflicting factors pull at us when we try to set a fair fee that many of us end up using "instinct," a rather unscientific approach to a critical problem.

In making a fee decision, practitioners usually take into consideration a number of factors:

Time spent on engagement.

Technical importance of the engagement (the responsibility assumed).

Value of the services to the client.

Risk factors involved.

Staff availability.

Ability of the client to pay.

Maintenance of professional standards (attendance at conferences and additional education).

Maintenance of facilities (staff, office equipment, and library costs).

Reputation of the firm (whether it be enhanced by performing the services for the client).

"Life needs" (enough money to provide a desired standard of living).

Keeping pace with the national economic picture (rate of inflation).

Minimum fee factors (the going rate within the community; what was charged in former years or in similar circumstances).

Various ethical considerations.

Notwithstanding the significance of these factors, the "time value" is still the basis for initiating a fee. It is composed of three things:

A labor rate (usually based on some kind of formula).

Job difficulty.

A staff person's ability.

Although the last two components may appear to be variations of the same factor, they really are separate considerations and can be defined as such. Let's examine each factor separately.

The Labor Rate

Methods of determining a labor rate are myriad. A common one is the "reverse" formula. By starting at the back and working toward the front, you will have little difficulty in arriving at a labor rate for your efforts. For example, if you want to charge $35,000 a year for an employee's time and (ideally) the employee works 1800 chargeable hours a year (equivalent to 240 days at 7½ hours each), you must bill $19.44 an hour.

Another method of determining the labor rate is to take a percentage of the annual wages of each employee at that employee's daily rate and break it down into an hourly rate. For example, using a 1% formula, if an employee earns $24,000 a year and works an average of 7½ hours a day, the labor rate is $32 an hour. To arrive at this figure, multiply $24,000 by 1% and divide by 7.5.

A third way to determine hourly labor rates, which is similar to the percentage method, is based on a percentage of average monthly salary. Under this schedule, if a firm adopted a 1½%-of-the-monthly-salary yardstick, it would charge $30 an hour for the time of a $2000-a-month staff person.

The Job Difficulty

Although there is no way to determine definitively how difficult a particular job will be, we should be able to predict where each type of job will fall on a "scale of difficulty" set up on some arbitrary basis. For example, a firm may offer the following services: monthly auditing, tax-return preparation, data processing, and systems installation.

Among these four categories, only auditing is conceded to be a "general accounting" skill. Let's give it a base of 100% (although in some cases auditing is a highly specialized skill and would be given a premium value). Tax-return preparation is also relatively common but mostly seasonal and must be done on a deadline basis. Let's give it a value of 125%. Data processing is a special skill but can be handled on a routine basis. Let's assign it a value of 125% also. Systems installation work is highly specialized and comes up less frequently than the others. This and other subjective considerations lead us to assign a value of 200% to this service.

Some firms who keep their records on a computer can list as many as a thousand categories of service classification (although this is certainly not a common situation). You should have sufficient knowledge of your own practice to be able to set up enough categories to handle the services you perform. Don't forget travel, correspondence, telephone, research, secretarial work (for the client's benefit), and management services.

Staff Person's Ability

Here, as with the degree of job difficulty, you must use judgment. The job is made easier, however, by dividing your accounting staff into several broad categories—clerical, juniors, and semi-seniors. Within these categories each staff person's ability is judged against a norm that can be set up in any number of ways (by test, education, experience, and length of service). Only those who are better than average need be rated. Again, this is an arbitrary figure—125, 150, or 200% of normal—the norm, of course, being 100%. No one should be rated lower than 100%. If you find that someone on your staff falls below 100%, start looking for a replacement. Give additional weight to any specialties an employee may have. For example, if the employee has undertaken special training in programming, that individual should be upgraded for using such skill.

APPLYING THE ELEMENTS

When you have finished setting up the three bases of the rate formula the rest will be easy. From here on, you merely apply the elements of the formula to each job.

Multiply the degree of job difficulty and the degree of personnel variation by the labor rate and add the three together. If an average employee's labor rate is $16 an hour and the assignment has a difficulty factor of 125% you would add 25% to the $16 hourly rate and come up with a rate of $20 for the job. Another example is a complex job that requires the services of a highly skilled employee. Let us assume a labor rate of $24, a degree of difficulty of 150%, and a personnel evaluation rate of 150%. This computes to $24 for the labor rate, $12 for the difficulty factor, and $12 for the staff-ability factor, a total of $48 an hour for this particular job.

We are not, however, submitting this three-factor method as a panacea for formulating fees. Many value judgments can be made (and defended). But if you want a sense of order and a degree of uniformity, examine this approach seriously.

TIPS FOR BILLING

Submit bills promptly and frequently. For extended jobs with a large fee, bills should be rendered periodically. This is particularly applicable to management services.

Have a clear understanding with the clients from the beginning. They should never be surprised.

Don't "write down" or lower a bill after it has been rendered. Clients who haggle are not the kind needed to build a successful practice.

Don't "write down" a bill on the theory that you will "make it up next time." This never happens.

Don't "write down" a bill because you are afraid to lose the client. Billing in fear can lead only to a substandard income and substandard work.

Do the easy billing first. It's then easier to deliberate on the tough ones.

Don't charge more than you would be willing to pay yourself. When in serious doubt, err on the side of reasonableness (golden rule).

Don't charge more than you can collect. This implies a faulty arrangement with the client or failure to keep the client posted. But this has happened at least once to everyone.

In rare instances it may be well to show the billing records to your client to establish confidence in the fairness of the fee. The client will generally be impressed with the authority of the document itself. But never back in the door by asking the client to help you arrive at a fair fee.

Fixed fees should be reviewed with clients annually. Achieve a clear understanding of the services included.

Always try to "sell" the fee during the engagement. Prepare the client for the bill.

Never let a bill come as a shock to a client. To implement this

(a) when starting the engagement, inform the client of the probable cost (to the extent that you can do so);
(b) let the client know how much the bill is running (unless it is in line with the preceding year);

149

(c) prepare a weekly listing of clients for whom services were performed during the preceding week and for whom work-in-process charges exceed $500. Review this list weekly to determine which clients should receive an interim billing.

Before sending out a bill of unusual size, call or write to the client. The approach is always that of an advisor seeking to do work at the lowest possible fee commensurate with the client's needs—and with yours.

When engaged for the first time, the "first-time-through" expense should normally not be absorbed but passed on to the client. It is not necessary to bill at reduced rates during the first engagements, because it is then, if ever, that the client is most receptive to higher fees.

A client should receive the bill as soon after the first of the month as possible. This requires prompt submission of time sheets by your staff and prompt posting of work-in-process records.

Except for out-of-pocket expenses, do not use odd figures on invoices. Round them out.

TIMING OF BILLINGS

Timing is an important consideration in billing. For several good reasons, billing as often as possible is a good rule to follow:

1. The client remembers and appreciates the work performed in the preceding month more than work performed several months ago.

2. Frequent billings of small bills are generally more acceptable to the client than one large bill.

3. Frequent billings also help to improve your cash flow and

reduce the amount of money tied up in accounts receivable or work-in-process.

It takes more than technical competence to be a successful accountant. It takes ability to manage your business. It takes the know-how and determination to charge an adequate professional fee.

Your clients want to feel that they have hired an accountant who is successful in the field. Success is an indication of professional knowledge of the business.

All this is to say that the economic well-being of your business is extremely important. Knowing when and how to bill, when to charge a premium fee, and how to keep proper time records is vital.

Always keep in mind that your clients need your services and can therefore afford to pay for them. It's up to you to convince them of your value.

9

SALES TECHNIQUES FOR THE NONSALESPERSON

The marketing program is without a doubt the most crucial part of training for the establishment of a successful accounting business. If the ability to gain a clientele is lacking the rest is futile. An accountant is not required to be a seasoned salesperson, but must be sufficiently knowledgeable in accountancy to introduce a unique system. Nothing can be left to chance. The accountant who follows this system cannot help but succeed. When presented correctly the system almost sells itself, although nothing, in fact, ever does. It has been tested on small and medium-sized businesses and has succeeded.

The concepts and techniques of marketing offer the professional accountant direction in developing a service as well as promoting and pricing it. Neither technical competency nor a CPA certificate is automatically rewarded by a retinue of clients. The world does not beat a path to the door of the person with the "better mousetrap." The world needs to be informed and persuaded before making most purchasing decisions.

An appraisal of your development program from a marketing standpoint raises the following questions:

What services should and can be offered?

Who needs these services?

Who should render the services?

When, where, and how should the services be offered and rendered? At what price?

How can the value and availability of these services be communicated to those who need them?

Marketing's major function is to present the firm's range of services properly in a manner that will enable present and potential clients (target clients) to recognize its value. Value recognition comes when clients can appreciate the benefits that result from the services. Clients do not hire accountants; they hire the accountant's ability to increase cash flow, reduce inventory costs, decrease or defer taxes, and draw up statements. The client's basic motivation is to make money, reduce operating costs, or satisfy a legal or social obligation. Clients may not be the best judge of technical competency, but they do recognize the person who can identify, evaluate, and solve their organization's problems.

A SYSTEMATIC MARKETING APPROACH

Indeed, clients have a number of problems to be solved and a variety of benefits to be sought that will provide unending opportunities for the aspiring accountant. To realize fully this practice development, however, a systematic marketing approach must be used. Every employee and all facets of a firm's operation are involved. An identification must be made of the services required and the services that can, in fact, be delivered, given the resources the firm already possesses and can obtain. This identification raises several questions that will introduce the firm to marketing planning and strategy:

What are the capabilities that define the charter of the firm and set it apart from other firms?

Who are the firm's present and potential target clients?

How are these clients being served presently and how can the service be improved?

These questions create an equation that requires simultaneous solution, for an answer to one question interrelates with those of others; for example, the means by which present and potential clients may be better served give direction to the definition of the firm's future character.

The challenge lies in exploring, identifying, and defining the many ways in which accounting services can be used. The depth of a firm's services is defined and developed by matching its resources with the potential recognized in its chosen target markets. A small firm chooses a segment it can serve well and for which it can create a productive program. A larger firm may serve several markets and market segments and perhaps tailor a different marketing program for each. For the small or large firm marketing programs and appropriate personnel reward systems guide its effort to attract and serve its chosen markets.

THE MARKETING PROGRAM

Once it has been decided tentatively which clients should be approached and which services are appropriate for them, a marketing program can be planned. A marketing program consists of developing promotion and pricing elements to match the services to be offered. The effort expended in implementing it determines the effectiveness with which the firm will achieve its objectives. These objectives, among other things, state the dollar revenue figure sought, how many and what type of clients should be added, and what profit target is desired. Objectives are important, for, as the saying goes, "if you don't know where you're going, any road will get you there."

There are major differences among accounting firms in the elements of a marketing program to be emphasized. For instance, the burden placed on advertising to create awareness and provide information may vary from none at all to a substantial amount.

Promotion

Promotion is an important part of the marketing program in that it provides methods of communicating with target clients to inform, persuade, and remind them. Promotion can increase a firm's practice with marketing tools like personal selling, publicity, and advertising.

Personal selling is the essential element of the firm's promotional program. Accounting services must be sold personally by accounting professionals. Successful selling begins when the opportunity is found to translate a firm's capabilities into client benefits. The professional must be positioned in appropriate situations to initiate sales; for example, an accountant may take part in a discussion of taxes during which it may be pointed out that in certain situations estimated tax payments can be reduced or pension contributions stretched out. The purchase of an accounting service is not an act but a process, a "creeping commitment," that occurs over time. In fact, a bold attempt at the beginning of a relationship to circumvent this process usually does more harm than good. Some clients can be obtained in this manner but can subsequently be lost just as quickly. It is also important to note that selling does not stop when a commitment has been made, for ways are continually being sought to establish the firm's services firmly in the client's business.

Publicity is a nonpaid form of communication that can have a significant impact on maintaining "word-of-mouth" recognition. Even though publicity is not paid for by the sponsor (the article in the newspaper is written for its newsworthiness), time and effort are required to prepare press releases, write articles, and make speeches. Because of the time involved, these activities should be directed at selected audiences. It is important to remember that information should be transmitted to persons in one's own profession and community as well as to target clients.

Advertising provides the means of delivering a message to a large number of people. It also provides visibility through selected media and can increase the awareness of a firm among target clients who to some degree may be presold by an advertising campaign. A firm's image can also be transmitted to a preselected audience of readers, viewers, and listeners. Sometimes a large national firm will speak in its advertising to its staff and potential staff.

It is most important to identify target clients clearly so that the firm can plan and implement each aspect of the promotional program. Basically, a promotional program, a mode of communication, is developed to inform, persuade, and remind target clients and those who influence these clients. Accountants who transmit the message must be mindful that they are the professionals, not the target clients who receive the information. For most clients the ability to judge accounting services is at best underdeveloped. The client looks to the accountant, the person offering the service, to provide answers to certain questions:

Do I need accounting services?
If so, what service(s)?

Who should render these services and how should they be rendered?

Clients are not usually "accounting experts" and must be fitted with a "pair of spectacles" that will help them to see and judge value. Clients do not automatically recognize that the benefits received are greater than the fees paid. They should be assisted by education and by the establishment of a climate of trust. Unfortunately, attempts to educate them have their limits because clients normally have little time to devote to purchase decisions and the subsequent use of the product or service. This is true whether it is related to the acquisition of a computer system or the hiring of an accounting firm.

Therefore the client's decision to employ a firm or to expand the use of a firm's services depends largely on faith in the professional's ability to supply solutions to the client's problems. This faith derives from the reputation of the firm and from a rapport developed in areas of mutual understanding and interest such as golf, the stock market, or charitable endeavors. It is important that the professional be mindful that civic, recreational, and other activities make a significant contribution to the firm's marketing program. A client who is given the opportunity to establish a relationship with a professional can sense much more than is made apparent about the professional's ability.

Price

Pricing or fee setting should not be ignored in marketing program planning. A firm's profitability rests on the proper calculation of the contribution made by each assignment, client, and service. Present profitability can be foregone for the small growing business or for accounts offering training benefits for personnel. Even for the exceptional account, however, a price is established after basic knowledge is gained of the firm's costs and an understanding of the client's perception of the value of its service. Competition and the cost of performing the service are factors in the pricing equation. Cost normally establishes a pricing floor, whereas the ceiling is established by perception of the service's values.

The professional usually tends to minimize a discussion of fees, although it is understood that the client should always be kept informed of the charges. Yet a distaste for discussion of fees should never interfere with the opportunity to stress value. If a client is persuaded of the value of a service, price becomes less an element of consideration. The more a firm differentiates its service from those of others, the less it makes price a common denominator of comparison by the client; for example, differentiating factors are specialization, office location, and expert personnel.

The marketing program delineates how much marketing effort is to be expended to convert identified opportunity into revenue and achieve the firm's objectives. Marketing planning enables a firm to design a program that, when implemented, will minimize wasted effort and project a consistent image; for example, personal selling is orchestrated to avoid unnecessary duplication, and advertising and publicity express their messages in a manner that doesn't create conflicting public impressions. No matter how large the firm, time, if not money, is at a premium. If accounting services can be sold only by professionals, the use of the professional's time for selling is a resource that invites planning.

Once a marketing program has been set in motion the firm will obtain more control over its own growth and the nature of its business. The development and maintenance of an accounting practice by the implementation of a marketing program permits the firm to take the initiative rather than merely reacting to whatever business happens to come through the door.

Throughout the marketing planning process it is important to undergo a client orientation. The concept of marketing is actually a philosophy of business that holds that the problem of any firm is to develop client loyalties and satisfaction. Customer satisfaction, however, must be delivered while meeting firm objectives and maintaining professional growth and norms. The key to good marketing is to maintain a focus on client needs throughout your relationship. This concept establishes a point of view that, by education, persuasion, and reorganization, permeates the thinking of every partner, associate, secretary, and receptionist in the firm.

Today's efforts to persuade clients to use existing services should not obscure the long-run objective of identifying and creating better ones to serve tomorrow's clients. Marketing encourages strategic thinking. Like the tournament chess player, you are not moving where there is room, you are making room for your moves. A future-oriented strategy requires planning today for tomorrow's clients, recognition of the future impact of present decisions, and anticipation of change.

The emphasis is on marketing, not selling. It is a healthier emphasis for all concerned, for marketing's focus is on the buyer's needs, whereas selling's focus is on the seller's needs. Moreover, an overemphasis on volume and growth can eventually lower quality and long-term profitability. A sales-oriented strategy would start with existing services and attempt merely to stimulate clients to buy them in profitable amounts. The emphasis, however, should not be on today's revenue but on long-term profitability. A marketing-oriented approach starts with existing and potential clients and their needs; it plans the services to be offered and the effort required to meet these needs and generates revenue and profits by delivering client satisfaction. It is not marketing that is placed at the firm's center. It is not a winner/loser situation for the firm and its clients. The clients receive more value from services rendered than they paid for and the seller receives more in fees than it cost to deliver them.

An aggressive approach to small-business target clients is based on cold calls, direct mail, and telephone solicitation. With extensive testing we found that 30 hours a week of marketing produced 1.4 clients a week. By clients we are speaking strictly of write-up business clients and not the individual tax-return clients that also came in as a result of this marketing. Next, a telephone campaign for arranging appointments with prospective write-up clients should be instituted. We found that from every 100 phone calls made we could generally get six to eight appointments. As a result of these appointments 10 to 15% of the prospects became clients immediately; another 10 to 15%, after follow-up efforts, were eventually signed up.

It was our determination at this point that the best way to get in the door to talk to a prospect was by soliciting an appointment by telephone as opposed to an uninvited, unannounced cold call. Yet we found that on cold calls made in the field we saw a much greater percentage of owners and were able to obtain a much larger percentage of clients than with the telephone solicitation technique. However, the problem was that a person cold calling in the field could see on the average only 10 to 20 prospects a day, whereas the telephone solicitor could easily make 75 to 100 daily contacts. Therefore in the marketing system that works best the solicitor obtains an appointment by telephone and then calls on the prospective client. This marketing program should produce two to four clients a week.

You must consider the size of your market area and its density. Because our system utilizes the telephone as the best approach to prospects, we have found that the prefix section of the telephone book is an excellent way to determine market areas. Based on your knowledge of your business area, you can isolate businesses by telephone prefix as a method of allocating your markets. Make a calling list before placing your calls to help you keep your efforts organized. These lists should be filed away to be used again because their preparation is time consuming. Aggressive marketing of accounting and tax services is so new and so infrequent that a firm that undertakes to do so in the current environment has a potentially unlimited market in which to work.

The telephone marketing person, when it isn't you, should be the entry-level type to be trained from scratch. Obvious assets are a pleasant speaking voice and a comfortable manner. This trainee should be one who can communicate well and have no trouble handling unusual responses.

You must know from the start just what you will sell to a prospective client. In another chapter you will find a basic outline of an initial telephone approach. Begin by introducing yourself and the firm. Find out at once if you're talking to the owner and if not make an attempt to do so. If you find that you cannot, which is the case approximately 30% of the time, get the owner's name for a possible follow-up. If you are speaking with the owner you have a 15 to 20% chance of getting an appointment. Once you have established the identity of the speaker proceed with a discussion of the purpose of your call. If your accounting practice is new, tell the prospect that you are opening an office in the area to specialize in small and medium-sized clients and that you or an associate would like to drop off a brochure. Ask for a 10- to 15-minute interview. At this point the ability of the telephone marketing person to communicate effectively with the prospect becomes most important. The numerous responses that the owner may make are often subtle in form. It requires a perceptive person to deal with the numerous variations. Typical responses and counters to them are included in the section on sales calls. A good method of keeping on top of them is to type each one on a 3×5 card and file it in a flip-file for easy reference during a telephone call.

THE TELEPHONE MARKETING PERSON (TMP)

Hiring

Over the years our accountants have determined that the best method of recruiting the TMP is to place a modest ad in a major newspaper. The ad should appear under the Help Wanted and run on Sundays only. The applicants should be interviewed in person at your office or at some other prearranged location. Some of the qualities to look for during the interview follow:

1. Clarity of speech.
2. Vocal projections.
3. Aggressiveness.
4. Degree of interest in your service.
5. Available hours of work.
6. Work surroundings.
7. Educational background.
8. Experience, if any.

TELEPHONE SOLICITOR

Financial institution seeks part-time telephone secretary. Work from home. Salary plus commission. Experience preferred. Calling on businesses only. Unusual opportunity. Call _____ .

RUN AD ON SUNDAYS ONLY

The best time for a TMP to make calls to prospects on the computer list is between the hours of 9:00 A.M. and 2:00 P.M. The

TMP should break for lunch between 12:00 and 1:00 P.M., a period that normally coincides with the lunch hours of most prospects. You are looking for 20 hours of productive time a week, or four hours a day.

Work surroundings are important for both male and female telephone secretaries. It is important to stress that no distractions or background noise should be allowed to interfere with a smooth presentation. In essence, work surroundings must be conducive to the job requirements.

Frequently a young married person with some college education is better for this type of work.

In attempting to select the proper TMP, it is not always best to hire a person with years of experience in telephone soliciting, the reason being that these "old pros" have worked for many companies and sometimes tend to represent several firms at a time.

File all applications for future reference because you may not be lucky enough to find the right person at first. Your first TMP may work out but we have found that it is good practice to keep two or three in reserve.

Many compensation plans have been tried, but salary plus commission is by far the best system. In testing areas on the East Coast and in the Midwest we have discovered that the average TMP starts at a wage of $7.00 to $10.00 an hour and a commission of $75.00 for every new client obtained.

Because the TMP will be working at home, you must explain that the job is based on the honor system and that 20 hours a week must be guaranteed for the hourly wages paid. If the TMP wishes to work longer hours to increase the commission potential it would be to your benefit as well.

A good TMP can earn approximately $400.00 a week. You will find that you can obtain satisfactory work with this salary and bonus arrangement. In the section on training the TMP we discuss the importance of a trial period. You should expect appointments by the third day.

A word to the wise. Some accountants starting out on their new careers have failed in this vital area of telephone soliciting by attempting to use their spouses or relations. There are exceptions to every rule, but please give serious thought to the adverse conditions that may result from applying undue pressure on a relation or close friend. These persons may not qualify and because of their relationship to you will hesitate to admit that they cannot handle the job.

Training

Once you have hired your TMP you will begin extensive training. The first thing to do is to have the TMP sign a lead list receipt. This agreement will include a acknowledgement of the telephone presentation booklet and the computer lead list. In addition, the TMP will also agree not to divulge trade secrets or the names of any of the prospective clients. The presentation booklet can be put together in a three-ring, cardboard presentation folder available at any stationery store and should contain instructions regarding the required work schedule, follow-up, and compensation. To these is added the actual presentation sheet; all are enclosed in acetate sheets in the binder. Be certain to obtain all necessary information on the TMP for your files (e.g., name, address, telephone number, and social security number). Because the TMP is hired on a contract basis, most accountants do not withhold taxes but do provide a 1099 at year-end.

Before you supply live leads it is strongly suggested that the TMP practice the presentation by using the Yellow Pages for at least one day. Designate categories of small businesses that you would like the TMP to call. Try to monitor these calls so that you can offer constructive criticism. Many TMPs have made appointments from the Yellow Pages but direct-mail leads are best.

You are now ready to have your TMP work on live leads. A number of supplies will be needed:

1. A 3 × 5 card file (for call-backs).
2. Sales brochure.
3. An appointment calendar.
4. The current week's computer lead list.
5. Telephone presentation booklet.
6. Sample mailing piece.

The 3 × 5 cards are necessary for logging all call-backs. The TMP will experience many occasions to follow up to obtain an appointment. A healthy call-back file should be developed. It is worth money to both of you and its importance should be emphasized. The 3 × 5 cards are worked in conjunction with the appointment calendar. Call-backs may be made at a time after normal working hours and the TMP should not hesitate to try in the evening. This will maximize commissions.

It is important to explain the sales brochure to give the TMP a better understanding of the contents of the telephone presentation. Also familiarize the TMP with the mailing piece.

The appointment calendar should be coordinated with your appointments on a daily basis (this in addition to the TMP's call-back schedule).

At this point you will present the TMP with the computerized lead list, but not in its entirety. We have found by experience that it is advisable to make a photocopy of approximately 200 business names from the list; enough for one week of calls. You will, as previously mentioned, be mailing 200 leads a week; therefore the TMP should be making 40 contacts a day. A contact is defined as a presentation to the owner or principal of a business and not an associate or clerk. A telephone call is not considered a contact until the TMP actually speaks with the principal. You must supervise the TMP by scrutinizing the work to ascertain that a call has not been marked NG when the owner has not been reached. The 3 × 5 follow-up card should be used if contact cannot be made that very day.

Many good lead lists have been ineffective because of the poor supervision of TMPs by the accountant. You should touch briefly on each NG lead every day to help the TMP to overcome the same routine objections.

Exhibit 20 is a Lead List Receipt, which should be signed by the TMP.

Exhibit 21 is a copy of a telephone marketing presentation that I developed and have used with great success. Feel free to adapt it to your own personality.

The telephone presentation is captioned with the words "Be Enthusiastic." This is extremely important because the TMP's attitude is reflected in the voice. The TMP should study this presentation and all the important notations outlined at the end. The TMP will find good techniques for overcoming strong objections but common sense must be used. Again, as suggested before, the TMP should practice with the Yellow Pages until a smooth natural delivery has been perfected. Most important to remember is that the telephone presentation may be varied but not changed.

Train the telephone marketing person to speak to employees only to find out when the owner can be reached. If a spouse or partner answers state your business and determine whether an appointment can be made for the owner. Always suggest that the appointment be made at their convenience and at the prospect's place of business. If asked how long it will take say at least one hour to make meaningful suggestions for improving their record-keeping methods. When the appointment time has been

---

Date _____

Accountant's name
Accountant's address
City, State, and Zip Code

Dear Sir:

I agree to accept the following material and to return at any given time during my employment:

A. The telephone presentation.

B. Computerized lead list.

I also agree not to divulge any of the prospective clients' names or other material.

Signed _____

Date _____

Exhibit 20. Lead List Receipt

agreed on ask them to write it down. Be sure that everyone who is associated with the owner is included (spouse and/or partner who take part in day-to-day business decisions). Their absence is sometimes fatal to securing the client. The TMP should be prepared to detect problems that the prospect may wish to discuss. Listen carefully and make notes. Keep a 3 × 5 card with which to record the exact name of the business, the names of the owner and partners, and address and telephone number, and any other pertinent information. Ask for directions to remote or out-of-the way locations.

BE ENTHUSIASTIC

IT PAYS!!

Good morning! May I speak to the owner please?

(If the owner is "out" or "busy" ask the person who answered the phone for the name of the owner and the best time to call him back. Write the owner's name on a card. *Do not* give your presentation to anyone but the owner or the owner's spouse. When you have reached the owner say

This is _____ of John Smith & Associates. We sent you descriptive literature to acquaint you with our complete computerized bookkeeping, accounting, and tax work service. Our accountant in your area would like to call at your convenience to describe in detail how our complete monthly service will fit into the service your business needs.

Naturally there is no charge for his visit nor does it take long.

When is the most convenient time for us to make an appointment for you with our accountant?

It may be to your advantage to compare our *monthly computerized* service with what you are now using.

Besides maintaining a complete bookkeeping system for you we

(a) promptly prepare your monthly profit and loss statement, which includes an excellent analysis of your business by percentages;

(b) prepare *all* of your tax returns and *naturally* file them on time;

(c) we reconcile your bank account monthly;

(d) we furnish you with personal advisory counsel based on the experience of others in your type of occupation;

and

(e) of course, bring all of your backwork up to date.

We also offer an excellent computerized accounts-receivable application.

If the prospect interrupts and asks, "How much?"

ANSWER: It is based on volume of work. Our accountant will be able to give you an answer after he has talked to you and determines the amount of work to be done. The fees start at $115.00 per month.

Exhibit 21. Telephone Marketing Sales Presentation

If the reply is that they are currently doing their own work you may ask: Have you ever considered the work saving, income tax saving, and counseling aspects of a monthly computerized service?

Whenever possible, after following through on a question or comment with the prospect, continue with this: What I would like to do is arrange a time when our accountant could show you just how our service can be tailored to fit your particular needs.

(You might mention to the prospect that the gentleman who will be calling is an accountant and not a salesman.)

When the prospect agrees to see the accountant your reply should be: *Fine,* when is the best time for the accountant to talk with you in detail.

IF YOU RECEIVE A STRONG OBJECTION YOU MIGHT TRY THIS

Sir, we do not employ salesmen. The accountant calling on you will merely demonstrate our system; you will decide.

You see, sir, our computer system completely takes the bookkeeping responsibility out of your hands. There is virtually no bookkeeping required and the cost will be only a fraction of what you are presently paying.

You will have to vary from the calling procedure occasionally, depending on the development of your conversation.

REMEMBER: You may VARY but you may not CHANGE the procedure.

Exhibit 21. (Continued)

REMEMBER: Above all, supervise your TMP

GOAL: Get appointments.

Although the TMP is not an accountant, some training in the basic terminology touched on in the presentation must be given. Acquaint the TMP with a 941, general ledger, and tax forms.

Your success depends heavily on how well you supervise the TMP. If you merely drop off the presentation and a stack of leads you may be certain that the TMP in most cases will be a failure. Daily contact is necessary. Discuss all problems and above all assist in overcoming them. Never agree with the TMP that the leads are no good or that the presentation should be altered. If you do, you will have laid the groundwork for derailing the entire system. Always remember that the TMP looks to you for support. You must impress on the TMP that the "total system" does work and that patience will bring results. The TMP's *only* responsibility is to obtain appointments. If the performance is not satisfactory terminate immediately.

The following criteria are presented as a gauge of the TMP's productivity. If no appointments have been made after the third full day a conference should take place.

It is now imperative to determine whether the TMP has the ability to do the work or whether phone calls have even, in fact, been made. This is a management decision that you alone must make. By the third day some appointments should have been arranged; by the second week the average should be three a day. If by that time the TMP has come nowhere near the quota you will have no choice. Terminate. Refer to your file of applicants and begin selecting another TMP. This is a trial-and-error situation, for it is almost impossible to predict the outcome. You may have to make two or three attempts to reach your objective. Time is expensive and you cannot afford to drag out the employment of a nonproductive TMP.

Appointments

Next in the chain of events is preparation for the appointment.

Because your TMP will report appointments on a daily basis, it is important that your calendars be coordinated. In the early stages of your growth your total effort will be in the area of marketing. It is not wise at this point to confirm appointments because the prospect may take the opportunity to postpone or cancel.

Show up on time, fully prepared to offer your services. We have discussed preparation. Nothing is more irritating to the prospect than unpreparedness.

Preparation includes all the necessary forms and sales brochures. It also includes a proper mental attitude. It goes without saying that your overall appearance and manner should reflect the professional public accountant, by which is meant proper grooming and attire to complement the prestigious position you hold.

10

PROSPECTING FOR CLIENTS

Any successful enterprise that requires marketing testifies to the truth of the statement that "results equate directly to exposure."

Maximum profit is generated by defining customer profiles accurately, searching out segments of the total customer base with similar characteristics, and then soliciting and resoliciting these segments to realize maximum sales throughout the longest possible client life-cycle.

Harnessing direct marketing's power requires more than your in-depth knowledge of your services. Just as important is the market analysis and planning discipline that can systematically and repeatedly apply expertise to the solution of your selling or communications problems. In this way you will reach your objective consistently and predictably by transforming the art of direct marketing into a more scientific and reliable approach.

You will never master the science of selling unless you can get in to see the prospects. First of all, there is no way to effectively practice and improve your skills of persuasion without real live clients. Secondly, even if you could become such a master that you sell 50% of the people you see, if you only see two people, you'll only get one new client.

Many accountants underestimate the value of prospecting skills. However, there are many sales trainers and sales managers who overestimate the outmoded concept that in order to be successful in building a practice, you need to get "belly to belly" with 20 prospects every day. The problem is that it is a rare accountant who can do so consistently and effectively over any period of time. Furthermore, even if that were possible, it is a very inefficient use of time. The accountant's time is being compressed by longer sales cycles and greater service demands from clients. This is compounded by an environment in which clients are much harder to reach. Sales is no longer simply a numbers game.

One accountant had been using the old cold call method and tracking the results. The accountant discovered that it took dialing the phone 15 times for each meeting that was secured with a prospective client. Rather than 20 face-to-face appointments per day, the goal was only three to five. Even with a smaller goal, it still took 225 calls to fill up one week's itinerary.

As competition grows and each sale becomes more complicated and time consuming, both accountant and client are becoming more time conscious. Neither can afford to spend as much time on low potential activities. Simple axioms like "see more people to sell more people" no longer apply. Today's accountant needs to discover new ways of getting the most done with the least amount of effort.

The most important quality for an accountant selling today is no longer persuasiveness. The new password is "strategy." Efficient prospecting which sets you up with high potential clients is the first strategic step.

COMPREHENSIVE RESEARCH NEEDED

To obtain and sustain profitable long-term growth of your accounting business you must start right away to provide comprehensive research and planning. You will find that the effort to gather the basic information and the insights you will need from your employees, consultants, agencies, government, and association sources—even your competitors—will stimulate all of them to become more creative.

Your key people will "see" response relationships that they may have overlooked.

It will force a "three-dimensional" exploration of the many combinations of marketing approaches and vehicles.

You will have to assign priorities to your objectives in terms of their probable bottom-line impact. Some will be attainable at little cost; others may be long-term, and some may be basically in conflict and will have to be modified or abandoned.

Your staff and suppliers will be forced to provide you with "up front" program specifications and schedules that will give you a running start in the control of quality and deadline performance once your actual program gets underway.

Benchmarks of expected return and profitability at each state in the life-cycle of your clients can be established to specify in advance acceptable measurements of the success or failure of a program.

The several expected consequences of each marketing decision can be spelled out in advance, thus allowing you to select the most profitable paths for testing.

A new perspective on options in planning will be disseminated to your staff and suppliers; they will learn to think in terms of overall relationships rather than of one-by-one unrelated steps.

As part of a continuous, cooperating system your associates

will do their work more enthusiastically, creatively, and consistently.

You have only limited resources, no matter how large your operation. People . . . time . . . thought . . . creativity . . . money are the foundation on which you've built your business. When you harness each of these elements systematically within the discipline of an overall structure to attain, step by step, your long-term objectives, you'll be maximizing the factors that have led to your initial success without sacrificing the creativity, spontaneity, and even the genius that you will expend to build your business.

If you're going to succeed, get your message across to prospects who are also being approached by your competitors, and bring in those prospects and sales leads in ever increasing numbers. You can't keep operating out of your back pocket. In these inflationary times even a "flattening out" of responses indicates a slump in profitability. Growth is more important than ever and can be sustained over the long-run only by increasingly complex planning.

This planning is definitely cost-effective, even over the short run, and the time, effort, and money spent will show up on the bottom line. Beyond any question, a superior and comprehensive direct-response marketing plan is a prerequisite to maximizing profits.

Far too many accountants spend too much of their time and energy trying to set up meetings with prospects by convincing them that they need the accountant's services (whether they do or not). There are several problems with this approach:

1. You usually don't know what their need is until you have the sales meeting in the first place. It's the old double bind: you can't get the meeting without demonstrating that you'll meet needs, but you can't demonstrate that you'll meet needs unless you get the meeting.

2. The prospect may already have someone in mind who can meet their needs.
3. You have still done nothing to predispose the prospect to listening to you in the first place.
4. Even when it works, you risk spending too much of your time dealing with low potential clients.

RESPECTING YOURSELF

If you believe in what you have to offer, then you have to believe that your time is just as valuable as your prospective client's. Don't waste it on low potential prospects. In other words, don't see people just because they're willing to see you. First make sure that they qualify to do business with you.

We will concentrate first on developing a "hit list" of high potential clients. Once your list is developed, we will work on how to gain admission to the client's appointment book by influencing their gatekeeper (a process called establishing "recognition").

DEVELOPING YOUR HIT LIST

Mining for High Potential Prospects

When the California gold rush started in 1849, many became wealthy just by showing up and looking around. (However, many also starved.) Today, finding new sources of gold takes highly sophisticated geologic surveys. These surveys are not done to locate isolated pieces of gold, but rather to determine areas of high potential for locating gold veins.

Selling todays presents much the same challenge. Honing your presentation skills and hitting the streets just isn't enough any more. You need to survey your market place for high potential prospects. In addition, rather than looking for the isolated sale, you'll need to find your selling veins of gold; business that leads to other business, and clients that lead to other clients.

High Potential Prospects:

1. Are predisposed to buying;
2. Can lead to other clients.

Predisposition

Since you won't know beforehand what your prospect's real needs that are related to your services are, this step becomes an "odds are" game. The idea here is to find the factors that most people who will need your services have in common so that you can develop your prospect list on that basis.

Business Predisposition

1. Companies in the following fields are more likely to need my services:

   _____   _____
   _____   _____
   _____   _____
   _____   _____
   _____   _____

2. Companies are more likely to need my services if their:
   A. Gross revenues range from _____ to _____.
   B. Profit range from _____ to _____.

    C. Other economic qualifiers: _____.

3. Companies are more likely to need my services if they employ:

    A. Between _____ and _____ number of people.

    B. Between _____ and _____ number of managers.

    C. Other employment qualifiers: _____

4. Odds are better that a company which is currently using the following products/services will need my services:

5. The companies that buy my services are more likely to be found in the following geographic areas: (Can be broken down by city, county, zip code, etc., or by the zip code areas within your territory where the income level of prospects most closely matches the requirements for your services.)

6. Odds are that a large percentage of the people that are members of the following clubs could benefit from my services:

7. Odds are that a large percentage of my potential clients subscribe to one of the following publications:

       _____   _____

       _____   _____

       _____   _____

       _____   _____

       _____   _____

8. Odds are that the decision maker I will need to contact has the following title:
   A. Primary decision maker   _____
   B. Secondary decision maker   _____
   C. Screen   _____

9. Odds are that the above decision makers will belong to one of the following clubs or associations:

       _____   _____

       _____   _____

       _____   _____

       _____   _____

10. Odds are that a large percentage of the above decision makers subscribe to one of the following publications:

       _____   _____

       _____   _____

       _____   _____

       _____   _____

11. Odds are that my prospective client will have the following needs/problems:

       _____   _____

       _____   _____

       _____   _____

If you have filled out the previous work sheets, you will have developed a profile of high potential prospects. The information can now be used to search for new names for your list.

WHERE DO YOU FIND THEM?

1. You already have them: Many accountants already have files full of leads that they never seem to find the time to follow up on. If you're one of them, take the time now to go through that file and see if you can further qualify them by using the factors identified in the work sheets. If you don't have the information necessary to qualify them as high potential prospects, you may want to consider using a telemarketing survey to get this information.

   Since this will be a survey (you will not be attempting to secure a meeting or a sale) anyone in your office can conduct it for you. If you have sufficient numbers (usually approximately 500 or more) it is cost effective to pay a telemarketing service to conduct this survey for you. A good service is fast, efficient, and doesn't use up your time or the time of others in your office.

2. Purchase a list: You can find a good list broker in your local Yellow Pages that will be willing to sit down with you, review the factors you've identified on your work sheets, and discuss options and lists available for you to rent or buy. If you decide to take this tack, you'll want to wait until you've finished the direct mail prospecting portion of this book so that you can discuss with your list broker how you'll be using these names.

3. Trade associations or clubs: Trade associations or clubs which prospects may belong to often are willing to give, rent, or sell their membership lists.

4. Publications: Publications to which your prospects may subscribe are often willing to sell or rent their subscriber lists.

5. Present clients: It is surprising how many accountants fail to follow up on present clients who can refer you to someone else who may be ready to engage you.

6. Newspapers: Skimming your local newspapers with a highlighter pen in hand can uncover a gold mine of prospects that are predisposed to buying your services.

7. The Yellow Pages: If you sell to specific classifications of businesses, this could be a good starting point. However, you'll have to dig deeper to get names and other information you need. You can call your phone company for copies of the directories for areas that you call. There are specialized directories available, such as street and cross-street directories and listings by telephone number sequence, that might fit your marketing needs.

IDENTIFY SUPER HIGH POTENTIAL PROSPECTS

Now that you've got your list compiled, go through it and ask the following questions:

1. Will my services solve a problem or fulfill a need for them?

2. If I establish a good relationship with them, can this lead to other business?

If you can answer "yes" to both of these questions, give that prospect an "A" rating. If you can answer "yes" to one but not both questions, give that prospect a "B" rating. If you can't answer "yes" to either of those questions, give the prospect a "C" rating.

Now divide your list into those three areas. Only go after the "B" rated prospects once you have exhausted all of the "A" rated prospects and deal with the "C" rated prospects only if they approach you first.

You've isolated a hit list of high potential prospects. In order to tap into that potential you'll need recognition so that you can get through the door. In this chapter, we'll work on the three most effective ways of establishing recognition. It's all based on positive exposure to your potential client. When the prospect is thinking, "I've heard of this person," he's a lot more likely to grant you a meeting. In addition, when handled properly, these three methods will also give you credibility by enhancing the value of that exposure. If "I've heard of this person" makes it easier to get in the door, then just imagine what "I've heard this person's good" will do for your chances!

The three methodologies are:

1. Direct mail prospecting: This is a strategic approach designed to keep your prospecting alive every day, but with a minimum of effort.
2. Referral prospecting: This step uses key centers of influence to establish credibility and gain admission into your prospect's appointment book.
3. Visibility prospecting: This is the ultimate in credibility builders and is the most effective way to get the client to come to you.

THE SECRET TO GREATER SALES SUCCESS

Make effective prospecting your daily habit. Once you've completed all the work in this chapter, the system itself will be very easy to follow. By making a commitment to sticking with this system, you will develop a prospecting mentality. Within two to three months your sales will start climbing and you'll never have to make another cold call.

DIRECT MAIL PROSPECTING

Do you remember the story about the race between the tortoise and the hare? The over-confident hare gets off to an early lead. He covers a lot of ground fast and then decides to take a nap. While he's napping, the tortoise covers a smaller amount of ground every day and, because of his consistency, wins.

The prospecting efforts of many accountants can be compared to the hare's racing strategy. When there is very little or no business they gather up many leads and fervently go about contacting these prospects. With success, more time is dedicated to concluding the sale and servicing the client, leaving less time and less motivation to continue searching for new clients at this inflated pace. Consequently, prospecting takes a nap while current business is being handled. This is how sales slumps are created.

For example, if the sales cycle (the process of going from first contact to signed engagement agreement) typically takes two weeks, and your prospecting efforts are reduced while you attend to current accounts, especially with backwork to bring each account up-to-date, when you're finished with those current accounts and start prospecting again, you've got yourself caught up in a two week sales slump. To combat this you need to develop a system that allows you to continually bring in new leads even when other selling and client service activities are high.

The direct mail prospecting system has been developed to help the accountant gain recognition with the prospect before calling to ask for an appointment. It is also an effective method of getting to large numbers of prospects with minimal time invested each day. It therefore serves as the foundation for your prospecting efforts.

THE BASIC SYSTEM

1. Send out five pieces of direct mail each day to new prospects.
2. Send three to four letters to each new prospect before attempting to contact them personally. Space these letters 7 to 14 days apart.
3. Follow up with a phone call approximately five days after their receipt of your last letter.

This system works for many reasons. First, it achieves recognition. Direct mail studies indicate that it takes three exposures before the customer begins to recognize your name. A good portion of these prospects won't even recall how they recognize your name. They'll just know that they've heard of you (and everything they've heard is good because you wrote it). It also works because it is the most consistent and efficient method to get at a large number of prospects effectively.

For example, if you mail four letters to each prospect spaced one week apart and choose five new prospects every day, you will reach 100 new prospects every month. Since you'll have all of these letters prepared and ready to mail ahead of time, you'll need to spend less than one hour per day implementing the system.

The following schedule shows how this works:

Direct Mail Prospecting Schedule

First week: Mail the first letter to five new prospects each day.

Second week: Mail the second letter to the five prospects that recieved their first letter last week.
Mail the first letter to five more new prospects each day.

At this point you will be mailing ten letters per day. By the end of the second week, you will have initiated contact with 50 new prospects.

Third week: Mail the third letter to your first group of prospects.

Mail the second letter to the second group of prospects.

Mail the first letter to five more new prospects each day.

You will now be mailing out a total of 15 letters per day. By the end of week three, you will have initiated contact with 75 new prospects.

Fourth week: Mail the fourth and final letter to your first group of prospects.

Mail the third letter to the second group of prospects.

Mail the second letter to the third group of prospects.

Mail the first letter to five more new prospects each day.

You will now be mailing a total of 20 letters per day. By the end of week four, you will have initiated contact with 100 new prospects.

Fifth week: Begin phoning your first group of prospects who have by now received their fourth and final letter.

Mail the fourth and final letter to your second group of prospects.

Mail the third letter to your third group of prospects.

Mail the second letter to your fourth group of prospects.

Mail the first letter to five more new prospects each day.

> Your efforts will now have stabilized at 20
> letters and five phone calls per day. This should
> take from 20 to 60 minutes depending on the
> number of calls that get through and the length
> of each conversation.

By the end of the fifth week, you will have made contact with
125 new prospects and phoned 25 of them to ask for meetings.
Keeping this system going will ensure that in less than one hour
per day, you will be able to contact 100 new prospects every
month.

Finally, what makes this system so effective is the persistence
factor. It will come as no surprise to you that the higher the level
of executive you are trying to reach, the more difficult it is to get
through. It is also true that the higher the level of executive, the
more likely they are to be the kind of person that appreciates
persistence.

You will constantly hear such comments as, "I wish all my
people were as dedicated as you are," or "I figured anyone as
persistent as you are deserves fifteen minutes of my time," or
even, "I thought I better give you the appointment or you'd
never leave me alone."

"What do I do when I run out of leads?" Remember to be
persistent. Cycle the ones you weren't able to get through to
back into the system for your next set of mailings. However,
remember to eliminate prospects from your list that prove to be
"low potential." At the same time you should be looking for new
leads.

Planning for Long-Term Profits

The effective creation of a direct-marketing plan affects your
long-term profit more than any other factor. Consequently your
organization must force itself to provide adequate time, money,

and personnel to develop a comprehensive marketing plan by the task method.

Expressed in one sentence, a direct-response marketing plan is the base on which to build your profits; incorporate it into your business life in the months ahead.

Negative Marketing Conditions

Some of the major conditions that contribute to and prohibit the growth of your practice are the result of distractions, so begin by setting your goals. Some accountants have been completely overwhelmed by minor problems that could have been by-passed, so they could have surged forward to the goal of obtaining new clients. Some of these major "problems" are:

1. Negative outside influences, such as a telephone marketing person's comments that the presentation does not work.
2. Clients who do not believe in computers.
3. Inability to manage the business and keep sales appointments.

If you concentrate on all the reasons for failure you could no doubt come up with untold excuses. The most important thing to keep in mind is that the system outlined in this book works for the majority of accountants.

Remember the formula that is paramount in our marketing system: CALLS equal LEADS equal SALES.

MOTIVATION

The first phase of an accountant's practice requires a heavy expenditure of time. Processing and marketing are full-time jobs in themselves. Thus the accountant must work the equivalent of two jobs. In so doing you will have the satisfaction of knowing that every hour you work is for yourself, not for someone else. The sooner you obtain enough clients to justify hiring a processing clerk, the quicker you will succeed. The amount of time you spend on marketing will increase with corresponding growth in the practice and profits. In short, you must focus on marketing and maintain processing.

After one year the motivated accountant who follows our system will have approximately 60 clients. You cannot stop your marketing campaign here. The entrepreneur who gains a certain share of the market and rests on laurels will soon lose clients to more motivated practitioners. You must continue to market to maintain your position. Even the best accountant will experience attrition. Your clients will declare bankruptcy or default on payments. When you experience this attrition you must acquire referrals simultaneously.

Growth leads to success! The accountant who does not aim at perpetual growth becomes complacent. The only sure thing in business is change. You will find that a practice will rarely maintain a level dollar volume. The direction you should follow is obvious.

The client expects the accountant to be active in servicing and processing work on time. The ideal accountant is one who never forgets the client and who never ceases to look for new clients to help the practice grow. This accountant provides quick and accurate results, friendly service, good advice, and an aggressive manner with equal success.

A successful accountant constantly *thinks* growth. You must also *think* success. It is not determined by your good looks, your mental capacity, or heritage but by your impact on the people with whom you come in contact. People cause people to act in a predetermined fashion. You are what you think you are.

To have an effective impact on the people you will meet on a day-to-day basis your mental attitude must be healthy and positive. Look on each appointment as a visit. Be cheerful, confident, and poised. You may call on a businessperson who has had a busy, troublesome day. You will set the tone of your meeting when you walk in the door with a handshake and a smile. Be friendly and calm and you will dominate the mood.

To feel confident you must know your marketing plan step by step. Practice is the common word between all professionals—doctors, lawyers, engineers, and accountants: practice, rehearse, practice. A professional marketeer plans what to do and what to say.

Your success in marketing is based on your ability to maintain your credibility:

1. Keep appointments. Have no fear of rejection that will put you in an attitude of skipping calls and finding yourself sitting at your desk sorting and shuffling your lead cards.
2. Keep good appointments. Enjoy yourself, make your visits pleasant, something to look forward to, not a chore.
3. Call on good prospects. This is a matter of organization. Use the referral method to find new clients and remember that the best appointment is the one someone else makes for you.
4. Be in the right state of mind. Feel good about yourself.

The knowledge that your sales approach is effective should give you confidence in your presentation. Work smarter, not harder. Never leave a sales presentation you did not close wondering what you did wrong—remember what you did right. You must do the "right" thing next time. Do not waste your energy analyzing what went wrong. Concentrate on what is right. Be a "Pro"! Have conviction, realize your capacity for work, and always remember to be constantly on top. Be aware!

DIRECT-MAIL PIECES

No magic is involved in direct-mail campaigns. The magic lies in the term *follow-up;* the second factor in our formula is the telephone marketing person. You will see as we progress into marketing how important a part the telephone secretary plays in helping you to achieve the necessary exposure among prospective clients.

Exhibits 22 and 23 are reproductions of direct-mail letters I have used successfully. They will provide a basis on which to develop your own letters.

The Client Lead Lists

There are hundreds of lead-list companies. Use one close to you. Ask for leads to small and medium-sized businesses prepared "pressure sensitive" labels. Also ask for a computerized printout that carries the telephone numbers. Telephone numbers are extremely important.

You must submit your order by zip code only. This is necessary for your bulk-rate mailing campaign. All bulk-rate mailings must be bundled by zip code.

The leads must meet certain standards for use in a successful campaign. We therefore stress the importance of obtaining reliable computer lead lists.

No direct mail campaign achieves a 100% return. Do not let this disturb you. We talk of exposure and basically this is what we are trying to accomplish. It is, of course, suggested that you review the list and remove the obvious labels such as governmental agencies that would never be prospects, but they'll slip through occasionally. The purpose of review is to save postage and printing costs.

Jack Fox Associates

Suite 550   4520 East-West Highway   Bethesda, Maryland 20814   (301) 656-7629

Accounting   Tax & Financial Consulting

Dear Business Owner,

How does your business stack up against its competition?

Do you fully understand your financial capabilities? What income data do you currently maintain on your net sales, cost of sales, gross profit and operating expenses? How about ratios: What are your assets to liabilities? Sales to receivables? Cost of sales to inventories?

No matter what business you're in -- we serve wholesale distributors, home improvement specialists, retail stores, travel agencies, general contractors and tradesmen, automotive service centers, non-profit organizations and associations -- you need customized financial reports every month in order to manage your business successfully. From carry-out restaurants to chimney sweeps, our expertise provides small businesses with the fast, accurate and concise financial records they need to top off their bottom line.

Computerized Financial Services, Inc., offered through Jack Fox Associates, brings a wide variety of business management and tax services to the small business owner at a minimal cost, including: income tax preparation, tax counseling and planning, accounting systems and bookkeeping records, loan packaging, new business start-up assistance and financial support in the critical areas of marketing, sales management and data processing.

We're in business to help solve the many problems confronting small business owners....so they can better manage their operations. You're in business to make a profit; we're in business to help you maximize that profit.

I'd like to send you a free current statement study including comparative historical data and other sources of composite financial information on your specific industry. Published by Robert Morris Associates, this comprehensive analysis will help you to better assess the efficiency of your own business operation....and learn how you rate in comparison to your competitors.

Just return the enclosed postage-paid business reply card for your free statement study and a personal presentation of our services--there's no cost or obligation!

However small your business, I'm sure you'll find that Computerized Financial Services can make business dollars and sense.

Sincerely,
Jack Fox Associates

Jack Fox, President
Computerized Financial Services, Inc.

encl.

Exhibit 22. Direct Mail Piece

"QUARTERLY TAX DEADLINES:"

- FEDERAL PAYROLL (941) TAXES
- STATE PAYROLL TAXES
- STATE UNEMPLOYMENT TAXES
- RETAIL SALES TAXES
- PERSONAL & CORPORATION ESTIMATED TAXES

ARE YOU MEETING THESE CRITICAL "TAX DEADLINES"?
IS YOUR PROFIT PICTURE WHAT YOU'VE ANTICIPATED?

If not, is it because you as a small or medium-sized business can't afford the high priced ACCOUNTANTS, SPECIALISTS AND CONSULTANTS the large corporations retain?

Wouldn't it be advantageous to have all the financial services of these experts at your finger tips for ONE INCREDIBLY LOW MONTHLY FEE!

Our firm of highly trained accountants with offices in your area can offer you this 5 step program at an economical monthly fee. Allowing you the needed time to concentrate on managing your business and free you of the burdensome "BOOKKEEPING AND TAX DETAILS".

OUR 5 STEP PROGRAM:

1) PERSONAL INTERVIEWS
2) COMPLETE TAX SERVICE
3) MONTHLY COMPUTERIZED "PROFIT & LOSS STATEMENT"
4) ALL BOOKKEEPING & LEDGERS MONTHLY
5) BUSINESS CHECKING ACCOUNT RECONCILED MONTHLY

The attached PROFIT & LOSS statement is an example of what todays small to medium-sized business man relies on as a management tool in order to control his business and compete with tough competition. This P & L statement shows your Cost of Sales including monthly and year-to-date PERCENTAGE figures. Allowing you the needed comparison to other similar businesses.

Included with your monthly P & L Statement are complete monthly computer reports showing detail of every check written for instant reference to controll excess spending in Cost or Overhead areas, before spending gets out of hand

Our Computers will process ALL your Ledgers ELIMINATING the need for your keeping Ledger Books, Payroll Records, Bank Reconciliations, quarterly Payroll Tax filings etc.

All Accounting and review of your Financial Statements are done monthly by the Accountant in an office servicing your area. He will prepare ALL Taxes and complete any backwork necessary to bring your records and taxes up to date confidentially. He is only a telephone call away and will stop by for a Personal interview to periodically discuss your needs and offer assistance.

Because of our unique IBM Accounting Computer System we can offer all of these services performed by an accountant assigned to you for a low monthly fee that you as a Small to Medium-sized business man CAN afford.

The ease of conversion to our system by the Accountant is effective and fast so as not to interrupt the day to day activities of your business

Our Accountant is interested in your business and would welcome the opportunity to stop by and explain the "NEW CONCEPT IN LOW COST RECORD KEEPING" and the "5 STEPS TO PROFIT" program at no obligation of course.

Please call our office at the above number or use the self addressed reply card. Our accountant will call for an appointment that is convenient for you.

Yours truly,

AHF/lar

P.S. — We offer complete computerized Accounts Receivable billing Systems with automatic ageing of accounts to cut the high cost of manual preparation and timely billing (important to a healthy Cash Flow).

Exhibit 23. Direct Mail Piece

Permits and Licenses

It is essential that you obtain a Bulk Rate and First Class Permit Numbers for prepaid postage.

The First Class Permit Number is used for 9 × 12 business-reply envelopes and business reply cards.

The 9 × 12 business reply envelopes are supplied to clients on an on-going basis for mailing their material to you each week. Under tested conditions it was found that clients won't address envelopes and affix postage. These envelopes have great marketing value and must be used.

The Bulk Mail Permit must be applied for at the Post Office at which you will mail your letters. The cost is currently $65 and must be renewed annually. This permit allows you to mail identical mailing pieces at a greatly reduced postage rate, provided you include at least 200 pieces per mailing and package them by zip code. There is also an additional one-time fee of $60 for the privilege of pre-printing the bulk rate permit number.

The two permit numbers can be obtained together from your local post office. It is important that you explain in detail their purpose so that the postal agent can issue the correct numbers. These permit numbers must be sent to the printer before any work can be initiated.

Direct-Mail Package

The following items are required in your direct-mail campaign:

1. Business name.
2. Business address.
3. Business telephone number.
4. Permit numbers.
5. Signature on mailing piece.

Business Name

You should be trading as John Smith & Associates. Most accountants prefer to use their own names on financial statements and sales brochures.

Business Address

This address should reflect an actual street location as opposed to a P.O. box number. Clients and prospects hesitate to respond to an unidentified box. The P.O. box number can be used in conjunction with the street address. The business address is printed on the tax mailer in the upper right-hand corner and also on the business reply card; your return address will appear on the number 10 envelope.

Business Telephone Number

This number must be shown on all direct-mail pieces and business stationery.

Signature on Mailing Piece

Accountants have taken several approaches to the printed signature on direct-mail pieces. Many will use their own names, with or without title. Some use a firm name. The name, of course, must be submitted along with other information at the time the printing is ordered.

All five of these items must be sent at the same time or your order will be returned, incomplete.

The direct-mail package consists of four parts: a business reply card, quarterly tax mailer, profit and loss statement, and a number 10 envelope. The mailing technique, used in conjunction with a prospect label list, is discussed later.

Exhibits 24 and 25 are reproductions of the business reply card and brochure used in direct mail solicitations.

Sales Brochure

One of the most important sales tools is your sample of the financial package which is part of the sales presentation. This

Dear Jack,

☐ **YES!** Please send me my free statement study and contact me so that I can learn more about the financial services offered by Computerized Financial Services, Inc. I'm especially interested in:

BOOKKEEPING	TAXATION	MANAGEMENT SERVICES
☐ Financial Statements	☐ Personal and/or	☐ New Business Start-Up Assistance
☐ Bookkeeping Services	☐ Business Tax Returns	☐ Loan Applications (SBA & Other)
☐ Payroll Taxes & Records	☐ Estates & Trusts	☐ Systems Design & Implementation
	☐ Tax Planning	☐ Business Evaluation (Sale/Purchase)

Name   Title   Type of Business

Address   City

State   Zip   Telephone

NO POSTAGE
NECESSARY
IF MAILED
IN THE
UNITED STATES

BUSINESS REPLY MAIL
FIRST CLASS   PERMIT NO. 44   GAITHERSBURG, MD. 20760

POSTAGE WILL BE PAID BY ADDRESSEE

**COMPUTERIZED FINANCIAL
SERVICES, INC.**
SUITE 201
3930 KNOWLES AVENUE
KENSINGTON, MARYLAND 20895

Exhibit 24. Business Reply Card

200

Why Do Smart Businessmen Lose Their Business ?

Because of poor financial management, some small businesses fail. Others struggle to keep out of the red. Still others stay in the black only because their owner-managers are willing to work for low pay.

According to the Small Business Administration, poor business results are caused, in many cases, by inadequate financial records. Other times, the owner-manager lacks the ability or experience to use these records wisely. "In achieving effective financial management, the services of a public accountant are helpful," SBA says. "He can design records, set up ways for maintaining them, draw off vital information, and help relate it to a profitable operation."

If you're spending more time with your books than your business, you need CFS — Computerized Financial Services, Inc.

Why CFS

CFS was founded on the belief that, in order to run efficiently and profitably, all businesses—particularly small ones—need the comprehensive, single-source financial services not usually available at a reasonable cost.

From recording and synthesizing financial data to producing the related journals, general ledgers, payroll summaries, financial statements and tax returns, CFS accountants are specifically trained to serve the special needs of small businesses.

Our streamlined procedures can help to organize and control your financial data by translating it into concise and meaningful information which supports your daily business operations.

Simply send us each month your: payroll listing, bank statement(s) with cancelled checks and checkbook stubs, sale summaries and monthly tax forms. In return, every month, we'll:

- Balance and reconcile your checking account
- Prepare all journals and ledgers to conform with IRS requirements
- Prepare Profit and Loss Statements and Balance Sheets
- Update payroll records and prepare the quarterly 941 form

Special Features

The benefits of our accounting and tax services are manifold. They include:

- Evaluation of your present record-keeping system and recommendations to ensure that your business has up-to-date financial information
- Preparation of accurate financial reports to provide the information you need for responsible decision-making
- No-charge telephone consultations. Answers to questions are as close as your telephone—without a stopwatch or billings for "conference" time
- Cost-effective data processing services for payroll, job costs, labor/cost distribution, personnel reporting, accounts receivable and sales analyses
- Federal, state and local tax preparation—both business and personal

Exhibit 25. Brochure from Jack Fox Associates

Our Philosophy

You're in business to make a profit. We're in business to help you maximize that profit by tailoring useful financial records to your specific business needs.

At CFS, we enjoy our work. we believe that you should enjoy yours, too. Most small businesses are overburdened (and over-taxed!) with the work which we take pleasure in doing. CFS believes that you should have the time to do what you originally went into business to do—to make a good living.

Like you, we're business people. We know that an accountant has to be more than a person who's good with figures. It's essential that we understand business itself. Your business. And that extends beyond mere accounting and auditing procedures.

The Bottom Line

The total cost of our monthly bookkeeping/accounting services starts at only $115. A one-time computer set-up charge of $185 is made when our services begin. All of our fees are completely tax-deductible. There are no hidden costs and no special equipment or materials to be purchased. We require no binding contract or annual prepayment fee to guarantee our services at this modest fee.

By effectively matching our specialized programs — the result of years of accounting expertise — with the limitless capabilities of the computer, we are able to offer so much for so little.

Isn't it time to move your bottom line up to the top? Just return the enclosed postage-paid business reply card for a personal presentation of our services. There is absolutely no cost or obligation. Do it today! You'll be glad that you did.

Other Services

Tax Preparation. You don't have to "cheat" on your taxes to save money. CFS can show you dozens of perfectly legal "loopholes" you're probably now overlooking. There are scores of perfectly legitimate tax deductions, credits and shelters just waiting for you to take advantage of them. From payroll and sales taxes to unemployment and personal taxes, we specialize in preparing your returns to provide the greatest deductions allowable by law.

Loan Packaging. We'll assist in the preparation of a package for a lending institution or the Small Business Administration, which guarantees up to 90% of a loan. Utilizing a wide range of collateral for repayment, we can help you locate capital for equipment purchase or expansion . . . at attractive rates and maturities. In many cases, we can even introduce you to the lenders themselves!

Consulting. We can analyze your capital needs and recommend strategies to get you the financial help you need. From applying for loans or credit to preparing government reports, our years of experience can make the difference between boom or bust, success or failure.

CFS also specializes in:
- Management Analysis
- Financial Planning Seminars
- Venture Capital Financing
- New Business Start-Up Assistance
- Entrepeneurial Development
- Business and Financial Newsletter Publishing

Jack Fox Associates

Suite 550	4520 East-West Highway
Bethesda, Maryland 20814	(301) 656-7629

Exhibit 25. (Continued)

brochure is designed to show your clients exactly what they will receive. It is a crucial item in the five-point presentation. Once you have selected a data center have the sample financial statements printed and bound. This binder will also contain sample sales and tax forms. It is the heart of the sales presentation.

Bank Authorization

The purpose of the bank authorization form is to secure permission to have your client's bank statements and cancelled checks forwarded directly to your firm. Exhibit 26 is a sample letter. It should be signed by the client.

Sample Checkbook

The system uses duplicate checks, which are custom printed by the client's bank, to show payroll code numbers; it also makes provision for split checks (See Exhibit 27.)

It is imperative for many reasons that you standardize your entire practice by using these duplicate checks. This system allows the client to keep the original stubs and precludes the need for time-consuming calls to the accountant for information contained on them. These duplicates, a source document for key punch, eliminate the possibility of loss of the original records.

If your client objects to the added cost of duplicates because of the supply of original checks on hand, it is suggested that you pay for the initial order.

The duplicate-check system contributes to the overall standardization of your practice. Its value cannot be underestimated. With sufficient effort, if properly explained, you should have no difficulty in persuading your new clients to accept these checks as a means of streamlining their bookkeeping.

Date: _____

_____

_____

_____

_____

Attention: Bookkeeping Department

Dear Sirs,

Effective immediately, will you please change the mailing address on the bank statement and cancelled checks only on the following account # _____

From: _____

_____

_____

_____

_____

To: _____

_____

_____

_____

Very truly yours,

Signed: _____

_____

Note: Do not change the mailing address for NSF checks, debit memos, notes, etc. The above address change pertains to bank statements and cancelled checks only.

Exhibit 26. Bank Authorization

It is understood, of course, that in gathering up backwork and bringing their books up to date, you will have to code their original check stubs.

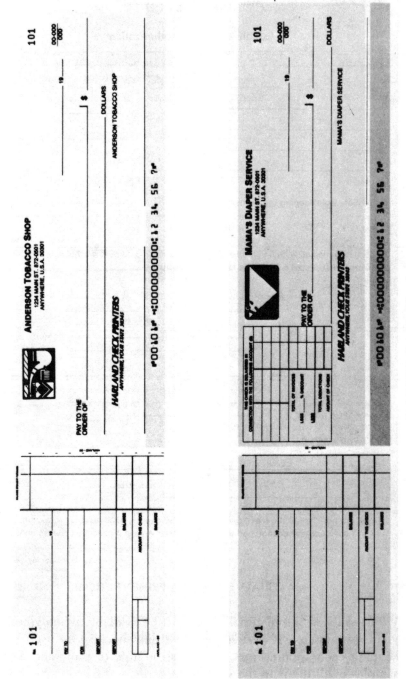

Exhibit 27. Sample Checks

PROSPECTING FOR CLIENTS

CLIENT DATA

FIRM NAME _____

ADDRESS _____

CITY _____

STATE _____ ZIP _____

TELEPHONE _____

PRINCIPALS

Name	Address	Position
_____	_____	_____
_____	_____	_____
_____	_____	_____
_____	_____	_____

BUSINESS STRUCTURE

☐ Sole Proprietor   ☐ Partnership   ☐ Corporation   ☐ Sub

VITAL DATA

Nature of Business _____   Date Established _____

Disposition of Income _____   Fiscal Year—Date _____

Number of Employees _____   Average Number of Checks _____

Number of Checking Accounts _____   Average Number of P/R Checks _____

Name of Bank _____   Previous Accountant _____

RECORDS NEEDED

☐ Last Balance Sheet   ☐ Sample Check ☐ Reg. ☐ Invoice   ☐ Payroll Data
☐ Current Check Stubs   ☐ Signed Mailing Authorization   ☐ Accounts Receivable
☐ Current Sales Records   ☐ Last Tax Return   ☐ Other _____

Client will receive following:

☐ Detailed General Ledger   ☐ Balance Sheet
☐ Employee Payroll Register   ☐ Profit & Loss
☐ Federal Returns   ☐ Sales Tax
☐ Excise Tax   ☐ U.C. Tax
☐ Bank Reconciliation   ☐ Form 941
☐ Accounts Receivable   ☐ State Tax

Client will provide following:

☐ Completed Sales and Cash Receipts Form
☐ Duplicate Checks Stub
☐ Preprinted Tax Forms
☐ All Information on a Weekly Basis

FEES

Monthly Fee $_____   Installation Fee $ _____ *

Year End Fee $ _____   Backwork Fee $ _____ **

Backwork Will Include _____

Fee is Effective _____   Special Fee $ _____ Type _____

* Installation fee is payable with order
** Backwork fee is payable ½ with order —Balance on completion

It is understood that no information obtained either verbally or through records shall be disclosed by any member of   and will be held in strictest confidence. The services detailed above are to be performed currently on a month to month basis and the monthly fee shall become due and is payable monthly on first of the month in which the services are performed. It is further understood that this agreement may be terminated by either party upon submitting a thirty day written notice.

By: _____   Accepted: _____

CLIENT   DATE

Exhibit 28. Client Data Sheet

206

Client Data Sheet

The client data sheet serves a dual purpose. It is used to close the transaction between the client and practitioner and to record the new client's data. (See Exhibit 28.)

MATERIALS FOR SALES PRESENTATION

We have listed the materials that must be available when you make your presentation. It is suggested that this checklist be used before keeping each appointment. You must be able to show and explain samples of all items in the sales kit.

Items to be carried in your briefcase for your sales presentation:

Sales book (sales and tax forms)
Postage paid envelopes, self-addressed
Bank authorization
Sample checkbook
Appointment book
Client data
Brochure samples
Business cards
Lead cards
Pen, pencil, legal pad, carbon paper, paper clips

11

ADVERTISING AND SALES PROMOTION

We've all heard that there is no such thing as free lunch, but public relations offers a relatively inexpensive way for the accountant to be noticed and remembered. Sought intelligently and creatively, publicity may not be absolutely free, but recognition gained by skillful public relations may save some advertising dollars.

Within a consistent promotion program (including advertising and personal selling), public relations can help a small firm to build sales. In today's ever tightening economy the small businessperson must struggle for recognition.

Public relations can be defined as "the projection of a desired image." Large corporations employ numbers of people who devote themselves entirely to this purpose; many retain outside counsel to tell them how to build their images. But the principles used by large organizations to communicate with millions of people around the world can be adapted by the corner grocery store owner to attract his neighbors down the street.

CHOOSING YOUR IMAGE

In developing your public relations program, the first step is to choose an image that will reflect the uniqueness of your business—the features that make it different from those of your competitors. It goes without saying that the face you decide to present must be a true one. A false front won't hold up.

Ask yourself, "What do I want my customers to think about my business?" decide on the overall impression you would like to make and write it down. This will fix the image clearly in your mind.

Remember, the image you choose must be tied to the program that will promote your business. There should be complete agreement between that image and the one you project in your advertising.

SELECTING YOUR PUBLIC

Not everyone will need or be interested in your services. Therefore the next task is to select your public, the people with whom you will want to communicate.

Ask yourself: "Who are my present customers? Who are my former customers? Who are my potential customers? Who are the other people that should know about my business?"

This last question is often overlooked. The concept of "opinion leadership" is well understood and used by communications experts and can be valuable to the small businessperson.

This group of opinion leaders should include people who influence the opinions and attitudes of others—for example, the mayor and city council members, business leaders, legislators, civic-club leaders, area media representatives (newspaper editors and publishers, television and radio station owners and managers), school board members, teachers, and student leaders.

These people may never need your services, but they can influence your public. Opinion leaders also wield legislative control of the operation and regulation of all businessses.

CHOOSING YOUR MEDIA

Next, choose the media through which you will communicate information about your firm and its image. Ask "Where do my customers obtain information?"

A sample list includes trade publications, television, newspapers, radio, brochures, special events (such as grand openings, tours, and contests), slide presentations, speeches, personal letters, and meetings.

A discussion of some of the media will shed further light on those you may want to use.

Newspapers

Local newspapers offer many opportunities to tell your story. First, get to know the news and city desk editors. These people decide what items are newsworthy. Find out who the editors are and introduce yourself. Try also to get some idea of the subjects that are regarded as newsworthy.

The best way to feed information to an editor is in a news release or fact sheet. Standard practice is to ask yourself the who, what, where, when, why, and how of the event or topic and answer these questions in the news story. Mention the more important items first—for example, what is happening, where, when, and to whom.

For those who feel that they could never write a good news story, a simple fact sheet serves much the same purpose. On the left side, list the topics or questions you will answer. On the right, give a short explanation of each of them.

Some of the items you can write about are personnel announcements, the opening of branch offices, introduction of new services, or any event that can contribute to the image you wish to present.

A photograph of the event, firm, or person in the story may be of interest to the newspaper. Papers will also take their own.

You won't get worthwhile coverage in any medium unless your story is interesting in itself or is presented in such a way that it becomes newsworthy. Study your local papers and note what is featured on radio and television. Use your imagination.

Television and Radio

Most television and radio stations have morning or afternoon talk shows on which topics of interest are discussed. Call the host and explain your services and what you could discuss or demonstrate that might attract viewers. This cannot be an advertisement for your firm but it can deal with topics of general interest.

In light of activities like these, people will begin to recognize you and your associates as experts in accounting and may seek you out.

Direct Mail

You will often have a message for a special group or segment of your public. In this case, direct mail can be the key medium.

Outline this information you want to send. Sometimes a simple flier, folded to fit into a number 10 envelope, will suit your needs.

If you foresee making a number of mailings, a small print shop will print, collate, and mail the flier.

Select your mailing list carefully and keep it up to date by adding and deleting.

These fliers can be coded with numbers. By asking customers to return the flier for a discount, you will have a built-in method of evaluating its success.

Check with a printer and your local post office before undertaking a direct-mail campaign. These sources can offer valuable advice including information on bulk-mail permits, regulations, and costs.

Speeches and Demonstrations

A sure way to become recognized as an opinion leader in your area of business is public speaking and making "how-to" demonstrations.

Study current material in your field. Trade publications (magazines and newsletters from associations or companies in the industry) are excellent sources. The local public library is another.

Select a topic of interest to segments of the general public— for example, business owners. Prepare a short 15 to 20-minute presentation or demonstration that will explain the topic in terms nonexperts can understand. Cover curent trends in particular. You may also wish to show slides or photographs to illustrate your talk. If equipment is needed, practice with it and check it over thoroughly before each use.

Approach civic and business clubs and women's groups to see whether they would be interested in your presentation.

Anticipate questions that might be asked by the group. Prepare a short flier that will outline the general information to be included. Add your name, address, and telephone number for the benefit of people with further questions.

Community Involvement

Another method of becoming known is by community service. A note of caution here, however. It is easy to become overly involved in community activities. Select those clubs, organizations, or projects that will gain you proper exposure. This means exposure to opinion leaders and potential users of your product or service.

Trade Publication Publicity

Magazines and newsletters that deal with your area of business or trade can be a worthwhile means of gaining recognition.

Trade publications accept information regarding new employees, growth announcements, feature and success stories, and new services. Look over those publications and note the kinds of story they contain.

ORGANIZING A PLAN OF ACTION

After you have chosen your image, identified your public, and selected your media, organize a plan of action. This plan should include several long- and short-range goals, time limits, and methods of acquiring feedback by which you can evaluate its success.

In the selection of your firm's image, you have identified its unique points—those that make it different, better, more reliable, of greater service—in the eyes of your public. Keep in mind how these points position your firm among all companies like it.

Begin organizing your plan of action by stating the long-range objectives. The short-range goals can be given similar treatment. Continue to evaluate them to make sure that they fit your particular needs.

Next, list in chronological order the projects you wish to undertake. A sample list might include a news release on planned expansion, an appearance on a local television or radio show, a direct-mail flier, and participation in a fund drive.

Plan each project separately. Consider the time, place, and date of the event, the participants, the projected budget, the means of publicizing, and the substance of the event itself.

At first, undertake only one project or event at a time until you begin to feel more confident. Then go for maximum impact in a concentrated effort, because one isolated event or a few fragmented attempts will probably attract little attention.

Each of these activities should make your public more aware of your product and services and should serve to support the image you have selected.

EVALUATING YOUR SUCCESSES

Research tools for evaluating your program can be simple yet effective. Personal interviews with customers, short questionnaires mailed to prospects, a suggestion box, question and answer session at demonstrations or speeches, talks with neighboring firms, return-mail postcards included with services delivered, and telephone surveys can all be helpful.

The more feedback received from your public, the better your understanding of your position.

PART OF THE WHOLE

Careful and realistic selection of a company image, identification of key segments of the public important to the firm, choice of media, formulation of a plan, and evaluation may well provide the competitive "edge" needed by the smallest and largest companies.

Your public relations program (and the publicity it generates) must be coordinated with your advertising and personal selling. It must complement them; they must complement it. All must grow as your business strengthens and your knowledge of your own markets increases.

What your particular public thinks about you and your business directly influences its decision to buy. Herein lies one of the advantages of public relations.

DEVELOPING A DIRECT-MAIL PROGRAM

Consider your overall marketing picture and list your company's objectives. Be specific. If your objective is to increase sales, state how and assign a target date.

Determine how many different ways you can use direct mail to support your business—keeping your objectives in mind.

List your best prospects by kind and size of business.

Decide which of your prospects to approach.

Consider realistically your geographic limitations (if any). Which areas can you service effectively and profitably? Will you select your mailing list by state, county, standard metropolitan statistical area, zip code?

Create and test various direct-mail packages. The layout and copy should be in line with your markets and objectives. Try business reply cards and other inserts and different offers.

Analyze your results by your respondents' lines of business, geographic location, and amount and frequency of purchase.

Test . . . test . . . and retest! Try mailing at different times of the year and to different lists of prospects.

Direct response offers you the following:

1. Precise Measurability and Research Capabilities. You no longer need to rely on personal opinion concerning the effectiveness of your advertising. Direct response brings the order back to you almost immediately; it offers the quantitative feedback you need to control your organization's marketing policies.

2. Precise Selectivity of Your Defined Target Markets This means highly controlled messages to controlled audiences. By supplementing your overall marketing communications to include highly controlled messages to highly controlled target audiences, your organization becomes a much more personalized entity. Each actual or potential client can be developed in an individual and cost-effective way.

3. Action-Orientation. Direct response always asks for action and gives the reader a way of responding without leaving home.

By taking your organization to the client, instead of waiting for the customer to come to you, you are generating new business.

CHECKLIST FOR APPLYING THE SIX BIG KEYS TO DIRECT-MARKETING SUCCESS

The following checklist contains broad considerations that are applicable to any business. Some of the entries apply to certain financial services, others to services or products or subsidiaries.

1. Your product and service:
   ( ) Is the product or service offered a good value?
   ( ) How does your product or service compare with that of the competition?

( ) Does your product or service possess unique characteristics?

2. The media you use.
   ( ) Is your own customer list update? Are the addresses corrected on a regular basis?
   ( ) Have you segmented your list by recency, frequency, and
   dollar amounts to target different audiences with different
   offers?
   ( ) Have you considered other products or services that may
   appeal to your customers?
   ( ) Do you mail to your customers often enough to maximize
   the sales from this group?

Prospect Lists

( ) Have you ever tried to use outside mailing lists to develop
new business?

Print:

( ) Have you measured the results of print media?
( ) Have you determined how often you can use the same
print media successfully for a particular offer?

Broadcasting

( ) Have you measured the results of the broadcasting media?
( ) Have you selected the best media and the best time to fit
your objectives?

3. The offer you make.
   ( ) Are you making the most attractive offers bound by the
   rules of good business?
   ( ) Do your offers lend themselves to the use of response
   incentives—installment terms, trial offers, gifts, or contests?

( ) Does your offer lend itself to the development of an automatic repeat business cycle?

( ) Does your offer lend itself to a "get a friend" program?

4. The formats you use.

( ) Are your mailing packages in keeping with your image?

( ) Have you developed the ideal format for your mailings by testing?

( ) Do your letters reflect the appropriate tone of the particular offer and target audience?

( ) Are your circulars in keeping with the complete mailing package?

( ) Does your response form restate the offer and does it grab attention?

Print

( ) Are your ads in keeping with your target markets and the services you're offering them?

( ) Have you determined the efficiency of stand-up announcer commercials versus staged commercials?

( ) Have you explored the efficiency of noted personality endorsements?

5. Your testing procedures.

( ) Do you constantly test the critical elements—the products or services you offer and the media and formats you use?

( ) Have you determined the most responsive geographical areas?

( ) Do you constantly test new mail packages, ads, and commercials against control ads?

( ) Do you follow your test results to the final conclusion—net revenue?

( ) Do you analyze your results by zip code and demographics?

TARGETED MARKETING: YOUR ANSWER TO TODAY'S CHALLENGE

Your marketing program can be improved by turning it into a targeted marketing program.

Try these following seven basic steps on your program to improve its sales effectiveness. (See Exhibit 29.)

1. Constituent identification.
   □ Establish your marketing data base
2. Market segmentation.
   □ Target your key selling constituencies

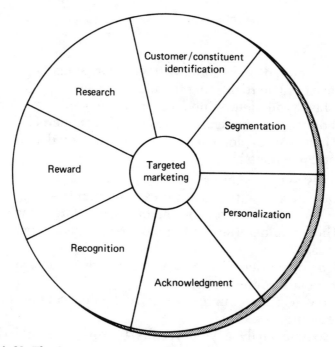

Exhibit 29. The Seven Key Components of a Targeted Marketing Program

3. Personalize your program.
   □ Develop your classic approach
4. Acknowledgment.
   □ Develop your response formula to their buying action
5. Recognition.
   □ Formalize your valuation of them through a special recognition program
6. Reward their buying action.
   □ Develop an incentive for them to deal with you
7. Research their needs.
   □ Track and analyze your successes to perfect your program.

DESIGNING THE MAILING

The same elements that make a personal call successful will make your direct mail pieces successful. To foster a successful sales call or direct mail piece, go through the following steps:

Step 1. Attract the prospect's favorable attention.

Step 2. Keep the prospect's interest.

Step 3. Show the prospect how he/she will benefit from your services.

Step 4. Close the sale.

Let's take a closer look at these elements.

GAINING FAVORABLE ATTENTION

In a direct mail piece you get the prospect's attention with your envelope. Your envelope needs to stand out in a way that will make your prospect want to open it. However, you do not want it to stand out in a way that will make your prospect prejudge you. The best way to accomplish your desired result is to take the personal approach.

Stay away from flashy symbols and clever manipulative devices. A multi-colored starburst on the envelope may attract attention, but it also makes your package look like a slick sales piece. The words "personal and confidential" on the outside of the envelope will probably get it opened, but they will also irritate your prospects when they find that there is absolutely nothing confidential about the enclosures. There is one especially effective way to ensure that your envelope gets opened by the largest possible number of prospects:

Hand address the envelope!

Hand addressed envelopes have a personal flair and almost always get opened. On the other hand, the surest way to the circular file is to use mailing labels. Mailing labels are impersonal and scream out to your prospect that "this is junk mail."

Another effective way to personalize your envelopes and to increase readership is to hand stamp them. A postal metered stamp detracts from the personalized appeal.

CONSTRUCTING THE LETTER

Interests and Benefits

A well constructed sales letter will pique the prospect's interest. Addressing his or her needs and problems will keep the prospect involved. This is the part that seems to stump a lot of accountants. Even many accountants who can stand face-to-face with a client and make an eloquently persuasive presentation seem to forget how to put two sentences together when it comes to writing the sales letter.

Don't think that you can cop out and just send a brochure. You are not asking for a meeting between them and your services. You're asking for a meeting between them and you. Besides, research shows that direct mail packages containing a letter pull greater response than those that don't. In this chapter, you'll learn the basic elements that make for an effective sales letter. You will get step-by-step instructions for constructing the letter and some work sheets to use in writing your own letters.

THE BASIC INGREDIENTS

In order to know how to design your sales letter, it is important to understand how people will read it. Direct mail studies indicate that most people do not read direct mail word for word, beginning to end. Rather they skim the letter in a particular order:

First, they look at the letterhead to see who sent it.

Second, they look at the salutation to ascertain to whom it's addressed!

Third, they look to see who signed the letter.

Fourth, if there is a postscript, they will read that before going back to the body of the letter.

Fifth, they will read your heading or opening paragraph.

Finally, if you've attracted their attention and piqued their interest, they will read or skim the balance of the letter.

WRITING THE SALES LETTER

A sales letter is a person-to-person conversation. It is your message to your prospects, in which they will learn how they can receive certain benefits by granting you a meeting.

```
SELLER'S
LETTERHEAD
                                     ┌─────────────────────────┐
                                     │ 1st thing they look at  │
                                     └─────────────────────────┘
Prospect's Name
Prospect's Company
Address

Dear _____
                        ┌──────────────────────────────────────┐
                        │ 2nd thing they look at.              │
                        │   Use a word processor and personalize.│
                        └──────────────────────────────────────┘

Heading or 1st paragraph
                          ┌────────────────────────────────────┐
                          │ 5th thing they look at.            │
                          │ Determines whether or not they read on.│
                          └────────────────────────────────────┘

Body
                             ┌──────────────────────────────┐
                             │ 6th thing they look at.      │
                             │ Most readers skim.           │
                             └──────────────────────────────┘

Sincerely
J. F. Seller
                               ┌────────────────────────────┐
                               │ 3rd thing they look at.    │
                               └────────────────────────────┘

P.S.
                        ┌──────────────────────────────────────┐
                        │ 4th thing they look at.              │
                        │ First message opportunity.           │
                        │ Often the only part of the letter that gets│
                        │ read.                                │
                        └──────────────────────────────────────┘
```

Exhibit 30. Now the Sales Letter is Read by the Prospect

Sales letters work best when they are conversational. In this regard, it is important for you to remember the following tips:

1. Do not over-edit—Write it as you would speak it.
2. Avoid jargon and pretentious wording. When you use words

that make people run for their dictionary, you can be sure that they will find the trash can on the way.

3. Use personal appeal—An excellent technique is to think of one person you know in your target audience and write directly to him or her.

4. Don't reinvent the wheel—Before going to the trouble of writing all new letters, check to see if letters already exist that have proven to work well. If so, use them.

SALUTATION

It is best to use word-processed letters with the date of the letter and each prospect's name. If each letter cannot be personalized, the next best thing is to use as personal a salutation as possible. If you have targeted your prospects, use one of your targeting qualifiers.

Some examples:
    Dear Executive
    Dear Decision Maker
    Dear Fellow Small Business Owner

Stay away from generics like "Dear Sir" or "To Whom it May Concern."

Heading

Prospects often use the heading as a screening device. Therefore, it needs to attract attention and either state or refer to a strong benefit. Whenever possible, this should be accomplished in one or two sentences.

There are five techniques that have been found effective in sales letters:

A. "You" approach—Talk to the prospect about him/herself. This approach works especially well as a headline with explanatory text. The following sample shows how this works:

Dear Carole,

You'll never have to fill out another tax return! If you're like most people, you would rather chew on aluminum foil than spend days or weeks filling out tax returns. That's why I am letting you know about my tax preparation services . . .

"You" approach examples:
    We're so sure you'll agree that . . .
    You owe it to yourself to find out . . .
    If you're tired of . . .
    If you're like me, you . . .
    If you're like thousands of other _____ . . .
    We need your help . . .
    I'm writing because I have reason to believe that you're the
        kind of executive who appreciates . . .
    If you're worried about . . .
    You'll never have to . . . again

Use the above examples, or think of your own to construct two opening statements that you could use in your own letters:

1. _____
    _____
    _____
    _____

2. _____
_____
_____
_____

B. The "Question" approach—Ask a question related to the prospect's interests. This works well because it lends itself to brevity and gets your prospect involved immediately. You may recognize the following sample:

What would happen to your family, Mr. Jones, if all of a sudden you were unable to work?

It's not a pleasant thought, but unfortunately it has happened to millions . . .

Asking a question examples:
Are you tired of . . .
Would you like to be able to . . .
How long has it been since . . .
How many times have you thought to yourself . . .
What is it worth to you . . .
When was the last time . . .
Have you ever had _____ happen . . .
Does your family know what to do in the event of . . .
Do you remember how good it felt the last time . . .

Use the above examples, or think of your own, to construct two questions that you could use as openings for your own letters.

1. _____
_____
_____
_____

2. _____
_____
_____
_____

C. Extend an invitation approach—This technique can be very effective when your letter contains a special offer, as in the following example:

Dear Neal,
Please accept my personal invitation to attend our upcoming seminar, "How to Obtain Your Own SBA Guaranteed Loan." There is normally a $95.00 fee for this program, but . . .

Invitation examples:
Your place has been reserved!
As one of the few _____ who can really appreciate _____ , we would like you to _____ . . .
Here's a special invitation for you to . . .
To a limited number of executives we are sending this invitation to try, at no obligation, . . .
You're invited, Mr. Smith . . .
. . . to be one of the first _____ to . . .
Please accept my personal invitation to . . .

Can you come up with a few invitations for your own offer?

1. _____
_____
_____
_____

2. _____
_____
_____
_____

D. Quote someone else—Quoting someone else saying the same thing that you are is redundant, but it doubles your credibility. If the person quoted is famous, it triples your credibility.

A quote can be used to make a point or to reinforce one. For instance:

"Seeing's believing, but feeling's the truth."

Thomas Fuller

You've probably seen it on T.V., but I'm convinced that once you get your hands on the new XZ 2000, you'll become a believer. That's why I would like to extend a special offer for you to try . . .

There are many books available that are compilations of quotes, organized by subject matter. Here are a few examples and how they can be used.

"You never know what you don't need until you're right in the middle of needing to know it."

Frederick Lankard
from
"No Bull Sales Management"
by Hank Trisler

Anyone who ever started a new project on a personal computer can relate to that statement. That's why we've established a 24-hour hotline . . .

"The great end of life is not knowledge but action."

Thomas Henry Huxley

We don't try to impress you with all we know, we just get it done.

"It's a funny thing about life. If you refuse to accept anything but the best, you very often get it."

W. Somerset Maugham

If you agree with Somerset Maugham, then you'll want to check out our . . .

"There are two things to aim at in life. First, to get what you want and, after that, to enjoy it."

Logan Pearsall Smith

You work hard to save up enough money to buy a new car. How do you know that you will really enjoy that automobile? Or, will you spend far too much time going back and forth to the repair shop . . .

"Opportunity for distinction lies in doing ordinary things well and not in erratically striving to perform grandstand plays."

William Feather

We're not a lot of flash. We just get the job done.

"The world is full of willing people. Some willing to work, the rest willing to let them."

Robert Frost

When you become our client, we don't just drop the work off and expect you to do all the work. I will be there every step of the way to make sure . . .
Use one of the quotes above or one of your favorites to develop an opening you could use in your letters.

E. Using a metaphor—A metaphor is a figure of speech in which an analogy is made between a literally denoted object and something likened to it. A metaphor can be used to tersely make a point. A metaphor can be a simple, succinct statement such as "learning this information quickly is like trying to drink from a fire hose."

Famous stories such as Aesop's Fables can be very effective, because the reader frequently already knows the story and gets the point with little effort.

Remember, most people just skim sales letters and don't read them thoroughly.

The danger in using stories lies in the reader's impatience. Yet, the benefits can be well worth the risk. You can reduce the risk by making sure that the story is clearly set apart so that it's easy to skip the story and get to the point.

Exhibits 31 through 32 are samples of letters that employ different forms of metaphor.

You may find the following stories useful for your accounting services offering. If not, you still may find them amusing and good examples of things that can be used.

Two men erected like houses. They had the same aluminum siding, similar slanting roofs, identical heavy oak doors, and storm windows of the same model. Yet, a cyclone reduced one to a heap of rubble, but had little effect on the other. The reason for this extraordinary phenomenon could be seen immediately. The first person built her house on sand, the second on a foundation of solid rock.

Points to be made —The importance of a strong foundation
—What you've built your business on
—How you can help your client build on a strong foundation (e.g. financial services)

Abraham Lincoln won many arguments through sheer force of logic. On one occasion, having failed to make a stubborn opponent see the error of his reasoning, Lincoln said, "Well, let's see. How many legs has a cow?"

"Four, of course," was the ready reply.

"That's right," said Lincoln. "Now suppose we call the cow's tail a leg, how many legs would the cow have?"

June 10, 1990

Mr. Bob Banker
First National Bank
1234 Main Street
Anytown, CA 92075

ARE YOU TIRED OF TRYING TO FIT SQUARE PEGS INTO
ROUND HOLES?   STOP TRYING. . . . . .

Dear Bob Banker,

You're unique. Each of your clients is unique, as well. At my accounting practice, we go out of our way to recognize this and to deal with you and each of your clients according to your needs and desires.

Most of our banker friends have told us that their #1 desire is simply to generate more business. So, we've come up with several different services to assist you in doing that. I can develop a support plan just for you. The plan could include:

- SBA Loan Seminars
- Accounting consultations
- Tax assistance
- Many other services

If your needs are more client-service orientated, we can develop a custom plan for that as well. It is all done to match our available resources to your expertise and to the unique needs of your bank.

I believe that by working together in this way—by fitting you and your clients with the appropriate services—we create a smoother environment. With as few hassles as possible. . . square pegs go into square holes.

If you would like to receive more detailed information on our customized service, please call us at 619-555-1234.

Truly yours,

P.S. When was the last time you had a phone call returned within 30 minutes! Try us, we guarantee it or the pizza is on us.

Exhibit 31. Sales Letter Utilizing Metaphor

234

July 10, 1990

Mr. Bob Banker
First National Bank
1234 Main Street
Anytown, CA 92075

EXTRA ANTS SAVE GRASSHOPPER

All summer long the grasshopper played his fiddle and sang songs. It was a pleasant way to live. Everyone enjoyed his music. He had many friends. There was plenty of food, free for the taking, in the green summer fields. The grasshopper just nibbled a little here and a little there, and moved on.

The ants, on the other hand, worked hard all summer long, collecting food and storing it in their houses.

When it began to get cold, and the snow fell, the grasshopper shivered. His stomach was empty, so he went from ant house to ant house, begging for something to eat. "While you fiddled last summer," said the ants, "we worked hard putting grain away for the wintertime. Now we have just enough for ourselves. Let us alone. Go away."

Poor grasshopper, he was getting hungrier and colder and was beginning to think he would starve to death. Night came and the grasshopper started sadly down the road that led away from the town where everyone had cruelly refused him food.

Just then he passed the last house. Through the window the grasshopper saw some ants preparing for a holiday feast. Once more he knocked on the door to ask for food. This time, a friendly ant opened it and saw her summertime companion, the grasshopper. Before the grasshopper could say a word, she shouted to her family. "Look, Tonight we shall have music!" To the grasshopper she said, "Come in and play and be merry with us." The grasshopper thought to himself, "I'm so lucky to have happened onto my friend the ant. But from now on, I will think ahead, collect and store for the future."

Dear Bob Banker,

Together with your energy and cooperation, our accounting business will help you to celebrate a growing and secure future.

With your foresight in working with our accounting business, we will help you collect and store new business through our:

Exhibit 32. (continued on page 236)

- SBA Loan Seminars
- Accounting Consultations
- New business start-up workshops
- Tax planning seminars
- Many other services

In today's financial chill, the banks with the largest storehouse of clients and public visibility will be the ones secure in the coming frost. With our accounting business's help, you too can have a secure warm future.

With your increased storehouse of business, our accounting firm will grow and celebrate with you in a long and prosperous relationship. Please, at your convenience, send back the enclosed questionnaire or call me at (619) 555-1234.

Helpfully yours,

P.S. Call for our complete analysis of the new tax changes.

Exhibit 32. Sales Letter with Story and Metaphor

"Why, five, of course."

"That's where you make an error," said Lincoln. "Simply calling a cow's tail a leg doesn't make it a leg."

or

"If all you have is a hammer, then you see every problem as a nail."

Points to be made —When some competitors don't have the correct solution to your problem, they'll sell you the wrong one and call it the right one.

—We are specialists in small business accounting, when you need a _____, you get a _____.

—We customize.

A census taker was on his rounds and he knocked on one door to learn who lived behind it. He asked the woman who opened it how many children she had. She said: "Well, there's Willie and Horace and Esther. . ."

The censes taker interrupted: "Never mind names. I just want numbers."

"They haven't got numbers; every one of them's got names," replied the mother.

Points to be made —How some companies treat their clients like numbers.

—Our firm provides personalized service.

"I told you so," a parent once said to a 14-year-old son, "You would not have made that foolish mistake if you had used good judgement."

The boy said, "Well, how do you get good judgement?"

The parent answered, rather slowly, "By making mistakes, of course."

Points to be made —The value of experience.

—We've been around for a long time.

—We've already made and learned from our mistakes.

—Don't trust your business to someone who'll be getting their education from it.

—We may not be perfect, but we learn from our mistakes. Here's how that can help you.

Michelangelo was explaining to a visitor a number of refinements and alterations that he had made in a statue.

"These are trifles," said his friend.

"It may be so," said the sculptor, "but remember that trifles make for perfection and perfection is no trifle."

Points to be made—Looking after all the small details.
                     —Demonstrates commitment to quality.

After a sign reading "HELP WANTED" was hung in a store window, a long line of applicants queued up at the door. One especially anxious fellow scribbled a note which he quietly handed to the owner. It read: "Don't do anything until you've seen me. I'm last in line, but I've got the goods."

Points to be made —Don't make a decision until you've heard what we can do for you.
                     —Young aggressive companies competing against long established competitors.
                     —Lesser known companies.

A farmer's neighbor wanted to borrow an axe.
"Sorry," said the farmer, "I've got to shave tonight."
Later, his wife took him to task, saying, "Why did you give our neighbor such a silly excuse?"
"If you don't want to do a thing," the farmer replied, "one excuse is as good as another."

Points to be made —It doesn't matter to you how good our excuse is. When the work is not done on deadline, you suffer the same.
                     —You expect the best. We give good quality service, not excuses.

Which of the preceding stories can be used in a compelling way in relation to your services? If none of them work for you, can you think of a story (even from your personal experience) that will?

1. Subject of story:

_____

How I will tie it in to my services:

2. Subject of story:

How I will tie it in to my services:

BODY

The body of your letter should flow directly from the heading. This is where you make your case. You should no longer be trying to gain interest. If you haven't already accomplished this, they've already stopped reading. The body should serve to substantiate the claim made in your heading, to allude to additional benefits, and to elaborate on any special offers.

How Long Should it Be?

Contrary to popular belief, short letters do not sell better than long letters. It should be as long as it takes to get your message across. All letters should be organized for easy location of answers to individual questions for which the prospect may be "skimming." If the prospect can easily find the answers to the following four questions, you've done your job.

1. What will you do for me if I listen to your story?
2. How are you going to do this?
3. Who is responsible for the promises you make?
4. For whom have you already done this?

Conclusion

In the conclusion you will "close the sale" by stating (or restating) your primary purpose in terms of the client's needs. Some examples:

Before you make a decision on . . . ,consider . . .

If you would like to take advantage of . . .

Just fill in the enclosed reply card and put it in the mail today.

For a no charge consultation, or a free brochure, just fill in . . .

I'll call within a few days to see when it would be convenient to . . .

So, give yourself a chance to discover . . .

I hope you'll accept my invitation to . . . I'm sure you'll be glad you did.

Next you will emphasize your interest in helping and make it easy for your prospect to contact you:

If I can be of any further assistance, just call me at . . .

If I can answer any questions, just call me at . . .

Postscripts

The postscript is usually your first and often your only opportunity to get a message across. Therefore, it should stand alone or act as a teaser to entice the reader to want more information.

Examples:

P.S. Call for more information about our special . . .

P.S. Be sure to return the enclosed card by _____ to receive your free . . .

P.S. These programs have been filling up fast. For every person enrolled, two are turned away. Please respond promptly.

P.S. If you're a realist and a skeptic like myself, you're probably looking for one last solid reason to take advantage of this offer. You'll find it on the enclosed reply card.

P.S. If you're already using someone else for _____, you'll find us to be a great backup so you never have to worry about . . .

P.S. Today, more than ever, it's important to make your business operate as cost efficiently as possible, Our new lower rates could help you do just that. Call us or mail the enclosed postage-paid card today.

P.S. Don't forget, we can send you . . .

P.S. Ever wondered how to . . . or . . . Just send the enclosed reply card and we'll send you a complimentary copy of our _____.

P.S. If you can't wait to begin achieving . . ., just call me at . . . and I'll show you how to get started fast.

Using these as guidelines, construct two postscripts that you could use in your own letters. First, you'll need to think of a special offer or compelling benefit. An offer can be anything from a free brochure to a 30-day free trial. Some other ideas:

Brochure	Seminar (free or reduced rate)
Free trial	Discount
Sample	Additional information
	Free consultation

1. P.S. _____
2. P.S. _____

Critical questions for reviewing your letters.

1. Does the heading speak of benefits?
2. Is the heading more than two sentences long? (It sometimes needs to be, but usually not.)
3. Is the postscript your most compelling message, or does it allude to the most compelling message (teaser)?
4. Are your thoughts arranged in a logical order?
5. Is it easy for the reader to follow the entire letter without getting lost or confused?
6. Have you made your claims believable by offering some kind of corroboration (evidence, statistics, testimony, examples, etc.)?
7. Is it clear to the reader what you want him/her to do?
8. Does the letter use more words that mean "you" than words that mean "me"?
9. Is the letter conversational?
10. Are 75% of the words one syllable?
11. Does the letter contain action verbs rather than noun construction? (e.g. "I am very excited to . . ." instead of "It is with great excitement that . . .")

Make it easy on them.

Although your primary goal is to create recognition so that you can call back later and secure a meeting, there will be some prospects that like your message enough to want to contact you. You can increase the likelihood of this by making it easier for them to do so in the following ways:

1. Enclose a business reply card.

Direct mail prospecting is the foundation of your prospecting efforts . . This is the case, because it is a system that is under your complete control and one that you can easily keep up, even on your "off days." It is a way of turning cold calls into warm calls.

12

PRESENTING YOUR PRODUCTS

Today's business owners need help. In our increasingly complex world the typical small business can no longer be made successful by the owner's "hard work." Factual records and a professional advisor who can offer sound advice on financial management are basic requirements.

Here you fit in to provide the financial planning and advice necessary to success. By using established systems and counseling techniques you will help your business clients to grow and prosper, to gain confidence in their ability to avoid failure through financial mismanagement.

Ours is an exciting and rewarding challenge for those who want to build their own careers by working closely with the men and women who make up the business community.

WHO USES YOUR SERVICES?

The number is virtually unlimited. Take a look in the Yellow Pages and you'll find possible clients in almost every category. The Small Business Administration estimates that more than 3.7 million small businesses are operating in this country.

You can offer your service to such clients as hairdressers, contractors, fast-food chain operators, florists, photographers, realtors, service station managers, and all types of retail business and professional people. The list is endless. A successful physician may know little about financial management. A talented florist may need help with taxes.

HOW TO HELP YOUR CLIENTS

Financial management is a critically important aspect of every business. You are uniquely qualified to assist by

(a) tailoring the record system and monthly operating statement to the client's needs;

(b) assisting in setting sales and profit goals;

(c) preparing and assisting in planning for taxes;

(d) establishing financial controls and reporting systems;

(e) providing monthly profit and loss and other financial statements;

(f) analyzing the business and making specific recommendations.

You can provide your clients with clearheaded, goal-oriented financial management advice and the facts on which to base everyday business decisions.

You need not be a flashy, high-pressure salesman, but merely know your product and be able to present it in a professional manner. An accountant is a skilled person, well organized and detail-oriented.

Confidence in your self and your service, coupled with a smooth delivery, will classify you as a professional. Business people will recognize the service's worth, but the package's good qualities will be neutralized if the accountant who markets it lacks self-confidence. To give the system credibility you must present it knowing that what you have to offer is unique and the best there is for the client. The service itself should give the accountant confidence. The key to a product's success is the salesman's ability to distinguish it from its competition. You must be 100% sure that

(a) you have something to sell that is highly marketable;

(b) you are the best person for the job;

(c) your prospects are genuinely interested in you and your service and, if convinced of its benefits, will buy it.

The public wants a winner. Your package is one. Therefore, people will want to hear what the accountant who represents this winner has to say about the service and its provider.

Armed with all the tools necessary for your presentation and a healthy mental attitude, you are now ready to keep the appointment and present your case.

It would be wise before showing up for your interview to acquaint yourself with the prospect's type of business. It is important to be able to discuss it with some authority. Many governmental publications will provide you with valuable information of this kind.

When meeting the prospect, introduce yourself as the accountant who has established an office in the area.

Try to "break the ice." Approach the prospective client directly by asking: "May I call you John?" It is always better to be on a first-name basis. Be friendly. Allow your prospects to finish completely whatever is felt to be relevant. Even though their statements may have no relation to a particular situation, it is always good psychology to hear them out.

"Breaking the ice" lays the groundwork for a relaxed, meaningful meeting. If you find your prospect receptive to friendly conversation, take the time to chat. Talk a little about yourself in a general way, but be careful. Your prospect may be very busy, yet still show you that courtesy. Never overdo it. Your primary goal is to present your services.

When you are ready to show your product, start by saying, "Janice I'd like to explain how we can reduce your work load in the bookkeeping area, and what our service can do for you." Begin by telling the prospect two things:

1. What you can do for your client. State it in any way that is comfortable for you, but get the general meaning across.
2. What the client has to do for you.

THE PRESENTATION

This is the part that must be committed to memory, "The Five-step Presentation." After the introduction and general discussion, explain the duplicate checkbook (samples are obtainable from your bank). Impress on the prospect that the only requirements are

(a) to make out duplicate checks (Exhibit 27); the original stubs never leave the client's possession.
(b) to fill out a daily, easy-to-use sales form.

Conclude by presenting the 9 × 12 self-addressed, postage-paid envelope, in which the client must mail, once a week, the duplicate checks and all sales sheets and tax forms.

At this point take the sales brochure from your briefcase and inform the prospect that each month a complete set of computerized financial statements, bound as the brochure shows, will be supplied.

Now begin the five-step presentation.

Step 1. Start with the balance sheet (Exhibit 33) which lists all assets and liabilities. Explain it to the prospect.

Step 2. Most important is the complete profit and loss statement (P/L). In presenting this document, (Exhibit 34), point out the two columns, "current month and year-to-date," and draw arrows to emphasize them. Explain that sales may be broken down into any number of categories. Then move along to the cost-of-goods section and point out how direct cost with percentages may be compared with sales. Continue to the bottom of the P/L and show that the total net profit and/or loss for each month and the accumulated year-to-date figure are given, with percentages. Conclude Step 2 by stressing the importance of the percentages and that by glancing at them the prospect may discover immediately the problem areas in the organization. Use Advertising as an example by circling this account on the P/L; show that there were no advertising expenses for the month and that the year-to-date is $105.00. Illustrate by drawing a circle around these amounts and explain the difficulty of pinpointing problem areas without percentages on the P/L.

You are now ready to demonstrate the ease with which the client may trace back expenses and other P/L items in the detail general ledger (DGL) by going on to the next step.

```
                  ASSETS

CURRENT ASSETS
  CASH ON HAND AND IN BANKS              5,526.82
  ACCOUNTS RECEIVABLE                   82,429.02
  INVENTORY                            291,717.38
  PREPAID EXPENSES                       5,875.21
    TOTAL CURRENT ASSETS                              385,548.43

FIXED ASSETS
  FURNITURE AND FIXTURES                11,668.00
  MACHINERY AND EQUIPMENT              125,711.40
  VEHICLES                              22,584.00
  OFFICE EQUIPMENT                      75,725.55
  ALLOWANCE FOR AMORTIZATION            68,442.00-
    TOTAL FIXED ASSETS                                167,246.95

  TOTAL PROPERTY AND EQUIPMENT                               .00

OTHER ASSETS
  DEPOSITS                                  70.00
  GOODWILL                              50,000.00
    TOTAL OTHER ASSETS                                 50,070.00

  TOTAL ASSETS                                        602,865.38
                                                   ==============
```

Exhibit 33. Balance Sheet

```
LIABILITIES AND STOCKHOLDERS EQUITY

        LIABILITIES

CURRENT LIABILITIES
  ACCOUNTS PAYABLE                      71,501.17
  LOAN FROM STOCKHOLDER                116,590.20
  PAYROLL TAXES PAYABLE                  9,255.64-
    TOTAL CURRENT LIABILITIES                          178,835.73

LONG-TERM LIABILITIES
  NOTE PAYABLE TO BANK                 175,980.22
    TOTAL LONG-TERM LIABILITIES                        175,980.22

    TOTAL LIABILITIES                                  354,815.95

STOCKHOLDERS' EQUITY
  COMMON STOCK                          67,481.82
  TREASURY STOCK                        20,000.00-
  RETAINED EARNINGS                     19,611.70-
  EARNINGS YEAR-TO-DATE                220,179.31
    TOTAL STOCKHOLDERS' EQUITY                         248,049.43

    TOTAL LIABILITIES AND EQUITY                       602,865.38
                                                   ----------------
```

Exhibit 33. (Continued)

	----CURRENT---- 10/01/83 - 09/30/83	---%--	---CUMULATIVE-- 01/01/83 - 09/30/83	---%--
INCOME				
CONTRACT SALES	338,230.78	100.0	688,797.21	99.8
MISCELLANEOUS			1,290.31	.2
LESS DISCOUNT ALLOWED			104.36-	
ADJUSTED GROSS INCOME	338,230.78	100.0	689,983.16	100.0
COST OF OPERATIONS				
ART WORK & PHOTOGRAPHY			2,538.54	.4
BLANK TAPES AND REELS			8,041.11	1.2
COMMISSIONS			20,167.05	2.9
DELIVERY			837.35	.1
FILM CREWS			10,759.87	1.6
FILM PRINTS			15,059.90	2.2
FILM PROCESSING			17,676.05	2.6
FREELANCE CONTRACTS			49,709.15	7.2
PACKAGING MATERIALS			5,967.69	.9
POSTAGE			15,223.31	2.2
PRESSING OF RECORDS			21,863.58	3.2
PRINTING			12,646.80	1.8
STUDIO CHARGES			6,281.33	.9
TALENT PAYROLL			14,061.50	2.0
TALENT CONTRACTS AND CHARGES			2,314.03	.3
TAPE DUPLICATES AND DISTRIBUTION			5,826.28	.8
W.I.P. ADJUSTMENTS	272,887.06	80.7	104,518.76	15.1
EQUIPMENT RENTAL			2,716.08	.4
TOTAL COST OF OPERATIONS	272,887.06	80.7	316,208.38	45.8
GROSS PROFIT	65,343.72	19.3	373,774.78	54.2
OPERATING EXPENSES				
ACCOUNTING			9,050.00	1.3
ADVERTISING			105.00	
AUTO EXPENSE			1,276.41	.2
COMMISSIONS			17,575.00	2.5
DELIVERY EXPENSE			1,779.43	.3
DEPRECIATION			4,143.00	.6
DUES AND SUBSCRIPTIONS			880.80	.1
INSURANCE			5,199.72	.8
INTEREST			3,225.10	.5
LEGAL			514.25	.1
LICENSES AND PERMITS			681.27	.1
OFFICE EXPENSE			2,558.88	.4
RENT			15,158.50	2.2
SALARIES - OFFICE			69,319.32	10.0
TAXES			5,354.34	.8
TELEPHONE			4,079.85	.6
TRAVEL			12,694.60	1.8
TOTAL OPERATING EXPENSES	.00		153,595.47	22.3
OPERATING INCOME	65,343.72	19.3	220,179.31	31.9

UNAUDITED - SEE ACCOMPANYING DISCLAIMER OF OPINION

Exhibit 34. Statement of Income

Step 3. The advertising account will detail advertising. You must use this account to explain the DGL. Now show how it works. (Always remember that in most cases the prospect is not an accountant). With your pen draw a circle around Advertising and show how each disbursement is listed with the payee's name, the date the check was issued, the check number, the amount of the check, and the opening and ending balances of the account. Before you continue, be certain that the prospect understands the working value of the DGL.

Step 4. The monthly payroll register is then shown. Explain its importance by emphasizing the fact that payroll records need not be kept in our system. We enter all the necessary records, including the quarterly payroll tax reports and the year-end W-2s, in our computer. Start by showing where the prospect's business name will appear, the date of the report. Then proceed as follows: Show where the employee's name is entered, the employee's social security number, ID number, the date the payroll check was issued, check number, gross wages, all deductions, and, finally, net pay. Then explain that for each employee these figures will give totals for month, year-to-date, and quarter-to-date. Finally, point out that this report details all payroll totals to tie into the DGL. (All standard payroll systems work in this fashion.)

As you explain these items, make notations that will be helpful in review. You will be leaving this brochure with the prospect.

Step 5. The bank reconciliation is the final step in the monthly computer printout. Circle the item called "correct bank balance" and compare it with the balance per ledger. Next, point out the outstanding checks section and draw an arrow to the top. Any standard bank reconciliation form can be used for this purpose. Then draw a circle around the last stub and instruct the client to refer to that stub number and make the required adjustment to arrive at the correct bank balance.

If you have followed this procedure methodically and have presented the monthly computerized financial statement clearly and adequately you will be ready to begin the close.

Before we introduce this final step, some important tips are in order. We have touched briefly on control of the interview. We will now elaborate on its importance. A prospect's attempt to take the brochure from you and start thumbing through its pages before you have had an opportunity to present it is one example of what could go wrong. On this rare occasion, state calmly that you will leave the brochure with the prospect but would like to explain how it works.

Control is extremely important. Control is lost in an interview when the prospect causes you to lose the continuity of the five-step presentation. The result is confusion for you and the prospect. In time and with added confidence control of your delivery will become an easy matter.

Always remember to go completely through the step-by-step delivery, regardless of the interruptions you or your prospect may experience. For this reason, we stress the importance of memorizing the five-step presentation. It will allow you to pick up wherever you left off. If you are interviewing an extremely busy prospect, you may be bothered by frequent interruptions. Therefore, when concluding your presentation it is suggested that you review the five steps briefly to ensure your prospect's full comprehension of the total value of the service.

You will find that your prospect will have many questions. Answer to the best of your ability and then continue with the presentation. The one question that should never be answered before you conclude is, "How much is it?" Carefully avoid replying by explaining that the price is predicated on the volume of checks written and that you will show the price chart as soon as you have finished describing the service. You might add, at this point, a statement to the effect that the prospect may be pleasantly surprised at the reasonable cost of the total package.

MARKETING GUIDELINES FOR SALES PRESENTATION

These general marketing guidelines will give your presentation clarity and consistency.

After the general discussion, follow these step-by-step instructions:

1. Present duplicate checkbooks.
   Present daily sales forms.
   Present self-addressed postage-paid envelopes.
2. (a) Present the monthly financial statement incorporated in the five-step presentation:
   Balance sheet
   Profit and loss statement (circle Advertising)
   Detail general ledger (Advertising)
   Payroll
   Bank reconciliations
   (b) Present all tax forms, federal, state, and local (These should be part of your sales kit).

(c) Emphasize that WE DO ALL TAXES.

(d) Quote fees (installation, monthly, year-end).

3. Close

(a) Commence completion of client data form.

(b) Ask for void check (bank authorization).

(c) Ask for installation fee.

4. Go into backwork

When concluding with bank reconciliation, close the brochure and present it to the client with the commitment that 13 complete computerized statements with the company name on the cover sheet will be supplied. State that these records are all that is necessary, because they will provide an excellent audit trail of all transactions throughout the year. In addition to the client's copies, you will keep duplicates on file at your office. As a third backup, all totals will be held in memory in the computer. Be sure to stress that these 13 printouts will eliminate about 80% of the prospect's record keeping. Explain further that a 13-month adjusted year-end statement will be used to prepare tax returns.

SUMMARY

By now you will have taken the prospect all the way through your services and are about to explain your complete tax service. The close is such a critical part of the five steps that we have devoted most of the next chapter to this subject.

You will learn from experience that every call you make is a challenge. You will begin to build a backlog of follow-ups or call-backs. The call-back is most often more important than the initial presentation, because it represents a definite sale. Every call will demand your total attention, but the physical setup will vary immensely. You may be interviewing a prospective client at the rear of a dry-cleaning establishment or standing at the center of a foundry while the owner tries to listen to you and at the same time oversee the plant. Whatever the conditions, remember to keep your cool and the interview under control.

Next comes the close—MASTER IT.

13

ANATOMY OF A SALES CALL

Although, because of our high standards of professionalism, we do not advocate high-pressure tactics in the solicitation of a new client, we realize that at some point we must decide whether our service is really desired. Certain basic marketing rules must be followed if we are to experience a healthy growth pattern. One of these is that we must "ask for the business." Over the years it has been proved beyond the shadow of a doubt that there is one and only one low-keyed way to approach this basic issue. The overwhelming success strategy which results in a high close ratio is never to ask directly, but to assume that your service is wanted automatically. Hence, the widely accepted policy of the "assumptive close."

We begin this lesson with Step 5, by using the assumptive close.

THE ASSUMPTIVE CLOSE

After completing the presentation of the sales brochure, hand it to the prospect to thumb through. Answer any questions relating to it, but avoid prolonged conversation. Do not break the continuity of Step 5. At this point remove the sales presentation binder from your briefcase and show the client all the tax forms that are included in your service. Make it a point to show a dummy form 1120 or form 1065 or whatever tax return is appropriate to the particular business structure. Explain that your firm completes all taxes, payroll, business, and personal, and that the client need only drop the necessary data in the postpaid envelope. Your firm will take it from there.

Turn through your sales binder to the last page, the "recommended fee schedule."

Any opening remark will name the fee—for example, "And now for the best part, the cost." A suggested explanation of the fee structure is to show the prospect that many accounting firms base their charges on gross sales or company size, regardless of the amount of work required. Tell your prospect that your firm considers this criterion inequitable, because it is not a good yardstick and could result in over-charging. Some accountants charge by the hour, but neither is this method equitable because many clients will hesitate to ask for advice or assistance for fear of paying high hourly rates.

Now tell your client that your firm uses a flat monthly rate based only on the volume of work done and that this fee schedule applies to all clients, large and small. Explain that the fee will be based on the number of checks written. As an illustration, point to the charges for 60 checks and, depending on whether the client is a sole proprietor, partnership, or corporation, follow the line across the listed monthly fees. Then announce that "your monthly charge will be $____ and the installation fee is a one-time charge of $____." Explain further that the installation fee includes setting the system up, ongoing training, and continuous supplies. The year-end fee is for closing the books, running the final thirteenth month adjusted statements, and completing all tax returns, business and personal taxes (This includes two personal returns only). The year-end fee also includes all W-2s and opening the books for the new year.

The technique we are about to discuss is so critical that if not followed carefully it will have an adverse effect on your closing ratio. Our main objective here is to bring the client's checkbook out on the desk so that you may conclude the sale successfully. This is how it works. Ask the client approximately how many checks are written each month. Above all, suggest that the checkbook be taken out and the stubs, counted. It is extremely important that the checkbook be brought out in the open. Try to include as many months as possible to obtain a good average. Once the period of months has been decided on, make the calculation by taking the last check number, subtracting the first check number, and dividing by the number of months. You will now have obtained the number of checks. Ask the prospect if it is agreed that this number is a fair representation of the total.

Beware of split checks that show more than one general ledger (G/L) account number. If a check is split, each G/L number must be counted separately. Cash payroll disbursements should also be counted and added to the total to determine the fee. Count each employee as one check only. Remember to use the cash payroll slip. This slip should be coded and submitted to data processing for payroll updates.

Point to the recommended fee schedule (still on display). Write the fee on the face of the brochure that you will leave with the client and explain that this is a fixed fee, guaranteed for a year, and will not fluctuate from month to month. State that any charge after the first year would depend on any change in check count.

You have now accomplished two major steps, namely, you have quoted the fee and have caused the checkbook to be brought out. You will see how easy it is to close if you have followed this procedure with close attention.

You may now pause to feel out your prospect and answer any questions posed. At this point you may experience some form of objection. We cover objections at the conclusion, but for continuity we assume that no objections have been raised and that you have answered all questions.

Now remove the client data sheet from your briefcase. Point to the bottom and state: "We have no contract per se, but I should like to point out two basic items on our client data sheet. As you can see, everything will be held in strictest confidence. No member of our staff will divulge any of the information. This service is on a month-to-month basis and may be terminated by a 30-day written notice by either party." Also explain that as long as a client is satisfied no contract will be needed.

You may now assume that the prospect wants your service, although you MUST NEVER make it a direct question. If you do, you will be asking for a yes-or-no answer, which is certain doom.

The title of this section is assumptive close. There is absolutely nothing wrong with your assumption that this client desires your service, assuming, of course, that you have received no strong objections. After explaining the data sheet, turn it toward you, and, with a carbon inserted, begin to fill it out. Start by asking for the correct firm name and address. Naturally, it is understood that you already have that information but the psychology here is to obtain the client's participation.

Once the client begins giving you the necessary information, you will be well on your way to completing the close.

After obtaining the business telephone number, begin to complete the section entitled "principals." The owner's name, title, address, and home telephone number are inserted here. Explain that it is important to have the home number for use in an emergency and that it will be held in the strictest confidence. Mark off the structure of the business—for example, retail hardware or physician. Disposition of income is to denote whether all funds are deposited in the bank or whether heavy cash disbursements are customary. The number of employees is self-explanatory. Do not get into any discussion of this subject at this time, however. The name of bank is self-explanatory.Regarding the "date established," do not belabor the date and hour, but merely approximate the year. This will give you an indication of the number of prior tax returns that you must obtain. Ask for the fiscal year date on which the books are closed. (NEVER accept this date as final when setting up a new client because more often than not there is confusion regarding the actual end.) Rely only on the date of the corporation tax return. The average number of checks have, of course, been determined and should be inserted here (The same applies to the average number of payroll checks). The name of the former accountant is important. You will probably have to ask for earlier records.

RECORDS NEEDED

Declare what you will need from your client. In the box next to "last tax return," enter three years. Also state that you will need the preceding three business and personal returns. Do not attempt to obtain these records. Just check off what you will need.

The next two sections, "client will receive" and "client will provide," should be handled identically. Read through as you check off the appropriate boxes. Tell the client what to expect, but be careful not to mention items that are not applicable, such as the accounts receivable package or perhaps excise taxes. Proceed to a discussion of what the client will give you, and emphasize that all work must be transmitted in the prepaid envelope on a WEEKLY basis.

Because the fees have already been established, merely fill them in as you repeat the amount out loud for the benefit of the client. Fill in the monthly, the installation, and the year-end fees only. DO NOT ATTEMPT TO DISCUSS BACKWORK AT THIS TIME.

Backwork fees and the effective fee date are postponed at this time to allow you to obtain a void check and the installation fee.

We have described in detail the theory of closing by this method to give you a complete understanding of the importance of this sequence of events and why it is imperative. Experience has shown that to obtain installation and backwork fees simultaneously tends to overwhelm the prospective client. Therefore, you must stop at the installation fee and follow the next step.

After all fees have been filled in, explain that you need a void check to order duplicate checks. (Remember, the checkbook should be available.) Explain further that you must have the void check to make sure that the coded account number is properly reproduced. IMPORTANT: while the client is avoiding the check, and only then, say: "By the way, the installation fee is normally payable with the order." (Point to the single asterisk in the fee portion of the client data sheet.) "Would it be possible to give me the installation fee now while you have the checkbook handy?" This is the suggested wording but you may, of course, use whatever suits you best. If, however, you fail to ask for the installation fee while the prospect is cutting the void check, you will lose the opportunity for a smoother close.

Now that you have obtained the void check and the installation fee, have the client sign the change of address on the bank authorization form. As you will have noticed, the client has not yet signed the client data agreement. We purposely do not push for this signature, because we have not determined whether backwork exists. The next topic of discussion is the pricing out of backwork.

BACKWORK

We have now come to the point in the close that establishes the question of existing backwork. You must ask to see all books of original entry at this juncture. The response to this question will range from current financial statements to no records at all.

Many situations will reveal that records are not up to date and usually need to be adjusted from the last quarter ending or the last year ending when taxes were filed. You may have to go back one or two years to do all the backwork, quarterly payroll taxes, and year-end taxes.

Backwork is the rule rather than the exception. This is a lucrative part of your practice and a good revenue center, especially in the early stages of your growth pattern. The following procedure has proved to be successful in determining backwork fees.

Begin discussing the condition of the prospect's record keeping by examining the ledger and financial statements or whatever material is available. You must base your determination on the condition of the records. It will often be obvious to you and the prospect that backwork does exist, in which case the prospect will readily agree that the books must be brought up to date.

On rare occasions you may encounter a businessman who considers the company records current, even though they lack a current balance sheet and P/L. If this person is not willing to pay a backwork fee because of a sincere belief that the general ledger is correctly posted and that it is merely a matter of pulling the financial statements from the files, you must decide for yourself. It is important to stress here that if in your own opinion there is little to do to bring the books up to date and that the possibility of signing a client hinges on this backwork charge, it would be advantageous to waive the fee and gain a new client. Because situation vary considerably, we cannot set down hard rules to follow.

Now that you have determined the amount of backwork required, explain to the client that you can run the entire job in one printout to reduce computer charges. If this is acceptable, tell the prospect that you can discount the backwork fee by 30%. Then make a quick calculation of the monthly fee, multiplied by the number of months of backwork, less 30%, and insert the net amount on the line reserved for backwork fees. Under "backwork will include" enter the inclusive dates. Follow with the month and year the fee becomes effective. The effective date, of course, should be in the month immediately following the last month of backwork. The monthly fee will be billed in advance. At this point all the necessary information is completed.

Turn the client data sheet toward the client and ask for approval of the information it contains. As the client is signing, point to the double asterisks and state that normally the backwork fee is payable half with the order and the balance on completion. Ask if it would be agreeable to pick up a check that day for half the backwork. If the client suggests voiding the old checks and combining the payment, insist that it is not necessary.

After the client data sheet is signed, give the new client a copy of the agreement, put all paperwork and checks in your briefcase, and begin assembling the records. Be sure to get as many prior tax returns as possible (a minimum of three years). Go over all the details and generally discuss what you will be doing to bring them up to date and on system.

If the client is not busy and you both have the time, take this opportunity to complete the new account set-up form. It is recommended that you X in the accounts desired to give the client an immediate printout of the custom chart.

After deciding which sales form is appropriate for the new client's business, begin the training in its preparation. Leave one or two pads of the selected form and eight 9 × 12 postpaid envelopes, an ample supply for two months.

You must emphasize the importance of obtaining as many records as possible. It has been proved time and time again that the very fact of your taking records with you, as opposed to picking all of them up at a later date, creates a feeling of total commitment. This will give you the chance to begin at once.

SUMMARY

In summation, we can only reiterate that every call will present a different situation, but overall, if you maintain control of the interview, the presentation and closing will follow an established pattern. Be confident, speak with authority, and know your service.

Objections are covered in detail in the following discussion. Some time during the assumptive close or even before reaching that point you may experience an "objection." The objection is a natural part of gaining new clients and may range from "I don't like computers" to "I don't need an accountant." No matter what form it takes, there is always a logical remedy or answer. We delve into solutions to this problem and describe proven methods for obtaining new clients.

THE OBJECTION

It is virtually impossible to imagine or attempt to list every possible objection you may encounter. The list that follows is accompanied by solutions to some of these major objections:

1. I want to think about it.
2. I do not want to fire my present accountant.
3. I want quarterly statements only.
4. I want to wait until the end of the year.
5. The fee is too high.
6. I am not interested.
7. Call back at a later date.
8. I don't need a monthly statement (interested in profits only).
9. I need a decision from another party.
10. I am not ready yet.
11. I do not like computers.
12. I do not need an accountant.

I Want to Think About It. This is one of the most common objections. It is a normal response and, in many cases, is not the underlying reason. Agree immediately with your prospect by stating, "That is the proper thing to do. I would do the same in your position." But you are obligated to determine the actual reason for this indecisiveness. To overcome it, you must ask if there are questions that might help to clarify the situation. Further, ask what specifically is to be thought about. Sometimes the true objection will be brought out, but if the prospect has no specific reasons in mind, there is little you can do. It is your obligation to set a firm follow-up date to call on this prospect again.

I Don't Want to Fire My Present Accountant. Some of our accountants have experienced the reluctance of their prospects to discontinue the services of their present accountants, even though it has been established that these same prospects are interested in making a change and have agreed that what they have been receiving is inadequate. A feeling of obligation or unwillingness to terminate is at issue. This may be a valid reason or only an excuse if their payments are in arrears. In the latter instance, you may never get the true facts.

In any case, offer to alleviate the pressure by explaining to your prospect that this is quite normal and that, in similar situations, you have approached the former accountant on the client's behalf and have picked up the company's records.

If this is agreeable, suggest that you call the former accountant in the prospect's presence and make arrangements for the return. Instill confidence by reassuring the prospect that the transition will not be troublesome and that you will be able to pick up where the other accountant left off.

As an additional incentive, stress that from a businessman's standpoint personal feelings should not be allowed to intrude.

In conclusion, once you have agreed to pick up the records and terminate the other accounting firm, it should be done immediately or as soon as possible. The longer you wait to transfer responsibility from your competitor to yourself, the greater the possibility of losing your prospect.

If you do not sign this client because of a reluctance to change accountants, continue to call at least once every three months. You will find that eventually the service received will lack so much that a change will become obligatory.

I Need Quarterly Statements Only. In an effort to contain their overhead costs, many accounting firms will minimize their client's services by asking for quarterly statements only. Many prospects will feel that quarterly statements are sufficient and that the monthly service will cost more. Explain this misconception by stressing the importance of keeping up to date on a month-to-month basis. Quarterly statements are made after the fact; in any event most of the work, such as payroll, tax deposits, sales tax and tax reports, and bank reconciliation, must be done monthly. Explain how it can be done by your firm on your computer and how the savings in labor and current financial statements will be advantageous.

Finally, if the prospect insists that quarterly statements are all that is needed, agree that you can run quarterly statements as requested. Use your best judgement in allowing a small discount for quarterly statements, because your savings from processing quarterly will be insignificant. Do not, however, lose the client because of this minute detail.

I Want to Wait Until the End of the Year.   If the prospect indicates a desire to make the change and wants your services, but feels that it would be better to wait until the end of the year for the present accountant to close the books and do the taxes, respond in this manner. Tell the prospect that because you will be responsible for all his/her taxes and recordkeeping you would like to do the year-end taxes yourself. Tell the prospect that you are well qualified to do tax work and would prefer to study the earlier tax returns and do a complete job from the beginning.

Make further assurances that the transition to your system is an easy one and that your clients have joined you at various times during the accounting cycle. Explain that the sooner the transfer is made, the sooner it will allow an analysis of the month-to-month activity of their business.

Many times the objection is not a true one. By pursuing this strategy, you may meet another. In any event, attempt to discourage postponement of this decision.

If the prospect stands firm in the decision to wait, keep in touch until the end of the year. Then try to get things rolling again. It is suggested that you call at least once a month to ask if there is anything you can do to help. You may find, to your surprise, that the prospect may have decided to move earlier than you anticipated.

The Fee Is Too High. Normally this objection is made when the present accountant is offering a lesser service. About the only thing you can do here is to compare the work now being done with what you can offer. (If the prospect's present accountant is working for a considerably lower fee than your recommended schedule, the services that you have available, such as payroll registers and monthly financial statements, will not be included.) Try also to ascertain what other differences exist between the present accountant's services and yours. This information may be provided voluntarily by the prospect.

In the final analysis, after weighing the entire situation, you may find that it will be necessary to negotiate the price. We are reluctant to suggest this approach but feel obligated to discuss the possibility. This is a high-profit profession. If the system is followed you will have considerable flexibility in the area of gross margin. If a ten or fifteen dollar deduction in fee will sway the client your way, it may be to your advantage to reduce the fee to acquire a new account. This is especially true during the early stages of your growth.

A word of caution is in order. We are not suggesting that you give your valuable services away. However, we are merely pointing out that initially it is good to build cash flow and to scrutinize the profitability of your accounts later on.

Again, this is a business judgment. You, as the entrepreneur, must decide how much you are willing to handle the account for. It is basically a matter of striking a happy medium between the two extremes of pricing yourself out of the market or pricing too low to make a profit. Examine your charges carefully to give yourself a feel for the flexibility of pricing, but most important of all, please make note of the fact that the words "recommended fees" appear on the top of the pricing chart. Following these recommendations, you cannot go wrong. Remember to be flexible if the situation calls for it. A good rule of thumb is to keep in mind that you are working with a 50 to 70% gross margin. This will give you a good yardstick with which to negotiate price.

I'm Not Interested. In this instance you have not obtained a true objection. This one is somewhat similar in nature to, "I want to think about it." It is a general statement and will not be encountered often because the fact that the prospect granted an interview would lead you to believe that a certain interest existed. To reiterate, ask the reason for the lack of interest and whether any portion of the service is unclear. Again, if the prospect flatly states a lack of interest and refuses to give any other reason for objecting, there is little you can do. Express your thanks politely for the time allowed you and leave the sales brochure with your card attached. Ask to be called if you can be of any service in the future.

Call Back at a Later Date. "Call me in about a week" is closely related to "I want to think about it," and will be the response given most of the time. The experience of our accountants has shown that only 30 to 40% will actually buy your services on the first call. It is extremely important that this does not in any way influence your attitude.

You must make the attempt to sign the client on the first call; otherwise you will lose the 30 to 40% first-call closings. We feel, however, that we must be realistic by informing you that a good 60% of your presentations will be call-backs.

A request to call back can mean many things. It can be a put-off or an expression of genuine interest in pursuing your service. In many cases a call-back condition will arise when all the people involved in bookkeeping decision making are not present. It is obviously important to have all the decision makers take part in the interview. Pursue this matter before the presentation by asking if the prospect will make the decision alone or if others will be present.

You will experience call-backs. They are a critical part of your overall marketing campaign.

I Don't Need a Monthly Statement. Some prospects will express an interest in having only taxes, such as payroll taxes, kept current. The misconception here is that if there is money in the bank, a profit is being made and everything is going along fine. It is important that you point out the shortcomings of operating under the "I have a feel for it" concept.

An effective way of refuting this objection is to explain that although there is money in the bank and the prospect feels that profits are being made many advantages can still be obtained by the use of current monthly financial statements. Show that even higher profits and greater income can be gained by examining overhead factors and controlling costs more efficiently. Also mention the fact that good cash flow or "money in the bank" can be misleading, because the debt ratio can be high and the true picture may be entirely different from the one that the prospect considers a healthy financial condition.

It is most important to show how costs can be controlled, sales evaluated, and profit centers pinpointed. This will encourage better management and deeper analyses for future reference. Taxes are just one part of the overall management of a prospect's business. It should be realized that even though a profit is made, to ensure future profits, there should be constant analysis of assets and financial statements.

If it is insisted that monthly statements are not needed and you cannot sway this opinion, say that you will run at least quarterly statements, will be able to do all the tax work, and will assist them in all accounting problems.

You must understand, of course, that it is important to obtain the account even though it requires abiding by other rules. You may find later, after one or two printouts have been examined, that a sincere interest will develop in the overall financial picture and a decision will be made that monthly financial statements are needed.

In any event, yours is a full service firm, and the financial statements are only one part of your service. You can still give monthly service without submitting statements. Attempt to sign the client on any terms. You can actually run the statements and keep them on file for periodic review.

I Need a Decision from Another Party. If you have properly qualified your prospect, you should not be in the position of having to present your service a second time or to have the prospect explain it to another person. As stated earlier, you must determine whether your prospect is the one to make decisions or whether other people are involved. This does not always work, however. You will find occasionally, after the presentation, that it is necessary to talk to another accountant, bookkeeper partner, or associate.

In any event, it is important that you be the one to make the second presentation. Never rely on your prospect to present the package properly. This is sure disaster. Answer all questions that your prospect may have. The key here is to follow up on this account.

I Am Not Ready Yet. This is one objection that obviously should be overcome by responding with the statement, "But may I ask why it would not be feasible to change now?" In other words, attempt to determine the exact reason why the prospect is not ready but still wishes to change at a later date. Normally, this will be followed by another objection, such as "I want to wait until the end of the year." In many cases the prospect must be assured that the transition to computerized accounting is easy and requires little involvement.

I Don't Like Computers.   We have on rare occasions been told that the client does not like computers. Although the average accountant does not place much credence in this frivolous attitude, it might be a good idea to give you a quick answer. The best response to this objection is to state that you represent a full-service public accounting firm involved in management, accounting, bookkeeping, and tax work and that this is your major service. The computer is used only as a tool, a means to an end. Also explain that all the input is under your supervision and that many controls are built into the system.

Explain the computers have increased the efficiency and cut the costs of record keeping. Explain also that they are widely accepted and that your present clients rely heavily on the accuracy of their computerized monthly financial statements.

It is strongly recommended that you never process an account manually. It will stymie your growth and cause severe complications in your practice. You must understand that you are the only one who would be able to process this type of account. Your time is more valuably employed elsewhere.

I Do Not Need an Accountant.   It is a rare prospect who would grant you an interview and then tell you that he/she not need an accountant. The attitude of this prospect is overwhelmingly antagonistic. If signed, you may find that the account poses potential problems.

Attempt to be friendly and ask sincerely why the prospect holds this opinion. The response may be that all work is done personally and that an accountant is a waste of money.

You must never let a prospect offend you. You may rationalize by saying that you are involved in accounting and tax work on a day-to-day basis and can offer this expertise in addition to any other financial service that may be needed.

You will find that if you keep your "cool" and are friendly and sincere the prospect will warm up and show a change of attitude. In many cases, however, it is difficult to work with a client whose personality is basically negative.

SUMMARY

These objections are those that seem to be encountered more than others. Always remember that they are part of the thought process that assists a prospect in making decisions. You must realize that because you are met with an objection it does not mean that the prospect is not interested in your service or that you have no chance of gaining a new client. It is merely a means of communication between you and your prospect that you must accept until you reach the assumptive close.

One of the major problems noted in selling is the inability of some accountants to deal with objections. Sometimes a prospect will voice an objection instead of asking a question. It is a way of trying to learn as much as possible about your services. Never lose confidence or appear to be discouraged by an objection. If the prospect detects that an objection has destroyed your enthusiasm or confidence, confidence in you will be destroyed as well. The prospect is constantly assessing your attitude. Objections are part of the natural process. You must overcome them one at a time by maintaining your belief in your total system.

If you tackle all objections with a healthy attitude, you will find that it is a part of your marketing effort which leads to a higher percentage of closes. Approach objections with the idea that you are discussing your services openly and want to know how the prospect feels about them. If you go in armed with this attitude, you will overcome all objections successfully as part of a natural process.

We now discuss super sales techniques that really work. The goal of any successful marketing campaign is to obtain as many sales as humanly possible. We have taken you through a step-by-step procedure that presents the service, overcomes objections, and closes the account. Now we are ready to launch the easiest part of the entire marketing program—that of obtaining referrals and call-backs. Referal sales represent a major portion of your marketing. The "art of referrals" has been mastered so successfully by some accountants that they have determined by actual records that 35% of all sales were referrals.

We begin this section by discussing the two strategic times to ask for referrals. It is suggested that you study this section carefully if you wish to establish a rapid growth pattern.

REFERRALS

There is only one "best time" to ask for referrals and that is at the conclusion of a sale. After the paperwork has been completed and you are about to leave, ask your new client to recommend a friend or associate who might be in the market for your services.

Psychologically, this is the best time to ask for a referral. The new client, having made the decision to sign, feels that it was the correct one and won't hesitate to suggest a business acquaintance or friend as a likely candidate.

After taking the name of the referral, ask permission to use the client's name as a reference. In most cases, there will be no objection.

When a request for a referral is made, your client may be happy to introduce you by telephone or talk to a business associate about your service. On occasion, however, a wait-and-see attitude may be adopted before making a recommendation.

In the event that you do not obtain a referral at the installation stage, your job of acquiring referrals has just begun. This is an ongoing proposition and should be foremost in your mind. Many accountants have created physical reminders to follow through on referrals. A sign in their offices, a large notation at the top of each month on their calendars, and many other motivational techniques have been employed. It is easy to overlook the importance of referrals. Don't fall victim to this shortcoming. Always create some method of reminding yourself to ask for them.

At every opportunity, on every call, a subtle hint should be directed to your clients for new referrals. Always remember that these are business people who understand that your success is predicated on growth.

Your clients may feel that the referrals they have made obligate you to provide them with better service. In some instances accountants have offered one month's free service for each new client they gain as a result of a referral. They have also found that it is more impressive to present a client with a check rather than to give credit on the monthly statement.

You will be called on continually to perform additional services that may fall into the classification of consultation. There are two ways of handling this extra work. One is to charge an hourly fee if there is considerable involvement. If you feel that the request is a minor matter and can be done with little effort, it is suggested that you do it as a favor, but follow it up with a request for referrals. Never become too pushy but look for opportune times to remind your clients of your interest in gaining new ones. Any time that appreciation is shown for your services is a good time to ask for referrals.

The multiplying factors of an effective referral program are virtually unlimited. As new accounts are gained, your client base will yield more and more potential referrals. Your growth will be in direct proportion to how well you manage your practice, expand your staff, and pursue the "Art of Referrals."

THE CALL-BACK

Volumes can be written on follow-up without placing sufficient emphasis on one of the most critical facets of acquiring new accounts. You will find that although you are able to obtain many clients on a first-interview basis, the bulk of your new clients will come from call-backs. In studying the section on objections, it should be remembered that when you have exhausted all objections and cannot close the client at that first interview, you should never conclude the meeting without first obtaining a follow-up date.

You must realize, of course, that you have already invested your time at the initial interview and that the second or third call on the client is merely a summation of your services. You should run through the five points again before closing. Normally, if prospective clients grant you a second or third interview, it is obvious that they are interested and ready to acquire your services. Therefore, bearing in mind that most of your prospects will sign up on a subsequent call, follow-ups become more important than initial calls. It is suggested that a unique system of discipline be adhered to in which follow-up dates are logged on a 3 × 5 card and on your desk calendar so that full advantage can be taken of these valuable opportunities called "call-backs."

It is better to establish a time and date for a visit than to make a telephone follow-up. (You cannot sell a new client over the phone.) When conducting the second interview, it is imperative that you review your services briefly and, somewhere in the conversation, bring up any previous objections, whatever they might have been. Answer the objections adequately and go smoothly into the assumptive close by filling out the client data sheet.

No matter how many postponements your prospects may have made, they remain prospects until they actually tell you that they are no longer interested. Our accountants have acquired clients as much as a year later as a result of conscientious monthly follow-ups. You will find that with proper follow-ups, in addition to new appointments obtained on a day-to-day basis, you will have a wealth of prospects and should never find yourself in the predicament of having no one to call on.

COLD CALLS

Although cold calls are the least desirable and the most time consuming, it should be pointed out that many good accounts have been obtained by this method. It is not suggested that you pursue cold calling on a routine basis, but you should use your valuable time in any number of situations. As an example, if you are early for an appointment and have an hour to wait, visit the neighboring shops and businesses in the immediate area. Ask for the owner on a cold call. Introduce yourself as a local accountant. Leave your card for future reference. (But do not leave the brochure.) If the cold-call prospect shows interest and asks questions, answer them briefly and try to set up a convenient appointment. Explaining that you have a call to make in the neighborhood and need enough time to go into detail at a later date.

The merchants you patronize and the services you buy are another good outlet for cold calling. Without becoming repetitious, it should be enough to emphasize that you have an obligation to the success of your practice to inform every potential prospect of your full-service accounting firm by any means possible.

CIRCLE OF INFLUENCE

Become acquainted with the local bank officers (especially the loan officer), who are repeatedly in touch with small and medium-sized businesses in need of financial statements and bookkeeping assistance. It is suggested that you present the total system to these people. Another important contact is a good attorney. It seems all attorneys have contacts with accountants. When a client requests your assistance in locating a good attorney, you must not inadvertently expose your client to a strange attorney's accountant friend.

In addition to the referral system in the direct-mail campaign, the following list contains some other worthwhile methods of obtaining clients:

1. The local newspapers are a good source if the accountant will check daily under the heading of "Help Wanted—Bookkeepers." Because your system will eliminate 80% of the need for in-house bookkeeping, it is appropriate to point out when calling that your system can provide this service at great savings. Follow the same basic telephone presentation with some minor modifications.

2. It is common knowledge that most cities list new trader's licenses and/or permits in the local papers. Here, again, is a good source if followed up on a timely basis.

3. Be in constant touch with the local merchants you deal with personally. Do not hesitate to tell them that you would be

pleased to handle their accounts. Leave your card and some literature (if requested).

4. Any exposure you may develop creates a good opportunity to increase your growth pattern. Present your sales brochure to civic and professional groups, real estate boards, and petroleum and insurance associations.

As you can see, you are the manager of your time. If you are constantly on the alert, the marketing possibilities are virtually unlimited.

14

PLANNING FOR GROWTH

PRACTICE DEVELOPMENT

Still another advantage accrues to having a large number of small clients rather than a few large ones. The more clients you have, the more they will "advertise" for you. Clients who have an on-the-ball accountant like to tell their friends about it.

Experienced accountants agree that the best sources of referrals are the following:

1. Existing clients
2. Bankers
3. Lawyers
4. Personal friends and acquaintances

The agreement is general that the number one source is existing clients. The others will vary in productivity, depending on the individual situation, but it is rare to find an accountant who does not feel that existing clients are his/her best source.

A small client can be just as good a source of referrals as a large one—better, in fact, if he/she is enthusiastic. Some clients actually take pride in the amount of new business their accountants receive from their recommendations.

One point to remember. When new clients appear at your office, try to find out who sent them to you or what prompted them to come. This will give you a better idea of the origin of your referrals and an opportunity to express your thanks. It is good practice to write a thank-you letter if you haven't had the opportunity to call in person.

THE HUMAN INTEREST FACTOR

Small clients offer a unique opportunity. You will frequently develop a close relationship and make a definite contribution to the client's organization.

In many instances you will find that you are the client's closest and perhaps only professional advisor. You will be respected and shown sincere appreciation for the services you supply.

DEVELOPING AND MANAGING A TOP-NOTCH PRACTICE

Among the many constituents in the makeup of a successful accountant is the ability to develop and manage a practice.

"Practice development" refers to increasing the volume of the firm. An accounting firm must grow because only in expansion can greater opportunities be offered to qualified people. A growing firm can employ and promote good people, who, in return, will attract bigger clients, do more challenging work, and increase profits. Furthermore, clients are frequently lost through mergers, retirement, or death, thus making way for new clients and new sources of revenue.

It is well established that one's own clients provide the best opportunity for growth. Some practitioners tend to get so interested in obtaining new accounts that they overlook the present. Established clients can benefit from added services and, indeed, should be given priority. When considering practice development, remember that you owe your clients the best you can give and that they in turn are your best source of new business.

Accountants who excel in practice development generally have a plan of action—a program that gives better results than a hit-or-miss approach.

PRACTICE MANAGEMENT

Some accountants with growing practices devote too little time to the management of their organizations. They are more concerned with the work of their clients and find it difficult to devote nonchargeable time to their own responsibilities. This is a tough hurdle to overcome but it has to be done.

Some firms try to solve the management problem by passing it around each year to different partners or other associates. This is a certain path to poor management. The partner who inherits the job will look on it as an extra responsibility to be shed as quickly as possible. Furthermore, frequent changes in management will foster inconsistent policies and methods of dealing with staff. It is much more difficult to promote a smooth management function under this arrangement.

A sole practitioner naturally is responsible for the management of his own firm. Partnerships should assign one of its members to the manager's post. Management should be considered a specialty as important as the more technical functions of the business. The managing partner should study routines and work toward improvement.

Tradition has tended to make the senior member of the firm the managing partner. Based on experience, this is the logical choice,but it should be recognized that some people are not necessarily competent to administer the day-to-day affairs of an office. Some partners are better suited to and happier with client work. The choice of a managing partner should, therefore, be based on the individual's aptitude for and interest in management problems. If a younger partner is more suited to the job, so much the better.

CREATING A PROFESSIONAL IMAGE

The development of your practice is based to a considerable extent on what people think of you. Here are some guidelines to follow in creating your own professional image.

1. Reflect a desire to serve other people, to show a genuine interest in the problems of your clients and community.
2. Your standard of living should be in keeping with the image of a successful professional man.
3. Be self-confident. Develop a high opinion of yourself and the value of your work.
4. Your office should be modern, comfortable, and efficient.
5. Be known as a person who works on the professional level. Don't give the impression of bogging down in detail.
6. Be known as a person on top of your job. Don't give the impression of always being behind or snowed under.

PEOPLE MAKE YOUR PRACTICE GO

An accounting practice is as successful as the people who staff it. A group of talented people, properly managed, and motivated, can make all the difference in the quality and profitability of your practice. Three most important management functions relate to personnel—employing, training, and motivating.

It is well established that there is more to motivating employees than adequate salaries. Money is important, of course, but other factors are equally so. People like to feel that their work is useful and to receive recognition for their efforts. They want to be treated as human beings and not as cogs in the wheel.

How is this accomplished? Here are a few suggestions.

1. When an employee comes in to talk to you, stop what you are doing, look him/her in the eye, listen attentively, and show an interest in what he/she is saying.
2. Give employees an opportunity to make suggestions, to be creative, and to make their ideas and personalities felt in the organization.
3. Provide adequate office facilities, including good lighting, good equipment, sufficient space, and suitable private or semiprivate offices.
4. Let your employees know how well they are doing. At least once a year evaluate their performances and discuss them together. If possible, provide goals for the coming year. Don't forget to compliment them for jobs well done. When, on occasion, it is necessary to be critical, do so constructively and with dignity.

Develop a system for obtaining information about the performances of partners and staff. One important measure is fee production. The billings of the firm should be distributed among employees assigned to the work. An analysis of fee production should be part of the monthly financial statement.

LEARN ALL YOU CAN FROM OTHERS

It has been our experience that much of what we know about developing and managing our practices has come from other practitioners. The benefits of exchanging ideas cannot be obtained in any other way. Most practitioners are invariably willing to discuss management policies and techniques, matters that can be examined without revealing confidential information.

All practitioners should attend professional meetings and seminars and consider themselves fortunate to be members of a profession that provides so many opportunities to learn.

EVALUATE YOUR OWN PERFORMANCE

What guidelines can you use to measure your own performance? In a sense, this can be done by reviewing the results of your efforts—increased billings and the profits of the firm. To probe deeper, however, you must scrutinize your own performance in various areas of responsibility—fee production, public relations, client relations, technical expertise, management responsibility, and relations with staff.

An objective evaluation on an annual basis will help the accountant avoid complacency and keep him on his toes.

PRACTICE DEVELOPMENT CHECKLIST

I. Reasons for a client development program.
    A. Our office wishes to grow in size in order to

    (1) serve bigger clients;

    (2) render broader client services;

    (3) maintain high quality of service;

    (4) increase the firm's profitability.

B. We must acquire new clients in order to grow and to replace losses due to attrition.

C. We must provide the income and fee volume for staff advancement.

II. Limitations on program.

    A. We must at all times maintain and abide by the rules of professional conduct and the public accountancy laws of the various states. An active and successful program, can, however, be developed within these professional concepts.

    B. Define the characteristics of the client you want to attract.

III. Sources of growth.

    A. Growth of present clients.

    Although this category may at first seem to be beyond our control, it really isn't. Our program should include provisions for active participation in client growth by merger and expansion of geographic coverage.

    B. Additional services to present clients.

    We must continue to strengthen our programs of departmentalization and industrial specialization to be able to develop the in-depth experts needed to diversify our services. We should also review the needs of our clients to avoid overlooking service that we can supply. Some specific functions to watch for and methods to use are

        (1) pension and profit-sharing plans, including Keogh plans;

        (2) estate planning;

    (3) special audits not leading to an opinion, such as
        cash, inventory, and receivable audits;
    (4) systems design and changes;
    (5) EDP applications;
    (6) budgeting;
    (7) management letters with each audit;
    (8) use of specialists;
    (9) management audit questionnaire;
   (10) assistance in financing.

C. Client recommendations.

This seems to be the source of most of our new clients. Therefore, we must concentrate on enthusiastic clients, not just the contented. This can be accomplished best by showing a genuine interest in and understanding of the client's problems and needs. This applies to all clients, large and small. We never know where our next recommendation will come from.

We must plan our schedules to allow time to build close personal relationships with as many of our present clients as possible. This can be done by

    (1) lunches;
    (2) visits by clients to our office;
    (3) a friendly telephone call or visit;
    (4) parties at home;
    (5) outside entertainment, such as sporting events, hunting and fishing, and theater going;
    (6) remembrances at birthdays and anniversaries;
    (7) client newsletter;
    (8) congratulatory letters;
    (9) directory of offices and affiliates;
   (10) seminars and dissemination of business education material.

D. Recommendations from others.

To develop business from the recommendations of

friends and associates we must acquire as many acquaintances as time and energy permit by participation in various organizations such as
Religious and charitable
Civic
Social
Professional
It is not enough to be a name in a roster. We must participate actively and hold positions of responsibility. We should begin immediately to develop and maintain a record of the various organizations and associations in which we have members and then select others that we feel would be advantageous from the standpoint of client development.
Some suggested organizations in which we should become known are the following:
Professional
National Association of Accountants
CPA Societies
Administrative Management Society
American Management Association
Systems and Procedures Association
Business and Estate Planning Council
Estate and Financial Forum
Data Processing Managers Association
Internal Auditors Association
Civic
Chamber of Commerce
Junior Chamber of Commerce
Rotary, Kiwanis, Lions, etc.
Political parties
Neighborhood civic clubs
In addition to participation in formal organizations and associations, there are certain groups of business and

professional people who make the best sources of refer-
rals. A special effort should be made to catalog present
acquaintances and cultivate new ones in these groups
assiduously.
Attorneys
Bankers
Chartered life underwriters
Security dealers
Business executives
Chief accountants and controllers, particularly CPAs in
industry

IV. Operating procedures.
Meetings should be held to accomplish the objectives of the
program, probably not less frequently than semi-monthly.
In the beginning the program should be one of developed
partner participation, but it should ultimately be made
available to managers and other interested staff.

A. New client summary. (See Exhibit 35.)
This is an ongoing list of new clients prepared from the
data on contract forms with the following column
headings:
Date
Control partner
Client number
Client name
Type of business
Type of engagement
Source of engagement
Estimated annual fee

B. Lost client summary (See Exhibit 36.)
This is an ongoing list of clients lost, with the following
column headings:
Date
Control partner

Control Partner	Client Number	Client	Type of Business	Engagement	Source of Engagement	Estimated Annual Fee

Exhibit 35. New Client Summary

Date	Control Partner	Client	Approximate Annual Fee	Prospect For Return	Reason for Loss of Account	Follow-up Contact

Exhibit 36. Lost Client Summary

Client name
Approximate annual fee
Prospects for return
Reasons for loss of account
Follow-up procedure
C. Practice development report. (See Exhibit 37.)
This is a report of contacts made with people who are potential sources of business, including our present clients. It is to be maintained by each partner and has the following column headings:
Date
Person contacted
Title-function
Company/organization
Comments
D. The following agenda is suggested for these meetings:
1. Review new client summary.
2. Review lost client summary.
3. Review practice development report.

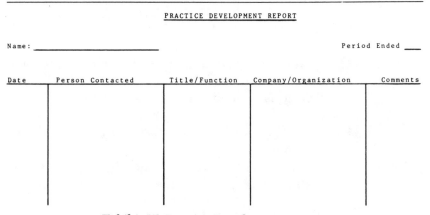

Exhibit 37. Practice Development Report

4. Review and list prospective new clients.
5. Review business section of newspapers.
6. Review progress of cataloging acquaintances among business and professional groups.
E. Review progress of cataloging representation among business, civic, and professional organizations.

Workload, Production, and Firm Responsibility
1. Fees produced by partner's clients.
.2. Profitability of work done for clients (write-downs, etc.).
3. Fees produced by partner individually.
4. Effectiveness of collecting client receivables.
5. Performance in and up-to-date knowledge of basic areas of practice (tax, audit).
6. Performance in and up-to-date knowledge of specialized areas (data processing, estate work, and pension plan work.)
7. Performance in contributing to the management of the firm.

Client Relations
8. Reputation for "attentive" service.
9. Ability to complete work promptly.
10. Availability to clients when needed.

Standing in the Community and the Profession
11. Image in the community as a top level citizen and professional man.
12. Positions of leadership in community organizations.
13. New clients brought in through individual contacts and efforts.
14. Standing within the profession (positions of leadership, etc.)

SOME BASIC GUIDELINES FOR CHARTING THE GROWTH OF YOUR PRACTICE

It is often said that you will become what you plan. When was the last time you took stock of yourself and your firm and made plans for growth?

A healthy, controlled, and growing practice requires planning. This includes (a) setting goals for the firm that coordinate with individual goals; (b) assigning actions to be taken; (c) setting schedules for these actions and for their periodic review; and (d) revising and updating the goals and plans.

Before goals can be set, you will have to take stock, to analyze your lists of clients, the services your firm provides, your organizational structure, and your market.

Begin your analysis with an overview of your firm. List its major strengths and weaknesses. An overview can also give you a profile of your clients, as shown in Exhibit 38.

Fee Range	Total Hours	Number of Clients	Total Fee	Average Hourly Rate
$ 0–$ 3,000	_____	_____	____	_____
3,000– 7,000	_____	_____	____	_____
7,000– 12,000	_____	_____	____	_____
12,000– 20,000	_____	_____	____	_____
More than $20,000	_____	_____	____	_____

Exhibit 38. Client Profile

303

Similar lists can be prepared for specific types of engagements; for example, audit, compilation, review, and taxes, the latter being divided into individual, corporate, fiduciary, and planning categories. Clients can also be viewed from other perspectives such as maturity, potential, and lines of business. These analyses can be especially useful in the identification of fruitful areas of specialization or in varying the firm's orientation to suit more of their client's needs.

Then look at your firm's organization. Who is responsible for policy decisions, administration, personnel, and tax, audit, small business practice? Describe staff members in terms of their current job responsibilities and their future. Are they "fast track" . . . "steady" . . . "comers"? Who provides backup for each of the key responsibilities?

Next do some market research. What is your market by geographical area and by type of service and specialty? Who are your competitors and what is their potential? What major factors will affect your firm in the next few years and what opportunities will be available in the near future?

With your market research completed, you are ready to set your firm's goals. Consider how your organization chart will change, how each person will develop in three or five years. Project ultimate potentials. Note areas of expertise to be developed. Employee income levels should be projected in anticipation of employee involvement in civic and professional activities. Determine whether this plan will meet the goals of individuals. Examine each person's professional interests, family commitments, and changing financial obligations (e.g., college costs). Try these projections for yourself three and five years away; detail family objectives, professional involvement, social interests, and a personal financial statement.

This exercise can reveal the holes in your firm's talent "mix," needed to satisfy the intent of the practice. It can also raise questions about finding people to fill the holes and how to acquire and motivate them.

Prepare tables for your audit, tax, and small business practices three and five years from now. Project financial statements for your firm. Reflect on their implications. Where will your new clients come from? Are you taking advantage of your "niche"? What specialties must be developed? Should you devise an "aggressive marketing" plan? Will your firm fill its internal requirements, participate in an association, or seek an appropriate partner in a merger? Is uncertainty so great that contingency plans are essential? Are there built-in inconsistencies between your firm's and your personal goals?

Exhibits 39 and 40 are forms for charting the quality of client contact performance and work assignments completed.

You might brainstorm a portion of the goal-setting during a partner retreat meeting. Yes, it is that important. If you want your staff to "buy-in," as a valuable source of input, they must be involved in the process and you must share the end product of your planning. It bears repeating that you become what you plan.

Practice Development Techniques

1. Perform services on a timely basis.
2. Get to the client's office on time.
3. Return telephone calls promptly.
4. When you write a letter on behalf of your client, send a copy to the client.
5. When preparing management letters at the conclusion of an engagement, don't make suggestions that will lead to increased costs until you have considered the offsetting benefits.

MONTHLY CLIENT CONTACT REPORT

CLIENT NAME	TELEPHONE #	FEE	JAN.	FEB.	MAR.	APR.	MAY	JUN.	JUL.	AUG.	SEP.	OCT.	NOV.	DEC.

Exhibit 39. Monthly Client Contact Report

MONTHLY WORK CONTROL

Bookkeeper's Name _____

Work Done in _____

MONTH _____ MONTH _____ YEAR _____

CLIENT NUMBER	Y/E	CLIENT'S NAME	FEDERAL TAX EXEMPT	REVENUE TAX DEDUCTED	DEPOSITORIES								QUARTERLY RETURNS					OTHER	DATE MATERIAL RECEIVED					
					Fed 941 AMOUNT	State 941 AMOUNT	Fed 940 AMOUNT	CITY AMOUNT					Fed 941	STATE 941 UC	Sent Rec'd				1	2	3	4	5	A

Exhibit 40. Monthly Work Control

6. Take interest in and listen attentively to a client's problems, even when they are unrelated to the audit.

7. If a client, or anyone else, asks you a question about matters appropriately handled by a CPA firm, and you don't know the answer, offer to find it and do so at once.

8. Answer your telephone promptly and don't leave the caller hanging on hold.

9. When visiting your office for an appointment, don't let your client wait without an explanation.

10. Spend some time with the person who actually pays your fee and not just the client's staff.

11. Let the client know your audit schedule well in advance. Have it approved and stick to it unless the client authorizes a change.

12. Give the client frequent progress reports. Don't wait until you are asked.

13. Never complain to the client's staff about their systems and methods. They are not responsible for the design or authorized to make changes.

14. Review the audit report, management letter, and other papers with the client, preferably in draft form.

15. Do not issue an audit report, management letter, or internal control letter that contains surprises. Prepare your client in advance for every item in a report. It is better to discuss these items during the engagement.

16. When you complete a management advisory services questionnaire at the conclusion of the audit, pass it on to your MAS department for consideration.

17. Use tact and diplomacy when dealing with a client who is uncooperative or dilatory. If you fail to observe this caveat, you will be the loser.

18. Do not conduct personal business at the client's office.

19. When working in the client's office, the accounting staff should hold personal conversations to a minimum, including those with the client's staff.

20. Offer frequent and sincere thanks to those responsible for referring new business to you.

21. Maintain your ties with the client after the engagement is completed.

22. In anticipation of a forthcoming engagement, make early contact with the client to let him know you are planning for and looking forward to working with him.

23. Do as much work at the client's office as possible to give the client the opportunity to review the actual time requirements of the engagement.

24. Send out client bulletins.

25. Conduct client and other seminars.

26. Carry on a formal practice development program.

27. Conduct formal meetings of the tax and accounting department staffs.

28. Keep up to date with the changes in professional affairs in a formal education program. Be sure that your clients realize that your services reflect the latest developments.

29. Provide adequate supervision of your staff when they work at a client's office. Don't let the client think that you or your staff are working aimlessly.

30. Prepare the client for increased fees and get his permission before incurring them. If you can't provide an explanation in advance, review the fee with him later by letter or in person, giving him full details.

31. When your schedule is full and you are rushed, never complain to the client.

32. If the client brings up the need for a service that you cannot provide immediately, make a note and get back to him promptly.

33. Maintain open and frequent communication between firm members to keep everyone fully informed.

34. If you need additional information from the client, prepare a list and make one telephone call instead of several.

GOOD COMMUNICATIONS IMPROVE CLIENT RELATIONS

It is our philosophy that good communication with clients is of primary importance, because it enables us to relate to them those things that we do best and to remind them that we are attentive to their needs. Communication breeds confidence. We can implement this philosophy in a number of ways:

1. Assign a partner-in-charge to each client.

2. Have a minimum of one annual review and planning conference with each client.

3. Establish proper lines of communication between the partner-in-charge and all personnel who work with the client.

4. Mail to each client a monthly newsletter of useful accounting and tax information and a calendar of current due dates.

QUESTIONS THAT WILL DEVELOP FREE THINKING ABOUT WHERE WE ARE AND WHERE WE SHOULD BE

I. Clients.
   A. Which clients are the most enthusiastic about us?
   B. Which clients have received the best service? Why?

    C. What clients did we lose? Who got the worst service? Why?

    D. What kind of clients should we seek?

    E. What kind of clients should we discourage or get rid of?

What to do: Decide who our clients should be, where they are, and how to reach them.

II. Kinds of Service.

    A. What is the best kind of work we do?

    B. What is the worst kind of work we do?

    C. What are we known for?

    D. What is the most profitable work we do? Why?

    E. What is the least profitable work we do? Why?

    F. What kind of work should we add or expand?

What to Do: Define the services we should be rendering and how we should concentrate on them.

III. Present Conditions.

    A. What is the current status of the profession?

    B. How will litigation change the profession?

    C. How do you feel about peer group reviews?

    D. What is the present status of the community in which we operate?

    E. What is the present status of the economy and how will it affect us?

    F. What are our clients looking for under today's conditions?

    G. What are our prospective employees looking for?

What to Do: Analyze what is going on around us.

IV. Future Conditions.

    A. What will our locality, state, and country be like in the next five years?

    B. What will international conditions be like in the next five years?

C. What will accounting practice be like in the next five years?
D. What services will clients need and how will we be able to satisfy their requirements?

What to Do: Project what we can expect in the future.

Here Are The Three Most Important Questions

What *is* our business?
What *will* our business be?
What *should* our business be?

15

BUYING OR SELLING YOUR BUSINESS

WHY PURCHASE A PRACTICE?

The acquisition of a good, well-established accounting practice at a reasonable price can be an excellent way to achieve independence and the other rewards that go with being one's own boss for the person who has some money and the necessary qualifications to attract and hold clients.

There are many reasons why it might be considered better to buy an established practice rather than a new one, not the least of which is that the buyer is not adding to the competitive state of the profession in the community.

THE CONFLICTING INTERESTS OF THE BUYER AND SELLER

The successful completion of the sale and the implementation of the agreement will usually involve considerable negotiation.

The buyer and seller occupy essentially adversary positions and their interests are often in conflict.

The seller wants the highest possible price. The seller wants to be assured of getting the purchase money. The seller also wants to be paid as soon as possible, consistent with good tax planning.

The buyer wants to obtain a good practice at the lowest possible price on favorable payment terms. The buyer also wants to obtain warranty protection against false statements of the seller and inaccurate financial data.

The buyer will want to arrange for the sale to take place immediately before the busy season. This will reduce the risk considerably and will produce the least strain on working capital. The seller will probably prefer to sell immediately after the busy season.

The seller is usually in a better position than the buyer. The seller knows what is being sold and how much value is being received. The buyer is facing several unknown quantities. On the other hand, if it is a forced sale the seller has less bargaining power; if the sale involves installment payments the seller in effect is sharing a large part of the risk with the buyer.

WHERE TO LOOK FOR A BUYER/SELLER

1. Consult other accountants, bankers, professors of business in local colleges, Chambers of Commerce, and local accounting society chapters.
2. Advertise in newspapers.

Accounting practice value is essentially a question of client value. Clients are a practice's most valuable asset and the most difficult to tag.

For the most part buyers of accounting firms pay prices determined by what others have paid. The prices are not generally related to conditions that exist at the time of purchase but are arbitrary computations agreed to by the parties. In addition, parties to accounting practice acquisitions have given little consideration to the time value of money.

An accounting practice should be valued at the time of purchase. In determining value, the point of view of the buyer should prevail. The recommended starting point in the negotiations to determine the value of an accounting practice should be 125% of its gross fees of the last year. This recommendation is based on the premise that an accounting practice has exchange value because future services are expected to be performed for its present clients. In arriving at the recommendation, consideration is given to expected annual gross fees, net income as a percentage of gross fees, an appropriate discount rate, and a reasonable period of time. An additional recommendation is that certain objective characteristics of the purchase be considered by the negotiating parties as reasons for increasing the suggested starting price and that other conditions be considered as reasons for decreasing the price. The amount of increase or decrease cannot be measured exactly for any of the characteristics. Also, subjective factors are considered by the buyer in setting the price he is willing to pay. These factors will not normally enter openly into the negotiations between the parties. Finally, a buyer should not pay a premium for seller assistance in the transfer of clients.

POINT OF VIEW TO CONSIDER IN DETERMINING VALUE

My recommendations consider value from the point of view of the buyer. This is a logical approach because the need for valuation arises whenever there is to be a change of ownership. The exchange value of a practice is directly related to the present and future benefits to be derived from the practice by the buyer. The recommendations are based on the anticipated net earnings, but the application to determine a specific price begins with the simpler figure of gross fees.

TIME TO DETERMINE VALUE

Ideally, an accounting practice should be valued at the time of purchase. Although any recommendation for practice valuation which estimates value at the time of purchase has to be based to some extent on opinion rather than on certainty of future performance, if this opinion is based on solid reasoning future parties to a purchase and sale of an accounting practice will welcome the recommendation. A lack of confidence in what will happen in the future has led to the common practice of making the purchase price contingent on future events. This practice is considered undesirable but necessary because of the nonexistence of any soundly supported recommendations for estimating value at the time of purchase.

A THREE-STEP APPROACH TO VALUE

An approach to the value of a practice to a prospective buyer is recommended in the following three steps:

1. A starting point applicable to all or most practices should be used in the price negotiations.
2. Certain objective characteristics of the purchase should be given consideration.
3. Subjective elements that affect the price a buyer is willing to pay but may not affect the negotiations should be given atten-

tion. The findings of empirical investigation and in the literature provide the basis for developing this three-step approach
to the value of an accounting practice.

A GENERAL RECOMMENDATION REGARDING THE VALUE OF AN ACCOUNTING PRACTICE

The starting point in the negotiation to determine the price of an
accounting practice should be about 125% of its gross fees of the
last year. This recommendation is based on the premise that the
value of a practice is principally the present value of its future
net income. In arriving at this recommendation, the following
factors were considered:

1. The expected annual gross fees from the acquired clients.
2. The percentage of gross fees that will remain after all expenses.
3. An appropriate interest factor or "cost of capital" rate.
4. A reasonable time period.

Gross Fees

The empirical investigation revealed that future annual fees
from retained clients will usually approximate past annual fees.
Several interviewees made the point that any losses in gross fees
caused by the nonretention of some acquired clients were recov-
ered by increased billings to other acquired clients. This obser-
vation is substantiated by a close look at the study results. The
total gross fees from 116 acquired clients in the year before the
purchase was $190,755. The total gross fees in the third year
after purchase from the 93 clients retained was $158,270 or 83%

of the fees from 116 clients for the year before purchase. However, the figures from one practice acquisition greatly distorted the study result. Five large bookkeeping clients belonged to this purchased practice and were included in the study. The fees from the five clients in the first year before purchase totaled $49,800. Three of the clients did not remain with the buyer. The fees in the third year after purchase from the remaining two clients were $23,800—a loss of $26,000. Two of the losses (fees of $18,000) were initiated by the buyer. In these two cases the buyer helped to obtain full-time bookkeepers for the clients. If these five clients are deleted from the study findings the fees from retained clients in the third year after purchase were about 95% of the fees from all clients in the first year before purchase. The total fees in the first year before purchase would be $140,955 ($190,755 less $49,800); the total fees in the third year after purchase would be $134,470 ($158,270 less $23,800). Therefore the assumption that future annual fees from retained clients will usually approximate past annual fees appears to be valid and past fees can be used in a determination of practice value.

Net Income as a Percentage of Gross Fees

The computation of net income should include as an expense an amount for the owner's salary. There were 13 firms in the investigation which had only one owner and no other professional staff. These firms are chosen because no provision for professional salaries was included in their net income percentages. Using firms with professional personnel other than owners would create the problems of determining how much additional salary is necessary to cover the services of the owner or owners of the practices. In the 13 firms chosen the owner performed all of the professional services. Net income, before a salary allowance for the owner, averaged 58.6% of the gross fees for the 13 firms. Most of the individual figures for the 13 firms were within a few percentage points on either side of 58.6%

There still remains the owner's salary. An accepted "rule of thumb" for billing is two and one-half times the direct salary cost. In other words, the direct salary cost should be 40% of the billings. Therefore net income for the firms included in the computation averaged 18.6% of the gross fees (58.6% less 40%).

Interest Rate

The interest rate that is used to discount future net receipts should reflect the buyer's cost of capital. There can certainly be disagreement on regard to proper rate. The rate used should vary with the cost of money. A lower or higher discount rate does not materially affect the result.

Time Period

Ten years is a reasonable time period to use in the present value computation. At least one noted writer uses a 10-year discount period when determining the value of goodwill. Although the buyer hopes the acquired clients will benefit his firm for a much longer time, he has to justify the purchase in the earlier years. Also, adding extra years does not materially change the result because the present value of net receipts from distant future years would be small. The use of a lesser number of years would not fully compensate the seller for his efforts in developing the practice.

Computation of General Recommendation

The computation that results in a valuation recommendation of 125% of gross fees is as follows: the present value of one received each year for 10 years, discounted at 8% interest, is 6.71. The present value of 18.6 received for the same number of years at the same interest rate is 18.6 times 6.71, or 124.81. This is easily converted to a percentage of the gross fees. The present value of 10 years of net income valued at 18.6% of the gross fees at an interest rate of 8% is 124.81% of the gross fees. Because the future annual gross fees are assumed to approximate the gross fees of the years before purchase, 125% of the gross fees for the year before purchase is recommended as a starting point in the negotiations to determine the value of accounting practice.

A change in the interest rate used to find the present value of future net income changes the recommendation only slightly; for example, if 6% is used to determine the present value the recommended point to begin negotiations is 137% of the gross fees. If a 10% rate is used the recommendation is 114% of the gross fees.

The recommendation of 125% of the gross fees varies; the gross fees formula dominated practice among the firms of the empirical study. This difference, however, should not affect the credence of the recommendation. The traditional practice of valuing firms at 100% of the gross fees or some other arbitrary percentage was established primarily on an intuitive basis without benefit of the kind of analysis involved in determining the beginning point for negotiations. On the other hand, the study recommendation of 125% is developed by applying logic to empirical findings which include gross fees, net income as a percentage of gross fees, an appropriate interest factor, and a reasonable time period.

OBJECTIVE CHARACTERISTICS THAT DIRECTLY AFFECT PRACTICE VALUE

Factors that determine the basic value of an accounting practice are given above. This section considers the purchase characteristics that directly affect the first or second of the four factors— the future gross annual fees from the acquired clients or the percentage of gross fees that will remain after all expenses.

Purchase Characteristics that Affect Future Gross Fees

As mentioned before, the future annual gross fees of an acquired practice should approximate the past annual fees, primarily because losses from the nonretention of some acquired clients are offset by increased billings to retained clients. In the empirical investigation client retention and client "performance" were considered on several bases with the result that retention and performance differed under the varying conditions of the purchases. Client retention was greatest when (1) the buyer and the client were in the same city, (2) the seller was a CPA, (3) the buyer had experience in managing an accounting practice, (4) the seller had served the client for more than three years before the purchase, and (5) the client had been served only by the seller. The results also indicated that practices purchased after the death of a practitioner and practices purchased with no transfer assistance from the seller resulted in better-than-average client retention. A comparison of client performance with the professional status of the seller (CPA or non-CPA) and with the three-year trend of seller's fees revealed a definite pattern. When the seller was a CPA or when the seller's fees had been increasing a majority of cases resulted in a favorable outcome for the buyer. On the basis of these findings, it is recom-

323

mended that the following conditions be considered by the parties to a purchase as reasons for possible increases in the suggested starting point of 125% of gross fees:

1. The buyer and clients are located in the same city, especially when the city is small.
2. The seller is a CPA.
3. The buyer has experience in managing an accounting practice.
4. The seller has served the clients for more than three years.
5. The clients have received accounting services only from the seller.
6. The seller's gross fees have been increasing.

On the other hand, the following conditions should be considered by the parties to a purchase as reasons for possible decreases in the suggested starting point of 125% of gross fees:

1. The buyer and clients are located in different cities.
2. The seller is not a CPA.
3. The buyer has not had experience in managing an accounting practice.
4. The seller recently acquired the clients.
5. The clients have received accounting services from accountants other than the seller, either before becoming clients of the seller or concurrently with those of the seller.
6. The seller's gross fees have been relatively stable or decreasing.

A definite recommendation cannot be made concerning the consideration to be given to the different means of seller assistance in the transfer of clients. The findings of the empirical investigation suggest, however, that the literature has overestimated the value of having the seller spend weeks or months with the buyer in a strictly client-retention role. Practices purchased after the death of the practitioner and practices purchased with no transfer assistance from the seller had better-than-average client retention. This finding of the empirical investigation supports the position of R. Sproull in *Accountants' Fees and Profits*. Sproull states that the selling accountant should act only to the minimum extent of making introductions. It is recommended that the buyer pay no premium for seller assitance in the transfer of clients.

Purchase Characteristics that Affect Future Net Income as a Percentage of Gross Fees

In addition to the selling price adjustments, which are suggested because of the consideration given to expected annual gross fees, deliberation should be given to any selling-price adjustments needed because of a net profit percentage that differs from the previously established norm; for example, a practice comprised principally of small-fee tax returns will have a low net-profit percentage. In fact, a given practice of this kind might be unprofitable—the costs to perform adequate professional services would exceed the fees. The tax status of the payment for clients is another variable that affects net income. If the payment is tax deductible the buyer's tax bill will be reduced; therefore his net receipts as a percentage of gross fees will be greater.

Because it is not possible to measure exactly the effect on practice value of any of these conditions, the recommended adjustments to the suggested starting point in the purchase negotiations do not carry dollar or percentage amounts.

Subjective Considerations that Affect Value

In a given purchase one or more factors will exist that are no less important to the buyer than the foregoing purchase conditions, but because of their subjective nature these factors will normally not enter into the negotiations between the buyer and seller. They include many of the reasons that the interviewees gave for acquiring additional practices:

1. To get a "foothold" in the profession.
2. To acquire clients needing a certain type of service, thereby complementing their present practice.
3. To offer better service to out-of-town clients.
4. To give mature staff people more responsibility.
5. To move into a certain location.
6. To justify additional staff.
7. To acquire personnel in the purchase.

Other subjective benefits to be derived from a purchase include the expectation of referrals from acquired clients and increased retirement security. A nonmonetary benefit is the additional prestige of having a larger firm. One interviewee stated that the purchase of a practice allowed him to employ more staff, which in turn gave him a chance to spend less time in his clients' places of business and more time in his own office, where he could fulfill his desires to be a "manager."

USE OF FORMULAS

Formulas that would determine mathematically a proper exchange price for any given practice cannot be constructed. Not only is it impossible to measure the exact effect on future fees of the objective considerations mentioned, but it is equally impossible to place a definite value on the subjective considerations of giving mature staff members desiring to get a start in public accounting and wanting the prestige of a larger firm more responsibility.

SOME SUBJECTIVE OPINIONS OF THE AUTHOR

The Purchase of an Accounting Practice as an Investment

After a few years many practices reach a stage of "diminishing returns." The right purchase is the best way to enlarge a practice, to get started in a new location, or to get a start in public accounting.

Sellers of accounting practices tend to undervalue their practices, and in most cases this results in the buyer getting a bargain.

Practice Management After a Purchase

Most client losses that can be related to a practice purchase will occur within one year of the sale. After one year client losses will be normal.

In the first year after purchase a buyer of an accounting practice generally should not increase or decrease the fees charged to acquired clients. Client retention is affected particularly in that first year; also the buyer will not yet know his cost of providing good professional service.

327

Tax Treatment Accorded an Accounting Practice Acquisition

Practitioners, in many cases, lack adequate support for the tax treatment accorded the payment for clients. The tendency is to take a deduction for the expenditure, regardless of the facts of the purchase.

Other

Practitioners generally do not make adequate advance arrangements for the continuation or sale of their practices in the event of disability or death.

Many practitioners, especially those with small practices, do not keep adequate time and expense records. This deficiency in recordkeeping is a major cause not only of lack of success in selling practices but also of practice sales that prove to be unsatisfactory to the buyer, the seller, or to both.

The purchase agreement is one of the most important considerations in a practice transfer. Many (if not most) accounting practice purchase agreements are deficient in one or more aspects. A common deficiency is inadequate support for the tax treatment of the consideration paid and received for clients.

BUYING A PRACTICE

Many of the complications involved in setting up new practices can be avoided in CPAs who have the opportunity to buy already established firms. Ads for the sale of accounting practices are abundant in classified sections of professional publications and journals. CPAs exploring this possibility will have no difficulty locating prospects.

The chief advantage in buying an existing firm is that it will normally yield an established client base. Instead of biding time as they wait for new referrals, CPAs who buy practices can often step right into the shoes of their predecessors, handling existing accounts and being paid their accompanying fees. Also, an established firm provides office space, furniture, equipment, supplies and, in some cases, a staff thoroughly familiar with the clients and eccentricities of the local area. If the CPA is lucky, an accurate typist will be part of the package.

Despite these advantages, veteran accountants often warn that newcomers should approach this move with caution. Picking up where another accountant has left off can be hazardous and expensive. Many practices are put up for sale by accountants nearing retirement or by the families of practitioners recently deceased. Frequently the accountant has had the firm for many years. Their clients of long standing are themselves bent on retirement and may harbor skepticism of young or new professionals they deem short on experience. Furthermore, a client following at the time of sale is no assurance that when the new shingle goes up those clients will remain.

Established fees can also pose a problem for the new practitioner. The fees of many older accountants have remained static for years. Thus new CPAs often face the uncomfortable task of explaining that "old rates" need updating and that service costs will rise. The news sometimes discourages older clients from returning.

When these potential pitfalls accompany the existing practice prospective buyers may retain considerable leverage with which to negotiate the terms of transfer. Normally the purchase price of an accounting practice is based on a percentage of that firm's annual gross profit; for instance, a firm grossing $75,000 may be advertised somewhere between $35,000 and $60,000. For an unusually attractive practice the price could run higher than the gross. Generally, the purchase is financed by the seller who will, in most cases, require a down payment and several annual installments until the balance has been paid. In a bargaining situation, instead of offering a set purchase price, the purchaser may ask for an agreement in which a down payment is made and percentages of the annual gross fees are paid over a specified number of years. Normally, such contracts do not extend for more than 10 years.

An older accountant about to leave a practice may invite the prospective purchaser into the firm on a trial basis—to teach the ins and outs of the practice and receive reassurance that the right person has come along to carry on. Younger CPAs are warned by experienced colleagues that such arrangements may go sour if the seller expects too much from the novice, becomes dissatisfied, and cancels the sale. "I don't know why," says one seasoned CPA, "but invariably something goes wrong and the young accountant has to back-track." Others advise would-be buyers to obtain a signed commitment from the seller which would specify the reasons for termination in advance of any "trial period."

Exhibit 41 is a checklist of general information that should be completed before acquiring an accounting business. Complete instructions for the client worksheet segment appear in Exhibit 42. Exhibit 43 is a worksheet to be completed for each client.

BUYING A PRACTICE

1. (A) Name under which
   Practice is carried on _____

   (B) Date Established _____

   (C) Above name used since_____

   (D) Other names used during past _____years:

Previous Name	From	To
_____	____	____
_____	____	____

2. Does the sale include rights to firm name?_____

3. Type of organization_____

4. (A) Method of Accounting_____ (B) Accounting Period _____

5.

Names of Partners	Age	%	Yearly Salary	Billing Rate	Partner Since	Reason for Selling

COMMENTS:_____

_____

_____

It is important to know the owner's reason for wanting to sell his practice. Frequently, the decision·to sell results from poor health or the desire to retire. If the owner is motivated even partly by any other external or internal factor, the buyer should consider carefully the possible effects the change of ownership will have on the practice.

Exhibit 41. Checklist of General Information

6.

Names of staff accountants and other employees	Age	Yrs. Exp.	Yrs. With Firm	Billing Rate	Salary	Willing to Stay?

The buyer will be concerned with the attitudes and feelings of the staff because it could be a source of substantial competition. A change of ownership is the kind of event which could encourage a strong staff member to go into practice on his own.

7. Nature of Community

    A. Industrial___ Suburban___ Mixed___ Rural___
    B. Many Small Businesses___ Few large businesses___ "Well Mixed"___
    C. Community is: Growing___ Static___ Declining___
    D. General employment is: Full-time___ Seasonal___
    E. Population:

        _____ 1990 population of: city___ county___
        _____ 1980 population of: city___ county___
        _____ increase/decrease. ___%increase/decrease.

8. Location of office:

    A. Date occupancy began _____.
    B. Owned___ Rented___
    C. Present space is: adequate___ inadequate___
    D. Space will accommodate _____ additional personnel.
    E. Compared to other office buildings in community, this building is: above average___ average___ below average___.
    F. Building located in: business district___ outlying area___ in between___.
    G. Area where office is located is: growing___ static___ declining___.
    H. Has the zoning classification of the area been changed in last year or two? ___ If so, consider effect on neighborhood.

Consult with the landlord about taking over the seller's lease - possible extension of lease - renewal clause - repairs - improvements - etc.

Exhibit 41. (Continued)

9. Other offices occupied during the past _____ years:

Address   From   To

_____   _____   _____

_____   _____   _____

10. Equipment and other assets:

   A. Obtain list of all equipment and other assets which are to be transferred.
   B. Appraise each item.
   C. Is it adequate for the practice? ____

11. Operating Statistics:

					Last Year
(A) Audit Fees					
(B) Tax Work					
(C) Write-ups					
(D) Mgt. Advisory Services					
(E) Non-Accounting income					
(F) Total Income					
(G) Total Expenses					
(H) Net Profit					
ADJUSTMENTS:					

   The chief value of the above table is to help evaluate the overall profitableness of the operation. It can be used to aid in determining the value of the firm by making whichever of the following adjustments are appropriate:
1. Use figures which relate only to present clients.
2. Eliminate non-accounting income.
3. Eliminate income from special, non-recurring jobs.
4. Add back expenses not connected with practice.
5. Add back partners' salaries.

Exhibit 41. (Continued)

12. Compute the ratio of operating expenses to total fees for each year under consideration.

				Last Year

In relation to total fees, have operating expenses tended to: increase___ decrease___ remain about the same___ .

What is the explanation for the increase/decrease?

_____

_____

_____

13. Circumstances existing during any of the years under consideration which tended to increase total fees or profits above normal.

A. _____

B. _____

C. _____

D. _____

E. _____

14. Circumstances existing during any of the years under consideration which tended to decrease total fees or profits below normal.

A. _____

B. _____

C. _____

D. _____

E. _____

Exhibit 41. (Continued)

15. Fringe benefits now offered to employees (include vacation and sick pay, bonus and profit-sharing plans, etc.).

A. _____

B. _____

C. _____

D. _____

E. _____

16. Principal source of new clients:

_____% Other clients _____% Other accountants

_____% Partners _____% Attorneys

_____% Banks _____% Other

17. Competition:

How many new accounting practices (including branches) have been started in the community during the past five years? _____

A. Is this more than should normally be expected considering population and industrial growth? _____

B. Can the community support the new practices? _____

C. How many practices have failed or moved from the community during the past five years? _____

D. What circumstances have been responsible for this increase/decrease?

_____

_____

_____

_____

18. Business & Bank References:

NAME	Rating (Generally)
A.	
B.	
C.	

Exhibit 41. (Continued)

335

The worksheet, which follows, was designed so that it can be used for a single practitioner as well as for a partnership. Some of the items may not be appropriate in some cases and in others the prospective buyer may want additional information.

It is felt that a minimum of three years' operations should be examined. If the practice is less than three years old, more caution and study will be required.

The instructions and comments below are keyed to the columns of the worksheet.

A. <u>Name of Client</u>. The complete name and address should be listed. May also add the name and title of the "contact" man, such as John Jones, Treasurer. This information will be very useful if the sale is completed. List charity and other non-billed worked.

B. <u>Date Acquired</u>. The date a client was acquired is important in evaluating the future potential of that client and the prospects of his remaining with the buyer.

C. <u>Services Performed</u>. Indicate the general nature of the services performed for each client; such as, auditing, income tax, write-ups, management advisory services and other. This will aid the purchaser in determining the knowledge and skill required to handle the accounts.

D. <u>Place of Services Performed</u>. Use "C" for client's office and "O" for the firm's office. This will aid in determining the amount of travel and outside work involved.

E. <u>Method of Billing</u>. Indicate whether retainer, per diem, or other. The adequacy of any retainers should be examined. When adequate, they may be more certain than the per diem estimates for future years.

F. <u>Any Unbilled Time</u>? Arrangements must be made for work in process. See discussion in Part III.

G. <u>Client Consent to Transfer Files</u>? This will assist the buyer in determining the prospects for retaining the various clients. It is improper for an accountant to transfer his working papers and the other confidential files of a client to another accountant without the client's permission. If such permission is granted, the prospects for the purchaser to retain that client are good.

Exhibit 42. Worksheet Instructions

H. Time Billed, This will aid in determining the trend of the clients' accounts.

I. Estimated Time Next Year. To determine staff requirements and workload.

J. Estimated Billings Next Year, Discount seller's opinion when necessary.

K. _____ Year Average. This will aid in evaluating the goodwill of the practice and should cover a minimum of three years. If a particular client has only been with the firm for, say two years, a two-year average can be shown but it should be circled or otherwise identified as being less than the number of years for which the average is being computed.

L. Amount Billed, Use whole dollar amounts. Does practice consist of a few large accounts or many small ones?

M. Remarks. List nature of client's business and fiscal year. List anything else that has a bearing on the value of the client's account or his future relations with purchaser.

Exhibit 42. (Continued)

A NAME OF CLIENT	B DATE ACQUIRED	C SERVICES PERFORMED	D PLACE	E METHOD OF BILLING	F ANY UNBILLED TIME?	G CONSENT TO TRANSFER FILES?

Exhibit 43. Worksheet

H							I	J
TIME BILLED							ESTIMATED TIME NEXT YEAR	ESTIMATED BILLINGS NEXT YEAR
					LAST YEAR	THIS YEAR		
JR.								
SR.								
TOTAL								
JR.								
SR.								
TOTAL								
JR.								
SR.								
TOTAL								
JR.								
SR.								
TOTAL								
JR.								
SR.								
TOTAL								
JR.								
SR.								
TOTAL								
JR.								
SR.								
TOTAL								
JR.								
SR.								
TOTAL								

Exhibit 43. (Continued)

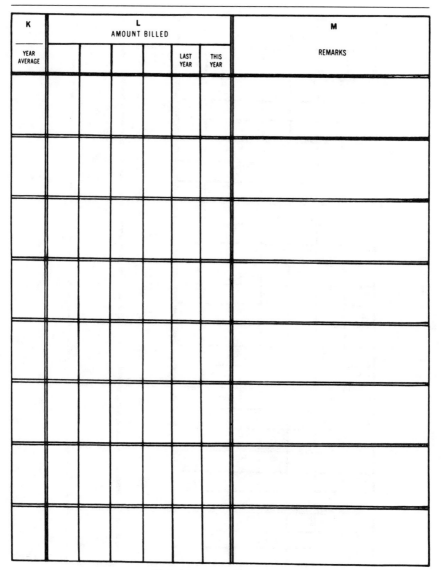

Exhibit 43. (Continued)

16

CONTINUING EDUCATION

Accounting, as a body of information, continually evolves. "So much so," reports a spokesman for one of the nation's Big Six accounting firms, "that knowledge gained in the field today will have practically no value within four years."

The short life of "current" accounting data makes it vital for the professional to be aware of all changes in tax laws, accounting principles, procedures, inventory evaluation, reporting earnings, auditing, ethics, and other professional trends that affect the accounting practice. Poorly informed CPAs may not only be a hazard to their clients but to themselves as well. Malpractice suits against CPAs have increased in recent years. Many suits for negligence have resulted from a lack of information on the part of the accountants involved.

Some professionals maintain that state-imposed requirements are not enough. They contend that accountants must pursue new information daily. Colleagues, say some, should put an hour of their time aside every day for reading current journals, tax service circulars, and accounting texts.

Some accountants have found it useful to form study groups with which to compare methods of handling various accounting tasks. Individual practitioners, in particular, find the study-group arrangement an excellent way to compensate for the lack of daily professional contact available in partnership firms. Some organize materials to be discussed into categories of interest. One accountant is responsible for reading in one area of accounting procedure, a colleague in another. On the date set for the meeting, each member shares with the others the information gained. Many approaches can be created.

Suggested Library

Accountant's Desk Handbook, 3rd. ed. Ameiss and Kargas. Englewood Cliffs, New Jersey: Prentice-Hall, 1988.

Accounting and Information Systems, 2nd. ed. John Page and Paul Hooper. Prentice-Hall, New Jersey: Englewood Cliffs, 1987.

AICPA Codification of Statements on Auditing Standards, Numbers 1 to 51. AICPA. New York, 1988.

The Art of Problem Solving. Russell L. Ackoff, New York: Wiley, 1987.

Auditing Theory and Practice, 4th ed., Roger H. Hermanson. Homewood, Illinois: Irwin, 1987.

Bankruptcy Tax Act of 1980, Law and Explanation. Chicago, Illinois: Commerce Clearing House, 1980.

Business Basics—The Profit Plan, 1001, Self-Instructional Module, Small Business Administration, Washington, D.C.

Business Basics—Capital Planning, 1002, Self-Instructional Module, Small Business Administration, Washington, D.C.

Business Basics—Understanding Money Sources, 1003, Self-Instructional Module, Small Business Administration, Washington, D.C.

Business Basics—Evaluating Money Sources, 1004, Self-Instructional Module, Small Business Adminstration, Washington, D.C.

Business Basics—Asset Management, 1005, Self-Instructional Module, Small Business Administration, Washington, D.C.

Business Basics—Managing Fixed Assets, 1006, Self-Instructional Module, Small Business Administration, Washington, D.C.

Business Basics—Understanding Costs, 1007, Self-Instructional Module, Small Business Administration, Washington, D.C.

Business Basics—Cost Control, 1008, Self-Instructional Module, Small Business Administration, Washington, D.C.

Business Basics—Credit Collections, 1014, Self-Instructional Module, Small Business Administration, Washington, D.C.

Business Basics—Job Analysis, Job Specifications, and Job Descriptions, 1020, Self-Instructional Module, Small Business Administration, Washington, D.C.

Business Loans: Bringing Other People's Money to You. Rick S. Hayes. New York: Wiley, 1989.

Buying and Selling a Small Business. Verne Bunn. Washington, D.C.: Small Business Administration, 1979.

Consulting Handbook. Howard Shenson. Los Angeles: Howard Shenson, 1982.

Corporate Marketing Planning. John Brion. Wiley, New York: 1967.

Cost Accounting, 6th ed. Charles T. Horngren. Englewood Cliffs, New Jersey: Prentice-Hall, 1987.

Current Value Accounting. Warren Chippindale and Philip L. Defiliese. New York: AMACOM, 1977.

Dress for Success. John T. Molloy. New York: Warner, 1976.

Earning Money Without a Job. Jay C. Levinson. New York: Seaver Books, 1987.

The Entrepreneur's Guide. Deaver Brown. New York: Ballantine, 1986.

The Entrepreneur's Manual. Richard White. Radnor, Pennsylvania: Chilton 1977.

Entrepreneurship and Small Business Management. Hans Scholl-hammer and Arthur Kuriloff. New York: Wiley, 1988.

Federal Tax Handbook (for current year). Englewood Cliffs, New Jersey: Prentice-Hall.

Guide to Working Capital Management. Keith Smith. New York: McGraw-Hill, 1979.

How to Form Your Own Corporation Without a Lawyer for Under $50.00. Ted Nicholas. Wilmington, Delaware: Enterprise, 1989.

How to Get Control of Your Time and Your Life. Alan Lakein. New York: Signet, 1989.

How to Increase Appointments and Sales. Mona Ling. Englewood Cliffs, New Jersey: Prentice-Hall, 1976.

How to Obtain Your Own SBA Loan. Jack Fox, California: Commercial Finance Real Estate Group, San Diego, 1990.

How to Pick the Right Small Business Opportunity. Kenneth Albert. New York: McGraw-Hill, 1980.

How to Put on Dynamic Meetings. Chester K. Guth & Stanley S. Shaw, Reston, Virgina: Reston Publishing Co., 1980.

How to Read a Financial Report, 2nd. ed. John Tracey. New York: Wiley, 1983.

How to Start Your Own Business . . . and Succeed. Arthur H. Kuriloff and John M. Hemphill, Jr. New York, McGraw-Hill, 1981.

How to Succeed in Your Own Business. William R. Park and Sue Chapin-Park. New York: Wiley, 1978.

Information Processing. 4th ed. Marilyn Bohl. Chicago: Science Research Associates, 1984.

Intermediate Accounting, 4th ed. Donald E. Kieso and Jerry J. Weygandt. New York: Wiley, 1983.

Manage Your Time, Manage Your Work, Manage Yourself. Merrill E. Douglass and Donna. N. Douglass. New York: AMACOM, 1985.

Marketing Tactics Master Guide for Small Business. Gerald B. McCready. Englewood-Cliffs, New Jersey: Prentice-Hall, 1982.

The Master Manager. R.G. Siu. New York: Wiley, 1980.

The Money Game. Adam Smith. New York: Random House, 1976.

Perfectly Legal. BARRY R. Stiner and David W. Kennedy. New York: Wiley, 1984.

Personal Financial Planning. G. Victor Hallman and Jerry S. Rosenbloom. New York: McGraw-Hill, 1987.

Portfolio of Accounting systems for Small and Medium-Sized Businesses. National Society of Public Accountants. Englewood Cliffs, New Jersey: Prentice-Hall, 1979.

Profitable Direct Marketing. Jim Kobs. Chicago: Crain, 1979.

The Seven Laws of Money. Michael Phillips. New York: Random House, 1974.

The Small Business Handbook. Irving Burstiner. Englewood Cliffs, New Jersey: Prentice-Hall, 1989.

The Time Trap. R. Alex Mackenzie. New York: McGraw-Hill, 1975.

Valuing Small Businesses and Professional Practices. Shannon P. Pratt. Homewood, Illinois: Dow Jones-Irwin, 1985.

Where to Find Business Information, 2nd. ed. David M. Brownstone and Gorton Carruth. New York: Wiley, 1982.

Working Smart. Michael LeBoeuf, New York: McGraw-Hill, 1979.

17

PREPARATION OF SMALL-CLIENT INCOME TAX RETURNS

REASONS FOR THE PREPARATION OF SMALL RETURNS

At the outset it is suggested that the accountant consider his responsibility in regard to the preparation of small returns. For our tax system to work it is necessary for taxpayers to have access to competent professional help. The accountant has an obligation to serve the public. It seems to follow, therefore, that preparation of small-client returns is a professional obligation and in the public interest.

This is not to say, of course, that the public must be served at a financial sacrifice. The practitioner should, and, indeed, can, prepare small-tax returns on a profitable basis. Later in this chapter we discuss methods of providing a profitable service.

Recent years have seen a new industry of commercial-tax-return preparers spring up around the country. These commercial firms are preparing tax returns on a profitable basis, and professional accountants should be able to do the same. Professional accountants may have to charge a higher fee than the commercial firms, but they can demonstrate that the quality of the service is worth the fee.

During the tax-filing season we deal with a much broader group of clients than during the rest of the year. Preparation of individual income-tax returns provides an opportunity to serve the general public, which is not the case with auditing, accounting, and corporate income-tax work. There is considerable satisfaction in assisting individuals with their income-tax problems.

The exposure to the general public enhances the accountant's reputation and image in the community and generates additional sources of referral. These referrals will frequently, but not always, be income-tax clients. On occasion an individual income-tax client will be in a position to refer a job of substantial size to his accountant. Always keep in mind that a large number of the accountant's new clients come because of the referrals made by satisfied customers.

SPECIAL PROBLEMS IN THE PREPARATION OF SMALL RETURNS

The most significant problem encountered in the preparation of individual income-tax returns is that of getting from the client the correct information in a form that permits preparation of the return without loss of time. The accountant can teach his clients how to assemble the material, but there are points to be considered and problems to be overcome in this connection.

One problem concerns the client who supplies incomplete information. The preparation of the return must be held up while you wait for the missing data. This interferes with the smooth flow of work.

Another problem concerns the client who remembers certain items after the return has been completed. This is even more disruptive to the work flow and certainly merits an additional charge.

Another factor that greatly influences the fee is the quality of the material submitted. Clients bring data in a tremendous variety of forms. Some provide all their bank statements, canceled checks, and paid bills. They feel more confident if the accountant examines all their material. Others, of course, simple prepare a list of assets and deductions from which the accountant can prepare the return.

Many of these problems can be overcome by patient education. Several of the computerized tax services that prepare returns for accountants provide organizers for the taxpayer's work papers and some even have the figures that were used last year entered in the computers. These materials greatly enhance the accountants ability to secure all the necessary data from the taxpayer in an efficient and time-saving manner.

FEE FOR THE PREPARATION OF SMALL RETURNS

Some accountants use higher billing rates for income-tax work than for auditing and accounting. They feel that it is more directly beneficial financially to the client and should carry a higher fee. Furthermore, the demand for service during an extremely short period of time is tremendous. The practitioner is required to staff his organization to take care of this peak work load and work long hours under hectic conditions, all of which justifies a higher fee than might be charged for other work under different circumstances.

If higher fees are charged for tax work the practitioner will have to decide whether to use a special billing rate or overbill his normal rate. A special rate complicates the accountant's procedures for recording time. On the other hand, it might produce more revenue by ensuring that the proper fee is billed. Many firms use special rates, many do not.

Another point to keep in mind when billing individual returns is the amount of incidental service required by the client during the year. When you bill income-tax clients don't forget that many of them call you from time to time with tax questions. Internal Revenue Service computers now generate an endless stream of notices to taxpayers and many clients ask their accountants to review any communication received. The fee you charge for the preparation of returns should make an allowance for these extra services.

HOW TO HANDLE THE TAX SEASON WORK LOAD

The tax season provides real opportunities and presents real problems. The work load increases substantially but the result is increased profits. Reorganization of the daily routine to cope with the extra work in an efficient manner is of the utmost importance.

Perhaps the ideal way to handle an influx of small-tax clients is to have a "small-returns department," staffed by a group of people who would be given exclusive responsibility for it. They could do a first-class job because they would be concentrating solely on individual returns and would become thoroughly familar with all procedures.

Setting up such a department, however, is easier said then done. In most firms the accounting staff is busy year-round with audit and accounting work and cannot be reassigned to small-tax returns. It might be feasible, however, to assign one accountant to this function. One person working exclusively with small returns could accomplish a great deal. If the volume of work requires more than one person, try using part-time people under the supervision of the full-time accountant. If there is a college in the community, junior and senior accounting majors could serve quite well. Office workers in other industries are sometimes interested in part-time work, and retired people may be available. Whether or not the accountant establishes a small-returns department, use of part-time personnel should be considered.

Overtime work during the tax season is universal among accounting firms. The range of hours worked is anywhere from 45 to 65 a week, but the trend apparently is to cut down on excessively long work days. Many firms are concluding that there is a loss in effectiveness when an accountant works more than 50 to 55 hours a week. We have worked about 50 hours a week in our firm for the last several years. It is clearly understood by everyone that these are the hours we will work and somehow everything is accomplished during that period of time. In more recent years we have worked a 10-hour day, five days per week, and closed the office on Saturday and Sunday. The time off over the weekend is appreciated by all concerned.

TECHNIQUES FOR MORE EFFECTIVE USE OF TIME

The practitioner is subject to interruptions and hectic working conditions during the tax season that can materially reduce effectiveness and productivity. It is important to arrange the work day to allow for certain periods free of interruption. The accountant cannot do justice to complex problems or meet deadlines without time for concentration.

It is desirable as far as possible to schedule appointments for specified hours. This leaves the rest of the day for direct productive effort.

Telephone calls are the principal interrupting element. It is wise to set aside certain hours of the day when calls will not be taken. They can be returned later and the secretary can handle some of them.

You have to remember, of course, the importance of being available to clients and staff. You cannot closet yourself for extended periods without disrupting the work flow. You do, however, need a limited time during the day that is reasonably free to concentrate on important work.

COMPUTER-PREPARED RETURNS

A recent development which has lightened the tax-season work load has been the use of computer-prepared returns. Many practitioners have taken this route and have found it advantageous. Computerized returns are neat and accurate and save the practitioner's time by eliminating detailed computations. In addition, the computer is programmed to check on certain elections, such as income averaging.

On the other hand, there are certain disadvantages. One, of course, is the cost factor. Ideally, the practitioner will have saved enough time to cover the cost of computer service. In actual practice, however, this is not always the case and the accountant must take a write-down or the fee must be increased.

Some practitioners object to the procedures for submitting information to the computer bureau. The preparation of the computer forms is in some respects almost as complex as the preparation of the return itself. The accountant must do a sizable number of returns by this method to become familiar with these forms. In fact, if an accountant is going to use computer-prepared returns it might be better to go all the way and put everything on the computer.

Some accountants prefer to do returns manually because little review is required after the work is completed. For computer-prepared returns it is necessary to review the work after it comes back from the bureau, which may be a week or 10 days later. This step is not necessary with manually prepared returns.

It seems clear, however, that more and more accountants will be using computer-prepared returns in the future. Undoubtedly, the cost will decrease and the quality and scheduling of the service will improve. Some firms are preparing returns on their own in-house computers, a method that also has increased possibilities for the future.

OFFICE PROCEDURES FOR SMALL TAX RETURNS

The most important factor to affect a smooth flow of returns is the interview itself. It is imperative that the interviewer obtain complete information to eliminate telephone calls and additional visits. It is easier to obtain complete information if the clients have been told what they are expected to supply. The interviewer must do a complete job, however, and must use a checklist as a reminder to ask the questions that might otherwise be overlooked. This checklist will also serve to record certain information concerning the preparation, processing, and delivery of returns. We prefer a one-page checklist because it is easier to complete. Although it is not so extensive as those of other firms, it serves our purpose. We revise it and run it on different colored paper each year. It is stapled to the front of our copy of each return and is easily identifiable by the color selected for the year.

When a client has called in for an appointment the secretary types in headings (name, address, etc.) on the current year's checklist and on all forms used on the client's return for the preceding year. This material is available in the file at the time of the interview.

Our returns are prepared in pencil on Internal Revenue Service forms and photocopied. Checking is, of course, done before copying and errors are corrected simply by erasing the pencilled information. We have found that the use of electronic calculators in preparing and checking tax returns is much faster than the use of conventional adding machines.

The appearance of returns is neater if headings are typed rather than printed. The typing can be done by a secretary, thus saving the time of the accounting staff. Headings and descriptions can also be typed for depreciation schedules and any other lengthy material.

CONCLUSION

The small client most frequently needs the accountant's service because of tax problems. The preparation of income-tax returns in a professional manner is the heart of tax work. The accountant must become familiar with the preparation of returns, be able to handle the tax-season workload, adopt office procedures that provide for efficient operation, and know how to charge a proper fee for this service. There is nothing more important in small-client service.

Exhibit 44 is a chart that may be used to manage the flow of income-tax preparation.

INCOME TAX CONTROL

Year End	*Structure	Client Number	Name	Client Info.		Called			Date Acct Closed	Computer Service						Date Mailed	Comments
				Rec'd	Addl Info	2	2	2		Pro Forma?	out	in	Rerun out	in			

* I - Individual S - Sole Owner P - Partnership C - Corporation X - Sub Chapter Corp

Exhibit 44. Income Tax Control

359

18

COMPUTER
GUIDE AND MANUAL

A generic manual of instruction for using computers in an accounting practice is a starting point before selecting your own accounting software and hardware. This chapter will familiarize you with the terms, phrases and conventions found in the computer environment.

Field	The purpose of any software program is to accumulate data, usually for manipulation and reporting. The computer stores each piece of information in a "field." The limit to the number of fields a program can have is limited by the language of the program.
Record	The program groups together in a record all fields related in a specific way. A record can have one field or dozens of fields depending on the amount of data to be collected. All

fields in a record usually relate through a common denominator.

File
The program groups together in a file all records related in a specific way. A file can have one record or thousands of records, depending on how many different items must be collected.

Tables
A table is a list of frequently used information. They are constant in use; the code used to identify information for one record is also the code used to identify the same information for another record.

Keyfield
Every record of information must have one field which is unique so that a specific record can be found.

Search Field
A search field is a keyfield (or its description) which has searching capabilities, so that if you press a function key, the system displays a list of records already in the file.

Keystroke
When the manual recommends a specific keystroke to enter data into a field, the key to be entered will be surrounded by v-brackets. For example, the function key F-1 becomes <F1>, the ESC key becomes <ESC>, the Page Down key becomes <PgDn>, etc. However, you need only press the key with that description found on it; do not include the <> (v-brackets).

Letters
Computer systems frequently require a single letter, which is the first letter of a word, as input. For example, in the prompt (A)ccept, (E)dit or (R)eject, the system accepts only an A, E or R. Do not include the () brackets when entering the letter.

Prompt   A software program uses a "prompt", generally in the form of a question or statement, to urge the user to enter the appropriate information.

Return Key   After input of data into a field, the Return or Enter key must be pressed before the system can accept the value entered. If the field is to be skipped or the default value inserted, still use the <RETURN> key.

Operating Features

The design of your accounting software should bring about an easy-to-use system, incorporating many features common to all modules. Function keys drive some of these features (F1, F2, etc.), editing keys drive others (insert, delete) and some are just by system design. The intention is to reduce keystrokes, improve accuracy and enhance user-friendliness.

Standard Features

A number of features found in most good accounting software packages are intended to simplify operation, create a user-friendly environment, and ease the input of data. The list that follows includes features found in all of the accounting software modules:

Menus   These are lists of available accounting tasks that prompt you to select one that is to be performed.

Input Screens   After selecting a task, the screen for input becomes a "form," and the system guides you through filling in the blanks.

Prompts   To guide you through filling in the input screen, all fields display a message to "prompt" you to enter the correct value requested.

Defaults   Whenever appropriate, certain "default" values are assigned to fields. These are values which tend to be constant throughout businesses, and are a tool to reduce data entry keystrokes. To accept defaults for a field, simply press the <RETURN> key. Default values display on all screens appearing in installation.

Express Entry   The "express entry" key or <TAB> key greatly reduces the time required to enter data. In instances where information to be entered into a screen is usually the same, the software automatically enters that information for you. To accept defaults for an entire screen, simply press the <TAB> key.

Function Keys   Special function keys make data entry and editing extremely fast.

ACCOUNTING SYSTEMS

Most good accounting software is divided into sub-systems or "modules". Each module deals with a different accounting function. You may not need all of them, depending upon the nature of your practice.

General Ledger: The storehouse of all financial transactions as contained in the general journal; financial statements evolve from this module.

Accounts Payable: Used in an accrual accounting system, this monitors debts owed by the client company.

Accounts Receivable: Used in an accrual accounting system, this records monies owed to a client company.

The General Ledger is at the heart of the accounting software, for it is the module which gathers, stores, and reports on the financial conditions of the client company. Most good general ledger software is designed for fast and easy installation. The systems automatically format financial reports conforming to generally accepted accounting principles. Many safeguards are included to deter mistakes commonly made and to force the operator to keep entries in a balanced condition.

Features of most general ledger software include the following:

A full year of journal detail may be stored.

Complete and useful audit trails through the trial balance report, journal detail list and outstanding journals waiting for inclusion in the general ledger.

Management tools are available through financial reports, budget and comparison reports, and statement of changes in financial position.

Repeating monthly journal entries can be stored and posted each month with a few keystokes.

Flexibility of account and department set up to satisfy even the most complicated client businesses.

Types of Reports

There are many reports generated by the General Ledger module which can be separated into four main categories: file list, audit list, audit reports, and financial reports.

File Lists   A print-out of raw data:
    Account list
    Departmental list
    Budget listing
    Prior year listing
    Recurring voucher listing

Audit Lists   The system prints audit lists after an input routine. They recap the information entered. Not stored permanently, these are working reports to be discarded when finished. The information they contain repeats on the audit reports. The audit lists are:
    Outstanding journal listing
    Work file audit listing
    Journal entry audit listing

Audit Reports   Print audit reports at the end of the month, or when there is a need to verify the entries en masse. They are usually permanently stored as the accounting records. The reports are:
    Trial balance
    Journal detail list

Financial Reports   Financial or management reports as follows:
    Income statement
    Balance sheet
    Change in financial position
    Budget variance
    Prior year income statement
    Prior year balance sheet
    Comparative income statement
    Comparative balance sheet

Report Descriptions

A closer look at the reports generated by the General Ledger software follows:

Account List	A list of the chart of accounts.
Department List	A list of the departments on file.
Budget List	A list of the budget amounts entered for each month of the accounts.
Prior Year List	A list of the previous year's account balances for each month.
Recurring Vouchers List	A list of the recurring vouchers on file.
Outstanding Journal Listing	A list of the transactions from the supporting modules which are waiting to be posted into the general journal.
Work File Audit Listing	A list of the transactions as you enter them into the entry routines. This report is only available immediately after exiting from an entry routine, but before you return to the menu.
Transaction Audit Listing	After posting outstanding journals to the general journal, the system prints an audit report of the transactions posted.

Trial Balance

The trial balance presents the accounting transactions sorted by range or all accounts, and can include detail or summary totals.

Journal Detail List

The primary audit report, this presents the detail contained in the general journal.

Income Statement

Also known as a Profit and Loss Statement, this calculates the net profit (or loss) by subtracting expenses from revenue.

Balance Sheet

This calculates the net worth of a business: the amount of capital obtained once you subtract liabilities from the assets.

Change in Financial Position

This is another management report which defines the sources and uses of cash and the changes in working capital.

Budget Variance

If you set up a budget for Income Statement accounts (revenue and expenses), this report will compare what was budgeted against the actual amount.

BACKUP!

Backing up your data EVERY DAY is crucial and will save you immeasurable time if you ever have the slightest problem with your computer. If you have ever had to reenter months, weeks, days or even hours worth of work lost because of a power surge you will never neglect the backup of data.

Backing up simply means making a copy of your data as a safety precaution. In the event the data files become unusable you can restore the data from a backup.

Backup all data files every day. A good routine is to name each set of backup disks by the day of the week. If using floppy disks for backup, each day will consist of several disks. Name each as 1 of 5, 2 of 5, 3 of 5 etc. If using tapes for backup, this same method will work except requiring only 1 tape per day. On Monday, take the set labeled Monday and proceed with the backup. On Tuesday, take the set labeled Tuesday, and so on and so forth.

The time of day for making backups has more room for flexibility. The end of the day is usually preferred, just after the days work has been entered. However, if backup takes sometime, lunchtime can be used. The important thing is that it is done every day. If you work in an environment that lends itself to frequent power drains, interruptions, or more severe problems, and your data input is substantial, make backups more frequently (two or three a day).

19

SOURCES OF FURTHER INFORMATION

The list that follows is a comprehensive buying and reference guide to the products and services you need to keep pace with the changes in accounting practices.

A major part of this chapter is devoted to computers and software. The reason is obvious. The computer revolution—fueled by the personal computer—is rapidly transforming the accounting profession.

AN ALPHABETICAL LIST OF COMPANIES AND THEIR ADDRESSES

ACCOUNTANTS' SUPPLY HOUSE
(800) 645-6588; (800) 632-6727 (in New York)
516-561-7700
514 Rockaway Avenue
Valley Stream, NY 11582

AMACOM
135 West 50th Street
New York, NY 10022

APPLE COMPUTER, INC.
(408) 996-1010
Personal Computer Systems Division
20525 Mariani Avenue
Cupertino, CA 95014

MATTHEW BENDER & CO.
P.O. Box 989
New York, NY 12201

CCH COMPUTAX INC.
(213) 540-3881
21535 Hawthorne Boulevard
Torrance, CA 90503

CENTER FOR ENTREPRENSEURSHIP AND SMALL BUSINESS MANAGEMENT
Campus Box 48
Wichita State University
Wichita, KS 67208

COMMERCE CLEARING HOUSE, INC.
(312) 583-8500
4025 West Peterson Avenue
Chicago, IL 60646

DAY RUNNER, INC
(800) 2 DAY RUN
3562 Eastham Drive
Culver City, CA 90232

DELL COMPUTER CORPORATION
9505 Arboretum Blvd.
Austin, TX 78759

DUN & BRADSTREET CREDIT SERVICES
(212) 285-7134
Dun's Financial Profiles
99 Church Street
New York, NY 10007

EPSON AMERICA, INC.
2780 Lomita Blvd.
Torrance, CA 90505

ESSELTE PENDAFLEX CORP.
Clinton Road
Garden City, NY 11530

JACK FOX ASSOCIATES
(619) 632-8595
109 Via Solaro
Encinitas, CA 92024

**HEWLETT-PACKARD
COMPANY**
(303) 227-3800
Desktop Computer Division
3404 East Harmony Road
Ft. Collins, CO 80525

IBM CORPORATION
101 Paragon Drive
Montvale, NJ 07645

**MITSUBISHI
ELECTRONICS AMERICA,
INC.**
991 Knox Street
Torrance, CA 90502

**MOORE BUSINESS FORMS,
INC.**
(312) 291-8221
1205 Milwaukee Avenue
Glenville, IL 60025

**NATIONAL ASSOCIATION
OF ACCOUNTANTS**
10 Paragon Drive
P.O. Box 433
Montvale, NJ 07645

**NEC INFORMATION
SYSTEMS, INC.**
1414 Massachusetts Avenue
Boxborough, MA 01719

NBS SYSTEMS, INC.
P.O. Box 321
Edwardsville, IL 62025

ODESTA CORPORATION
4084 Commercial Avenue
Northbrook, IL 60062

UARCO, INC.
(312) 381-7000
West County Line Road
Barrington, IL 60010

**WARREN, GORHAM &
LAMONT**
210 South Street
Boston, MA 02111

JOHN WILEY & SONS, INC.
One Wiley Drive
Somerset, NJ 08873

INTERNAL REVENUE DISTRICTS

ALABAMA
Birmingham, AL 35203

ALASKA
Anchorage, AK 99501

ARIZONA
Phoenix, AZ 85004

ARKANSAS
Little Rock, AR 72201

CALIFORNIA
San Francisco, CA 94102
Los Angeles, CA 90012

COLORADO
Denver, CO 80265

CONNECTICUT
Hartford, CT 06103

DELAWARE
Wilmington, DE 19801

DISTRICT OF COLUMBIA
Washington, DC 20009

FLORIDA
Jacksonville, FL 32202

GEORGIA
Atlanta, GA 30043

HAWAII
Honolulu, HI 96850

IDAHO
Boise, ID 83724

ILLINOIS
Chicago, IL 60604
Springfield, IL 62701

INDIANA
Indianapolis, IN 46204

IOWA
Des Moines, IA 50309

KANSAS
Wichita, KS 67202

KENTUCKY
Louisville, KY 40202

LOUISIANA
New Orleans, LA 70130

MAINE
Augusta, ME 04330

MARYLAND
Baltimore, MD 21201

MASSACHUSETTS
Boston, MA 02203

MICHIGAN
Detroit, MI 48226

MINNESOTA
St. Paul, MN 55101

MISSISSIPPI
Jackson, MS 39201

MISSOURI
St. Louis, MO 63101

MONTANA
Helena, MT 59626

NEBRASKA
Omaha, NE 68102

NEVADA
Reno, NV 89509
Las Vegas, NV 89101

NEW HAMPSHIRE
Portsmouth, NH 03801

NEW JERSEY
Newark, NJ 07102

NEW MEXICO
Albuquerque, NM 87101

NEW YORK
Brooklyn, NY 11201
New York, NY 10007
Albany, NY 12207
Buffalo, NY 14202

NORTH CAROLINA
Greensboro, NC 27401

NORTH DAKOTA
Fargo, ND 58102

OHIO
Cincinnati, OH 45202
Cleveland, OH 44199

OKLAHOMA
Oklahoma City, OK 73102

OREGON
Portland, OR 87204

PENNSYLVANIA
Philadelphia, PA 19106
Pittsburgh, PA 15222

RHODE ISLAND
Providence, RI 02903

SOUTH CAROLINA
Columbia, SC 29201

SOUTH DAKOTA
Aberdeen, SD 57401

TENNESSEE
Nashville, TN 37203

TEXAS
Austin, TX 78701
Dallas, TX 75242
Houston, TX 77002

UTAH
Salt Lake City, UT 84111

VERMONT
Burlington, VT 05401

VIRGINIA
Richmond, VA 23240

WASHINGTON
Seattle, WA 98174

WEST VIRGINIA
Parkersburg, WV 26101

WISCONSIN
Milwaukee, WI 53202

WYOMING
Cheyenne, WY 82001

IRS SERVICE CENTERS

States

ALABAMA
Atlanta, GA 31101

ALASKA
Ogden, UT 84201

ARIZONA
Ogden, UT 84201

ARKANSAS
Austin, TX 73301

CALIFORNIA
Fresno, CA 93888

COLORADO
Ogden, UT 84201

CONNECTICUT
Andover, MA 05501

DELAWARE
Philadelphia, PA 19255

DISTRICT OF COLUMBIA
Philadelphia, PA 19255

FLORIDA
Atlanta, GA 31101

GEORGIA
Atlanta, GA 31101

HAWAII
Fresno, CA 93888

IDAHO
Ogden, UT 84201

ILLINOIS
Kansas City, MO 64999

INDIANA
Memphis, TN 37501

IOWA
Kansas City, MO 64999

KANSAS
Austin, TX 73301

KENTUCKY
Memphis, TN 37501

LOUISIANA
Austin, TX 73301

MAINE
Andover, MA 05501

MARYLAND
Philadelphia, PA 19255

MASSACHUSETTS
Andover, MA 05501

MICHIGAN
Cincinnati, OH 45999

MINNESOTA
Ogden, UT 84201

MISSISSIPPI
Atlanta, GA 31101

MISSOURI
Kansas City, MO 64999

MONTANA
Ogden, UT 84201

NEBRASKA
Ogden, UT 84201

NEVADA
Ogden, UT 84201

NEW HAMPSHIRE
Andover, MA 05501

NEW JERSEY
Holtsville, NY 00501

NEW MEXICO
Austin, TX 73301

NEW YORK
New York City and Nassau,
   Rockland, Suffolk, and
   Westchester Counties
Holtsville, NY 05501

NORTH CAROLINA
Memphis, TN 37501

NORTH DAKOTA
Ogden, UT 84201

OHIO
Cincinnati, OH 45999

OKLAHOMA
Austin, TX 73301

OREGON
Ogden, UT 84201

PENNSYLVANIA
Philadelphia, PA 19255

RHODE ISLAND
Andover, MA 05501

SOUTH CAROLINA
Atlanta, GA 31101

SOUTH DAKOTA
Ogden, UT 84201

TENNESSEE
Memphis, TN 37501

TEXAS
Austin, TX 73301

UTAH
Ogden, UT 84201

VERMONT
Andover, MA 05001

VIRGINIA
Memphis, TN 37501

WASHINGTON
Ogden, UT 84201

WEST VIRGINIA
Memphis, TN 37501

WISCONSIN
Kansas City, MO 64999

WYOMING
Ogden, UT 84201

Possessions

AMERICAN SAMOA
Philadelphia, PA 19255

GUAM
Commissioner of Revenue and
   Taxation
Agana, GU 96910

PUERTO RICO
(or those excluding income
   under Section 933)
Philadelphia, PA 19255

VIRGIN ISLANDS
Permanent residents

Department of Finance, Tax
  Division
Charlotte Amalie
St. Thomas, VI 00801
Nonpermanent residents
Philadelphia, PA 19255

A.P.O. or F.P.O address of
Miami

New York
San Francisco
Seattle
Atlanta, GA 31101
Holtsville, NY 00501
Fresno, CA 93888
Ogden, UT 84201

Foreign Country

(United States citizens and those excluding income under section 911 or 931 or claiming deductions under section 913)
Philadelphia, PA 19255

STATE TAX RETURN ADDRESSES

ALABAMA
Department of Revenue
Montgomery, AL 36130

ALASKA
Department of Revenue
State Office Building
Juneau, AK 99811

ARIZONA
Department of Revenue
State Capitol Building
Phoenix, AZ 85007

ARKANSAS
Department of Finance and
  Administration
State Capitol
Little Rock, AR 72201

CALIFORNIA
Franchise Tax Board
Sacramento, CA 95867

COLORADO
Department of Revenue
Capitol Annex Building
Denver, CO 80203

CONNECTICUT
State Tax Department
470 Capitol Avenue
Hartford, CT 06115

DELAWARE
State Tax Department
Wilmington, DE 19801

DISTRICT OF COLUMBIA
Revenue Division
Municipal Center
300 Indiana Avenue, NW
Washington, DC 20001

FLORIDA
Department of Revenue
Tallahassee, FL 32304

GEORGIA
Department of Revenue
State Office Building
Atlanta, GA 30334

HAWAII
Department of Taxation
Honolulu, HI 96809

IDAHO
State Tax Commission
Boise, ID 83722

ILLINOIS
Department of Revenue
State Office Building
Springfield, IL 62708

INDIANA
Department of Revenue
State Office Building
Indianapolis, IN 46204

IOWA
Department of Revenue
State Office Building
Des Moines, IA 50319

KANSAS
Director of Revenue

State Office Building
Topeka, KS 66625

KENTUCKY
Department of Revenue
Frankfort, KY 40601

LOUISIANA
Department of Revenue
Baton Rouge, LA 70821

MAINE
Bureau of Taxation
State Office Building
Augusta, ME 04330

MARYLAND
Comptroller of the Treasury
State Treasury Building
Annapolis, MD 21401

MASSACHUSETTS
Income Tax Bureau
100 Cambridge Street
Boston, MA 02204

MICHIGAN
Department of the Treasury
Lansing, MI 48922

MINNESOTA
Department of Revenue
St. Paul, MN 55145

MISSISSIPPI
State Tax Commission
Jackson, MS 39205

MISSOURI
Director of Revenue
Jefferson City, MO 65107

MONTANA
State Board of Equalizatior
Helena, MT 59601

NEBRASKA
State Tax Commission
State Capitol
Lincoln, NE 68509

NEVADA
State Tax Commission
Carson City, NV 89710

NEW HAMPSHIRE
State Tax Commission
Concord, NH 03301

NEW JERSEY
Treasury Department
Division of Taxation
Trenton, NJ 08625

NEW MEXICO
Bureau of Revenue
Santa Fe, NM 87503

NEW YORK
State Income Tax Bureau
The State Campus
Albany, NY 12226

NORTH CAROLINA
Department of Revenue
Raleigh, NC 27640

NORTH DAKOTA
State Tax Commissioner
State Capitol
Bismarck, ND 58505

OHIO
Department of Taxation
68 East Gay Street
Columbus, OH 43216

OKLAHOMA
State Tax Commission
Oklahoma City, OK 73194

OREGON
Department of Revenue
Salem, OR 97310

PENNSYLVANIA
Department of Revenue
Harrisburg, PA 17105

RHODE ISLAND
State Tax Administrator
189 Promenade Street
Providence, RI 02908

SOUTH CAROLINA
State Tax Commission
Columbia, SC 29214

SOUTH DAKOTA
Department of Revenue
Pierre, SD 57501

TENNESSEE
Department of Revenue
Nashville, TN 37242

TEXAS
Controller of Public Accounts
Austin, TX 78774

UTAH
State Tax Commission
State Office Building
Salt Lake City, UT 84114

VERMONT
Department of Taxes
Montpelier, VT 05602

VIRGINIA
Department of Taxation
Richmond, VA 23282

WASHINGTON
Department of Revenue
Olympia, WA 98504

WEST VIRGINIA
Income Tax Division
Charleston, WV 25305

WISCONSIN
Department of Taxation
Madison, WI 53701

WYOMING
State Tax Commission
Capitol Building
Cheyenne, WY 82001

FURTHER SOURCES

ACCOUNTANTS' WEEKLY
P.O. Box 270828
San Diego, CA 92198-2828

ACCOUNTING & TAX NETWORK, INC.
400 Pinnacle Parkway
Suite 410
Norcross, GA

AMERICAN INSTITUTE OF CERTIFIED PUBLIC ACCOUNTANTS
1211 Avenue of the Americas
New York, NY 10036

AMERICAN WOMEN'S SOCIETY OF CERTIFIED PUBLIC ACCOUNTANTS
P.O. Box 389
Marysville, OH 43040

NATIONAL ASSOCIATION OF ACCOUNTANTS
10 Paragon Drive
P.O. Box 433
Montvale, NJ 07645

NATIONAL ASSOCIATION OF BLACK ACCOUNTANTS
256 Montgomery Street
San Francisco, CA 94104

NATIONAL SOCIETY OF PUBLIC ACCOUNTANTS
1010 North Fairfax Street
Alexandria, VA 22314

THE PRACTICAL ACCOUNTANT
40 West 57 Street
New York, NY 10019

UNITED STATES SMALL BUSINESS ADMINISTRATION

SBA Field Offices

REG	TYPE	CITY	ST	ZIP	ADDRESS		PUBLIC PHONE
01	RO	BOSTON	MA	02110	60 BATTERYMARCH STREET	10TH FLOOR	(617) 451-2030
01	DO	AUGUSTA	ME	04330	40 WESTERN AVENUE	ROOM 512	(207) 622-8378
01	DO	BOSTON	MA	02222-1093	10 CAUSEWAY STREET	ROOM 265	(617) 565-5590
01	DO	CONCORD	NH	03301-1257	55 PLEASANT STREET	ROOM 210	(603) 225-1400
01	DO	HARTFORD	CT	06106	330 MAIN STREET	2ND FLOOR	(203) 240-4700
01	DO	MONTPELIER	VT	05602	87 STATE STREET	ROOM 205	(802) 828-4474
01	DO	PROVIDENCE	RI	02903	380 WESTMINSTER MALL	5TH FLOOR	(401) 528-4586
01	BO	SPRINGFIELD	MA	01103	1550 MAIN STREET	ROOM 212	(413) 785-0268
02	RO	NEW YORK	NY	10278	26 FEDERAL PLAZA	ROOM 31-108	(212) 264-7772
02	DO	HATO REY	PR	00918	CARLOS CHARDON AVE.	ROOM 691	(809) 753-4002
02	DO	NEW YORK	NY	10278	26 FEDERAL PLAZA	ROOM 3100	(212) 264-4355
02	DO	NEWARK	NJ	07102	60 PARK PLACE	4TH FLOOR	(201) 645-2434
02	DO	SYRACUSE	NY	13260	100 S. CLINTON STREET	ROOM 1071	(315) 423-5383
02	BO	BUFFALO	NY	14202	111 W. HURON STREET	ROOM 1311	(716) 846-4301
02	BO	ELMIRA	NY	14901	333 E. WATER STREET	4TH FLOOR	(607) 734-8130
02	BO	MELVILLE	NY	11747	35 PINELAWN ROAD	ROOM 102E	(516) 454-0750
03	RO	KING OF PRUSSIA	PA	19406	475 ALLENDALE ROAD	SUITE 201	(215) 962-3750
03	DO	BALTIMORE	MD	21202	10 N. CALVERT STREET	3RD FLOOR	(301) 962-4392
03	DO	CLARKSBURG	WV	26301	168 W. MAIN STREET	5TH FLOOR	(304) 623-4317
03	DO	KING OF PRUSSIA	PA	19406	475 ALLENDALE ROAD	SUITE 201	(215) 962-3846
03	DO	PITTSBURGH	PA	15222	960 PENN AVENUE	5TH FLOOR	(412) 644-2780
03	DO	RICHMOND	VA	23240	400 N. 8TH STREET	ROOM 3015	(804) 771-2617

03	DO	WASHINGTON	DC	20036	1111 18TH STREET, NW	6TH FLOOR	(202) 634-4950
03	BO	CHARLESTON	WV	25301	550 EAGAN STREET	SUITE 309	(304) 347-5220
03	BO	HARRISBURG	PA	17101	100 CHESTNUT STREET	SUITE 309	(717) 782-3840
03	BO	WILKES-BARRE	PA	18701	20 N. PENNSYLVANIA AVE.	ROOM 2327	(717) 826-6497
03	BO	WILMINGTON	DE	19801	844 KING STREET	ROOM 1315	(302) 573-6294
04	RO	ATLANTA	GA	30367-8102	1375 PEACHTREE ST., NE	5TH FLOOR	(404) 347-2797
04	DO	ATLANTA	GA	30309	1720 PEACHTREE RD, NW	6TH FLOOR	(404) 347-2441
04	DO	BIRMINGHAM	AL	35203-2398	2121 8TH AVE. N.	SUITE 200	(205) 731-1344
04	DO	CHARLOTTE	NC	28202	222 S. CHURCH STREET	ROOM 300	(704) 371-6563
04	DO	COLUMBIA	SC	29202	1835 ASSEMBLY STREET	ROOM 358	(803) 765-5376
04	DO	CORAL GABLES	FL	33146	1320 S. DIXIE HIGHWAY	SUITE 501	(305) 536-5521
04	DO	JACKSON	MS	39269-0396	100 W. CAPITOL STREET	SUITE 322	(601) 965-4378
04	DO	JACKSONVILLE	FL	32202	400 W. BAY STREET	ROOM 261	(904) 791-3782
04	DO	LOUISVILLE	KY	40202	600 FEDERAL PLACE	ROOM 188	(502) 582-5976
04	DO	NASHVILLE	TN	37219	404 JAMES ROBERTSON PKWY	STE 1012	(615) 736-5881
04	BO	GULFPORT	MS	39501-7758	ONE HANCOCK PLAZA	SUITE 1001	(601) 863-4449
05	RO	CHICAGO	IL	60604-1593	230 S. DEARBORN STREET	ROOM 510	(312) 353-0359
05	DO	CHICAGO	IL	60604-1779	219 S. DEARBORN STREET	ROOM 437	(312) 353-4528
05	DO	CLEVELAND	OH	44199	1240 E. 9TH STREET	ROOM 317	(216) 522-4180
05	DO	COLUMBUS	OH	43215-2887	85 MARCONI BLVD.	ROOM 512	(614) 469-6860
05	DO	DETROIT	MI	48226	477 MICHIGAN AVE.	ROOM 515	(313) 226-6075
05	DO	INDIANAPOLIS	IN	46204-1584	575 N. PENNSYLVANIA ST.	ROOM 578	(317) 269-7272
05	DO	MADISON	WI	53703	212 E. WASHINGTON AVE.	ROOM 213	(608) 264-5261
05	DO	MINNEAPOLIS	MN	55403-1563	100 N. 6TH STREET	SUITE 610C	(612) 370-2324
05	BO	CINCINNATI	OH	45202	550 MAIN STREET	ROOM 5028	(513) 684-2814
05	BO	MARQUETTE	MI	49885	300 S. FRONT ST.		(906) 225-1108
05	BO	MILWAUKEE	WI	53203	310 W. WISCONSIN AVE.	SUITE 400	(414) 291-3941
05	BO	SPRINGFIELD	IL	62704	511 W. CAPITOL AVE.	SUITE 302	(217) 492-4416

UNITED STATES SMALL BUSINESS ADMINISTRATION

SBA Field Offices (Continued)

REG	TYPE	CITY	ST	ZIP	ADDRESS		PUBLIC PHONE
06	RO	DALLAS	TX	75235-3391	8625 KING GEORGE DR.	BLDG. C	(214) 767-7643
06	DO	ALBUQUERQUE	NM	87110	5000 MARBLE AVE., NE	ROOM 320	(505) 262-6171
06	DO	DALLAS	TX	75242	1100 COMMERCE STREET	ROOM 3C-36	(214) 767-0605
06	DO	EL PASO	TX	79935	10737 GATEWAY W.	SUITE 320	(915) 541-7586
06	DO	HARLINGEN	TX	78550	222 E. VAN BUREN ST.	ROOM 500	(512) 427-8533
06	DO	HOUSTON	TX	77054	2525 MURWORTH	SUITE 112	(713) 660-4401
06	DO	LITTLE ROCK	AR	72201	320 W. CAPITOL AVE.	ROOM 601	(501) 378-5871
06	DO	LUBBOCK	TX	79401	1611 TENTH STREET	SUITE 200	(806) 743-7462
06	DO	NEW ORLEANS	LA	70112	1661 CANAL STREET	SUITE 2000	(504) 589-6685
06	DO	OKLAHOMA CITY	OK	73102	200 N. W. 5TH STREET	SUITE 670	(405) 231-4301
06	DO	SAN ANTONIO	TX	78216	7400 BLANCO ROAD	SUITE 300	(512) 329-4501
06	BO	CORPUS CHRISTI	TX	78401	400 MANN STREET	SUITE 403	(512) 888-3331
06	BO	FT. WORTH	TX	76102	819 TAYLOR STREET	ROOM 10A27	(817) 334-3613
07	RO	KANSAS CITY	MO	64106	911 WALNUT STREET	13TH FLOOR	(816) 426-2989
07	DO	CEDAR RAPIDS	IA	52402-3118	373 COLLINS ROAD NE	ROOM 100	(319) 399-2571
07	DO	DES MOINES	IA	50309	210 WALNUT STREET	ROOM 749	(515) 284-4422
07	DO	KANSAS CITY	MO	64106	1103 GRAND AVE.	6TH FLOOR	(816) 374-3419
07	DO	OMAHA	NB	68154	11145 MILL VALLEY RD.		(402) 221-4691
07	DO	ST. LOUIS	MO	63101	815 OLIVE STREET	ROOM 242	(314) 539-6600
07	DO	WICHITA	KS	67202	110 E. WATERMAN ST.	1ST FLOOR	(316) 269-6571
07	BO	SPRINGFIELD	MO	65802-3200	620 S. GLENSTONE ST.	SUITE 110	(417) 864-7670

		City	State	ZIP	Address	Room	Phone
08	RO	DENVER	CO	80202	999 18TH STREET	SUITE 701	(303) 294-7001
08	DO	CASPER	WY	82602-2839	100 EAST B. STREET	ROOM 4001	(307) 261-5761
08	DO	DENVER	CO	80202-2599	721 19TH STREET	ROOM 407	(303) 844-2607
08	DO	FARGO	ND	58108-3086	657 2ND AVE. N.	ROOM 218	(701) 239-5131
08	DO	HELENA	MT	59626	301 S. PARK STREET	ROOM 528	(406) 449-5381
08	DO	SALT LAKE CITY	UT	84138-1195	125 S. STATE STREET	ROOM 2237	(801) 524-5800
08	DO	SIOUX FALLS	SD	57102-0517	101 S. MAIN AVE.	SUITE 101	(605) 330-4231
09	RO	SAN FRANCISCO	CA	94102	450 GOLDEN GATE AVE.	SUITE 108	(415) 556-7487
09	DO	FRESNO	CA	93721	2202 MONTEREY ST.		(209) 487-5189
09	DO	HONOLULU	HI	96850	300 ALA MOANA	ROOM 2213	(808) 541-2990
09	DO	LAS VEGAS	NV	89125	301 E. STEWART ST.	ROOM 301	(702) 388-6611
09	DO	LOS ANGELES	CA	90071	350 S. FIGUEROA ST.	6TH FLOOR	(213) 894-2956
09	DO	PHOENIX	AZ	85004	2005 N. CENTRAL AVE.	5TH FLOOR	(602) 261-3732
09	DO	SAN DIEGO	CA	92188	880 FRONT STREET	ROOM 4-S-29	(619) 557-7252
09	DO	SAN FRANCISCO	CA	94105-1988	211 MAIN STREET	4TH FLOOR	(415) 974-0642
09	BO	AGANA	GM	96910	PACIFIC DAILY NEWS BDG	ROOM 508	(671) 472-7277
09	BO	SACRAMENTO	CA	95814	660 J STREET	ROOM 215	(916) 551-1445
09	BO	SANTA ANA	CA	92703	901 W. CIVIC CTR DR	ROOM 160	(714) 836-2494
10	RO	SEATTLE	WA	98121	2615 4TH AVENUE	ROOM 440	(206) 442-5676
10	DO	ANCHORAGE	AK	99501	8TH & C STREETS	ROOM 1068	(907) 271-4022
10	DO	BOISE	ID	83702	1020 MAIN STREET	SUITE 290	(208) 334-1696
10	DO	PORTLAND	OR	97204-2882	1220 S. W. THIRD AVE.	ROOM 676	(503) 294-5221
10	DO	SEATTLE	WA	98174-1088	915 SECOND AVE.	ROOM 1792	(206) 442-5534
10	DO	SPOKANE	WA	99210	W. 920 RIVERSIDE AVE.	ROOM 651	(509) 456-3783

DO = DISTRICT OFFICE   BO = BRANCH OFFICE

389

INDEX

INDEX

INDEX